$7.50

THE NEW IMMIGRATION

edited by John J. Appel, *Michigan State University*

In the twenty years before the start of World War I, a floodtide of "new" immigration from Southern and Eastern Europe surpassed the old immigration to the United States from Northern and Western Europe. Except for the wartime interlude, this new influx continued until it was cut short by restrictive immigration legislation during the 1920s.

What significance did this new immigration have for the new homeland...for the mother countries...for the immigrants themselves?

In this new book, John J. Appel examines the causes and the consequences of this vast movement to the United States of Italians, Russians, Poles, and other national groups around the turn of the century... compares its impact with that of the earlier 19th century immigration from Northern and Western Europe. A carefully chosen collection of essays, articles, speeches, and book reviews written during the period presents a balanced picture of the new immigration as seen by a variety of contemporaries. Professor Appel fits this chapter out of our nation's past into the larger theme of American history. He shows how the nation hardened its national self-image and abandoned its policy of offering asylum to all in favor of a narrower 20th Century concept of national self-interest and ethnic exclusivity.

MAJOR ISSUES IN AMERICAN HISTORY

GENERAL EDITOR
A. S. EISENSTADT, Brooklyn College

John J. Appel is Associate Professor of American Thought and Language at Michigan State University. A long-time specialist in ethnic studies, Dr. Appel has been a visiting scholar at the Smithsonian Institution (1969-70) and a Harrison Fellow in American Studies at the University of Pennsylvania. Author of a wide range of articles and studies on immigrant and ethnic topics, he has also served as an advisory editor and a consultant for the American Jewish Committee and the Winterthur Museum. Dr. Appel received B.A. and M.A. degrees from the University of Miami and his Ph.D. in American Studies from the University of Pennsylvania.

A JEROME S. OZER BOOK
published by PITMAN PUBLISHING CORPORATION
New York * Toronto * London * Tel Aviv

THE NEW IMMIGRATION

EDITED BY

John J. Appel
Michigan State University

FOR SELMA AND MICHAEL

FOREWORD

The study of history in our classrooms too often
proceeds merely from the perspective of the present.
Hindsight becomes the great arbiter for settling the
past's problems. In our standard textbooks, we judge
rather than encounter the past; we instruct it with
lessons learned from later developments. In such
textbooks, the study of history tends to become a
tidy arrangement of certain consequences that arose out of certain
causes. As a result, the student can grasp only meagerly the sense that
every past was its own present, alive with its own problems, wavering
among the alternatives for solving these problems, uncertain about the
future. With the security of hindsight and distance, the student is not
sufficiently able to consider that a decade he sees as *then* was once
a vital and challenging *now,* that its roads into the future were many,
that there was nothing inevitable about the one it followed, and that
many voices spoke and many forces were at work in affecting its decision
to travel one road or another.

The study of American history has tended in recent decades, in
yet another way, to remove the classroom from the past itself. It is
not merely that we have been proceeding, in our textbooks, to perceive
the past from a perspective that is settled and certain, but also that,
in our supplementary materials, we have been reading not the past
itself but how our major historians are perennially changing their interpretations of it. In this way, too, we are supplanting a study of the
past with a study of latter-day commentators on it and, all too often,
of commentators on the commentators. The original, vital language of
the past itself has, it is fair to say, lost a good deal in the translation.

The *Major Issues in American History* series undertakes above all to restore the fresh, lively contact between the student of the past and the past he is studying. Each of the volumes in the series consists of fifteen or more essays written by earlier generations of Americans on issues of great importance in their times. The different volumes of the series tap a variety of primary sources, but mainly the rich store of our great periodical literature, in which the foremost leaders of American life, our publicists, literary figures, and statesmen addressed themselves to the major problems confronting their respective eras. The men and women who speak in these selections offer various reasons or qualifications for doing so: their intimate knowledge of the problem they are speaking of, their sophisticated perception of its nature, their deep persuasion about its urgency, their strong convictions about how to resolve it.

The selections in each volume seek to lay out the larger dimensions of the major issue with which it is concerned, to recapture the sense of the issue's contemporaneity and urgency, and to afford answers to questions such as the following: What are the nature and significance of the issue? How and why did the issue arise? How should it be resolved? What alternatives are there to achieve its resolution, and what difficulties does the pursuit of each of these alternatives present? Every age is alive with problems, doubts, and controversies, and the selections in each of the volumes seek to convey what these were, in the full measure of the immediacy and liveliness with which the age experienced them. In sum, the central aim of the series is to vitalize the study of the American past by means of *important contemporary essays on major issues.*

Each of the volumes has been edited by a specialist on the issue with which the volume is concerned. Each volume has several principal features designed to enhance its use by the student in his pursuit of a meaningful, rewarding study of the American past. The editor's introductory essay undertakes to present the issue in a broader perspective, indicating how it arose, what were its essential themes and substance, how the controversy it engendered proceeded, what proposals were made for its resolution, how it was ultimately settled, and what were its impact and historical significance. The headnotes for each of the selections extend the introductory essay, offering details about the author of the selection, what occasioned its writing, what the other sides of the controversy were, and the specific historical context in which the selection appeared. The bibliographical essay at the end of the volume offers a critical appraisal of the literature, primary and secondary, dealing with the issue under discussion. Selective rather than comprehensive, it affords the student the basis for a further exploration of the subject. Each volume has, moreover, a chronology which sets the major issue in the context of its times, relating it to the principal events of the age. It is a special point of the series, finally, that the selections have, wherever possible, been reprinted in their entirety. It is important that a spokesman of an earlier age be permitted to present his views in all their completeness and that the student give the past the full hearing it merits.

The *Major Issues in American History* series is meant for use in both basic and advanced courses in American history. The series extends the study of the American past in several ways. It takes the student beyond the confines of the textbook, with its pat formulations and neat divisions, to the reality of the past. Without in any way discounting the importance of what they are saying, it also takes the student beyond the perennial controversies among latter-day and recent historians about what the past signified. It sets the student down in the lively context of a major issue or crisis which earlier Americans had to face, and it compels him to take his place among them in facing and resolving it. Above all, it encourages him to venture out on his own into the realm of the American past and to develop those qualities of perception and judgment that make the study of history the challenging enterprise it is.

A. S. EISENSTADT
Brooklyn College

CONTENTS

A SELECTIVE CHRONOLOGY

1881–1901   Peak arrival years of immigrants from Germany, Great Britain, Sweden, Denmark, Switzerland, Portugal.

1882   First *general* federal law designed to exclude *individual* undesirables.

First Chinese Exclusion Act based on *racist* concepts.

1885   Foran Act excludes unskilled contract laborers but not skilled labor, domestic servants, artists, and friends of those already here.

1886   Haymarket bombings; blamed on foreign anarchists.

1887   The American Protective Association formed.

1889   House and Senate establish standing committees on immigration.

1890   Census Bureau announces disappearance of frontier.

1892   Federal inspection station at Ellis Island opened.

1894   Immigration Restriction League organized.

1896   Senator Henry Cabot Lodge introduces an immigration bill including a literacy clause; vetoed by President Cleveland.

1901   Assassination of President McKinley by Leon Czolgosz reinforces the stereotype of the "alien-as-radical" despite Czolgosz' American birth.

Anarchists and advocates of violent overthrow of government are denied entry.

Commissioner-General of Immigration placed under jurisdiction of newly-established Department of Labor.

1901–1910   Peak arrival years of immigrants from Italy, Greece, Austria-Hungary.

1907   Largest number of immigrants in United States history arrive: 1,285,349.

1907–1908	"Gentlemen's agreement" with Japanese government excludes Japanese laborers.
1911–1920	Peak arrival years of immigrants from Russia, Belgium, Turkey.
1914–1918	World War I interrupts mass migration from Europe.
1917	Literacy test adopted over President Wilson's veto.
	Beginning of twentieth century immigration policy based on selective "qualitative" group and racial criteria.
1919	Red Scare; Palmer raids; indiscriminate arrests of some ten thousand aliens—including citizens—suspected of radical activities.
1921	Emergency Quota Law ends era of unrestricted immigration.
1924	National Origins Act with discriminatory national and racial quotas adopted. Total quota for Southern and Eastern Europe: 24,222; for Northern and Western Europe: 126,053; Japanese excluded altogether. Debates postpone enactment until 1929.
1952	McCarran-Walter Act reaffirms principles of 1924 Act.
1965	Congress adopts legislation phasing out national origins system by 1968. National origins quotas abolished and replaced by numerical ceilings for immigration on "first come, first served" basis: 120,000 for natives of Western Hemisphere; 170,000 for those from Eastern Hemisphere. New preference categories: relatives, 74%; scientists, artists, 10%; skilled and unskilled labor, 10%; refugees, 6%.

THE NEW IMMIGRATION

Welcome! There is room for all in my ark. This cartoon by Joseph Keppler, which appeared in the German edition of *Puck* for April 28, 1880, reflects the welcome extended to immigrants in the early 1880s. *Puck* was published weekly in both English and German.

INTRODUCTION

The Immigrant is the title of a Charlie Chaplin film from the early days of silent one and two reelers. The film mixes generous portions of slapstick and buffoonery with some moments of acute social comment.

In one scene a boatload of prospective citizens of the land of the free shout, dance, and wave ecstatically as their ship glides into New York harbor past the Statue of Liberty. A few moments later, uniformed United States Immigration Service inspectors shove and kick the motley, expectant steerage passengers into line, rope them in like cattle, and subject them to rough, impersonal scrutiny before sending them ashore.

The movie captures some of the pathos and indignities of the steerage crossing and the confusion of the first hours and days in new, unfamiliar surroundings. Beneath its frantic comedy is the suggestion that the Americans already here are disdainful of the latest arrivals.

Instead of opening this introduction with a reference to the treatment of immigrants in a vintage Chaplin film, its topic could have been dignified by alluding to the Declaration of Independence, which charged King George III with restrictive immigration policies and "obstructing the laws for naturalization of foreigners." These two very dissimilar historical documents remind us that from the beginning of our national history, immigration and immigration policy have been prominent subjects of discussion and debate. And no single issue in American immigration history has been debated as hotly, or as long, or documented as voluminously (there are forty-one volumes of Reports of the Immigration Commission, set up by Congress in 1907 to investigate its nature and problems) as the so-called "new" immigration (1882–1924).

1

Antipathy to certain groups of immigrants, notably Quakers, Catholics, French radicals, and Germans, had flared up from time to time since the days of first settlement. But by 1860 even the most prolonged, best-organized outbreak of anti-foreign agitation, the so-called Know-Nothing movement, had largely subsided. During the Civil War, immigration had so slackened that Congress passed a law which authorized employers to contract for the services of prospective immigrants and prepay their passages. For two decades after the North and South had made peace, an expanding, optimistic nation solicited and welcomed thousands of arrivals each year for its growing cities, factories, mines, and farms.

For the most part, the newcomers were Germans moving chiefly to the Middle West; English, Welsh, and Scotch settling rather evenly throughout the country; Scandinavians heading for the agricultural regions of the upper Mississippi Valley; Irish who concentrated in cities of the northeastern states; Bohemians, French-Canadians, and only a scattering of other nationalities.

In retrospect, these settlers and their descendants were to be known as "old" immigrants, largely Protestant in religion except for many Irish and German Catholics and much smaller numbers of Jews. These immigrants came from the regions of western and northern Europe, close to the seaports from which they booked overseas passage. About five million who arrived before the Civil War and another ten million who landed after the conflict, belonged largely to this "old" migration.

Between 1882 and 1907, the years when post-Civil War waves of immigration crested, the national or ethnic[1] character of the newcomers changed decisively. Eighty-seven percent of all arrivals in 1882 were from northern and western Europe, the rest from southern and eastern Europe. In 1907, about eighty percent of arrivals were from eastern and southern Europe; they were "new" immigrants, most of them Catholics and Jews. Only about twenty percent belonged to the "old" migration from northern and western Europe. Whereas the "old" immigrants were mostly from Great Britain, Ireland, Germany, and Scandinavia, the new immigrants came from Austria-Hungary, Russia, Poland, Italy, and the Balkans, including Greeks, Rumanians, Croats, Serbs, Bulgarians, Montenegrins, Albanians, Slovenes, Slovaks, Ruthenians, and Turks; speaking a variety of languages and dialects until then seldom heard by most Americans. The "new" immigrants (like the old, but of course in propor-

[1] The extensive use of "ethnic group" for what earlier commentators called "race" seems to date from the 1930s, when it may have been introduced to counteract Nazi Germany's prostitution of the concept of "race." I use the term "ethnic group" to refer to groups identifiable by nationality and/or cultural traits such as religion, language, family-life patterns, food, and dress. In this sense, the Irish and the Jews are "ethnic groups." So are black Americans. Those belonging to an ethnic group do not always come from a politically organized state since nationality often preceded statehood. Ethnic group may therefore refer to a national origins group; the term may designate "race" as used loosely during the period covered in this book, it may refer to religion, or to a combination of these attributes.

tionately larger numbers) included many single men and many who were unskilled or planned to return to their European homes after working for a year or two in the United States.

As ever larger numbers of these newcomers with unfamiliar languages, customs, and religious practices congregated in the "ethnic" districts of American cities, "old" Americans — natives, "old" immigrants and their children — became alarmed and blamed the "new" immigration for lowering living standards, depressing wages, creating slums, crime, unemployment, delinquency, and spreading disease. And because the newcomers differed so widely in background and behavior from natives and "old" immigrants, they were seen as *racially* as well as culturally different from the already established majority racial or ethnic mixture.

Americans had long lived with traditions that relegated Indians and Negroes to racially inferior positions. The alleged racial inferiority of the Negro was cited to justify his servitude and, after the Civil War and emancipation, his *de facto* second-class citizenship. Racial arguments also supplied explanations for expropriating Indian lands, and forbidding entry to Oriental immigrants, or depriving them of legal and social privileges accorded members of "white" races.

In the 1880s, racial differences began to be mentioned as basic reasons for the alleged inferiority and unassimilability of Italians, Russians, Jews, Poles, Hungarians, Greeks, and Syrians.

Those who argued for the exclusion of "new" immigrants on racial or ethnic grounds overlooked or were ignorant of earlier periods of our history when the arrival of ethnically different groups had created tensions between the newcomers and old settlers. Thus the Catholic Irish, generally grouped with "old" immigrants, had crowded into eastern seaboard cities in the 1840s much as the "new" immigrants were to do half a century later.[2] The first "green" Irish experienced a compassionate welcome. But as thousands of their poor changed the character of entire neighborhoods, they were met by organized hostility. After their children became Americanized, there followed acceptance, at first grudgingly as fellow citizens, and, finally, as "old" immigrants.[3]

And while Catholic Irish were the chief targets of the organized political nativist movement of the 1880s and 1890s, the American Protective Association (A.P.A.), Irish-Americans had earlier, in the 1870s, aggressively and vocally opposed the Chinese, at first in California, and later wherever Irish-American votes, and occasionally fists, counted.

The Chinese, conspicuously different in race, culture, and language from Anglo-Americans, were the first group to feel the full force of

[2] Oscar Handlin, *Boston's Immigrants* (rev. ed., 1959); Ray Allen Billington, *The Protestant Crusade, 1800-1860* (1938); and John Higham, *Strangers in the Land: Patterns of American Nativism, 1860-1925* (2nd. ed., 1965) are definitive studies of nativism.
[3] For a discussion of the Irish in relation to "old" and "new" immigration, see Milton L. Barron, "Intermediacy — Conceptualization of Irish Status in America," in Barron, *American Minorities* (1957); originally in *Social Forces,* XXVII (March 1949), 256-63.

organized anti-foreign prejudice after the Civil War. After Congress passed the Chinese Exclusion Act of 1882, shutting off completely the entry of Chinese laborers, the "new" immigration bore the brunt of anti-foreign antagonisms.

In that year, a total of 788,992 immigrants entered, the largest number to arrive in a single year during the course of the nineteenth century.[4] The country receiving them was on its way to becoming the world's leading manufacturing nation. Spectacular railroad growth stimulated further industrial and agricultural expansion. Railroads took farmers and immigrants west and returned the products from field, mine, oil well, forest, and steel mill to the urban markets. The simultaneous growth of mass production and large cities were symptoms of both American opportunities and American problems. The frontier would last another eight years; then in 1890, the Superintendent of the Census announced its disappearance.[5]

Labor had to adjust to an impersonal factory system, yet public opinion remained largely hostile to unions and to demands for adequate wages, an eight (or ten) hour day, abolition of child labor, and unhealthful, dangerous, and degrading working conditions. Often the "new" immigrants were held entirely responsible for accepting or even creating substandard, dangerous, and "un-American" working environments in plants, mills, mines, and sweatshops.

Ruthless exploitation of labor and natural resources was justified by the prevailing business philosophy of *laissez-faire*. The Constitution, "science," and the Bible were invoked to prove that regulation of pools, trusts, monopolies, child labor, abominable working or housing conditions, hours of labor, and unrestricted immigration was wrong or foolish.[6]

As debates over the limitation of immigration moved from the seventies into the eighties and nineties, the changed character of the immigrants was emphasized. Many who repeated the traditional complaints that immigrants depressed wages, crowded natives out of jobs, or assimilated too slowly, also argued that the "new" immigrants were racially inferior.

Advocates of the exclusion of new immigrants on racial grounds included courageous, perceptive, and idealistic reformers in various areas of our social and political life. A conspicuous example of this type of man was the economist Edward A. Ross. A supporter of the welfare

---

[4] "Immigration," *Historical Statistics of the United States* (1949).

[5] The American historian Frederick Jackson Turner's 1893 essay entitled "The Significance of the Frontier in American History" advanced the thesis that the frontier had been the greatest molder of American democratic traits and institutions. Some of Turner's disciples, who wanted to exclude the "new" immigrants, found his thesis eminently suitable to support their position. The "new" immigrants, unable to go through the crucible of frontier and wilderness which had created the "old" American virtues, would therefore be less desirable additions to the American population than those whose ancestors had settled on the virgin lands. A succinct discussion of Turner's much-mauled ideas and their influence on the interpreters of American history and social psychology may be found in Carl N. Degler's *Out of Our Past* (rev. ed., 1970).

[6] Morrell Heald, "Business Attitudes Toward European Immigration, 1889–1900." *Journal of Economic History*, XIII (Summer 1953), 291–304.

state and fearless challenger of entrenched conservative views, he was dismissed from a teaching post at Stanford University for his unorthodox ideas.

It will be difficult then to deal evenhandedly and dispassionately with the issues of the times presented in this book and to form unbiased opinions about their spokesmen. To do so means to examine theories of race which often run counter to our convictions about ethnicity and the nature of American nationality and life. It means that we must try to fathom what social, psychological, economic, or political motives led a man to advocate doctrines and actions outmoded or discredited by subsequent events and by changing ideas.

Parallels with urban problems of the 1970s will be obvious. Then as now, thousands of newcomers arrived in congested cities to complicate and exacerbate already vexatious industrial and social conditions. Many of the migrants had little or no experience with the requirements of city living. They competed with native labor, worked for low wages, created health hazards, and changed the character of entire neighborhoods as well as of city politics.

But the new immigrants *alone* were hardly responsible for mushrooming urban predicaments: filthy streets, corrupt politics, unregulated slums, lack of municipal hospitals, defective and inadequate transportation, sewer and water systems, child labor, unregulated sweatshops, prostitution, and philosophies condoning subhuman working and living conditions for unskilled and semiskilled laborers. If the immigrants contributed more than their proportional share of slum dwellers and sweated labor to many eastern cities, it was because so many of them — men, women, and even children — were forced to take whatever employment, housing, and wages were offered.[7]

Another charge against the newcomers was their preference for city life. Few of them pioneered on farms and cultivated frontier lands. To do so would have meant to go against a worldwide trend of population movements from farm to city. Germans, Englishmen, and Scandinavians, who had always furnished many of America's farmers, after 1900 also found employment more readily in the industrialized East than the agricultural South and West. Greek and Italian immigrants from rural districts cleaned and cooked in restaurants in many American cities or peddled fruits and vegetables to city housewives who lacked efficient refrigeration and storage space for perishable foods.

Immigrant concentrations in certain districts and occupations made them highly visible and gave rise to some of the most enduring popular stereotypes of American folklore, stage, and magazine humor. Hungarians, Slovaks, and Poles predominated in some mining operations; Russian Jews in cigar making and clothing manufacture. Everywhere the "new" immigrants performed the common, unskilled labor. Yet the

[7] Oscar Handlin, *The Uprooted* (1951).

greatest number of industrial recruits for expanding plants and businesses came from domestic labor.[8]

What was new and disturbing in the 1880s and 1890s was not only the increasing ethnic diversity, which certainly added to the burdens of city officials and complicated urban reforms, but also the magnitude and complexity of the social issues confronting the nation. Their scale and spread, and the number of people involved, were beyond the capacity of existing local social and philanthropic institutions to handle.[9]

Labor unions had at first opposed only the importation of contract labor, but by 1896 the American Federation of Labor also opposed free immigration. Until the first years of the twentieth century, Southern and Western congressmen welcomed unrestricted immigration as a boon for their sections, but by 1907 they too supported restrictionist legislation. The accommodationist Negro leader Booker T. Washington urged Southern white leaders in 1895 to look to Negroes for the prosperity of the South rather than to "those of foreign birth and strange tongue and habits."[10] The American Protective Association, a secret, anti-Catholic organization which reached its peak political influence in 1894, appealed to native and "old immigrant" Protestants and supported immigration restriction.[11]

Some "old" immigrants like the Scotch-Irish, Huguenots, and British-Americans formed fraternal and historical societies to assure each other and their critics of their sturdy American loyalties and sometimes to publicize their differences from "new" hyphenates related to them by language, religion, or nationality. For instance, Scotch-Irish societies made a point to differentiate between Protestant and Catholic Irish. And American Jews of German descent preferred to be known as Israelites or Hebrews to avoid being lumped with East European Jews who crowded into the downtown quarters of many large cities.[12] Newly organized hereditary and veterans organizations like the Daughters of the American Revolution made patriotic and military ritual and instruction a kind of "secular religion." They warned against the foreign ideologies of anarchism, communism, and socialism which were associated in their members' minds with the "new" immigration.[13]

The most telling attack against the "new" immigration was mounted by a group of intellectual New Englanders and Midwesterners. These men taught in universities, were prolific contributors to popular

[8] William S. Bernard, *American Immigration Policy — A Reappraisal* (1950); Isaac A. Hourwich, *Immigration and Labor* (1912).
[9] Carl N. Degler, *Out of Our Past: The Forces That Shaped Modern America* (1959).
[10] "Atlanta Exposition Address," Leslie H. Fishel, Jr. and B. Quarles, *The Negro American: A Documentary History* (1967).
[11] Donald L. Kinzer, *An Episode in Anti-Catholicism: The A.P.A.* (1964).
[12] John J. Appel, "The New England Origins of the American Irish Historical Society," *The New England Quarterly*, XXXIII (December 1960), 462–75; and "Hansen's Third Generation Law and the Origins of the American Jewish Historical Society," *Jewish Social Studies*, XXIII (January 1961), 3 – 20.
[13] Wallace Evan Davies, *Patriotism on Parade, The Story of Veterans' and Hereditary Organizations in America* (1955); Wesley Frank Craven, "Differing Descendants," in *The Legend of the Founding Fathers* (1956).

magazines, represented their states in Congress, and, as has been noted previously, often were active in the reform-minded Progressive movement (c. 1890–1917).[14]

In 1890 Columbia University professor, Richmond Mayo-Smith, set the tone of discussions for many years to come when he distinguished sharply between "colonists" and mere "immigrants." An important supporter of the Immigration Restriction League founded by influential New Englanders in 1894, Mayo-Smith announced in his *Emigration and Immigration* that only Americans whose ancestors had arrived before 1783 belonged to the "proprietors" and were guardians of American institutions from alien influences. All others were immigrants, in the country "by invitation" of its original settlers. The League waged a persistent campaign for the literacy test and spread the notion that the "new" immigrants were inferior, hard to assimilate, and fundamentally different. Its aim was to check the "undesirable, illiterate" new immigrant without keeping out the immigration from northwestern Europe. The twenty-five-year contest over the literacy test publicized and gave respectability to the principle of selection by racial or ethnic origin. The literacy test clause was not incorporated into immigration legislation until 1917, when wartime fears, demands for "100 percent Americanism," and suspicions of "hyphenated" Americans enabled its supporters to override President Wilson's second veto of the bill. In the same year, just as America was about to enter World War I, Congress also passed an Immigration Act that codified all previously passed legislation and added other exclusions.

This legislation, adopted in an atmosphere charged with xenophobia and wartime emotions, marked the end of our traditional immigration policy.[15] The Acts of 1921 and 1924, described in the last selection of this book, began the policy of severe restriction through a discriminatory national origins quota system which lasted until 1965.[16]

Not all who wrote and lectured about the immigrants had lost faith in the assimilative capacities of American society or believed certain races to be "inferior." They pointed out that charges made against "new" immigrants had almost without exception also been leveled against "old" immigrants before they had had time to assimilate. Many asserted that the immigration problem was inextricably bound up with conditions fostered by uncontrolled industrial and urban growth; by the general lack of provisions for the protection of workers and the unemployed; by inadequate or nonexistent services to check, prevent, or alleviate overcrowding, industrial injuries, and health hazards; that neither native workers nor immigrants in the United States were protected by the social legislation eventually adopted by advanced industrial nations.

Besides, the shift in composition between "old" and "new" im-

---

[14] Barbara Miller Solomon, *Ancestors and Immigrants: A Changing New England Tradition* (1956).

[15] Oscar Handlin, *The American People in the Twentieth Century* (1963).

[16] Roy L. Garis, *Immigration Restriction* (1927) is a book-length, frankly pro-restrictionist study of opposition to and regulation of immigration into the United States.

migrants was gradual. The "new" did not exceed the number of "old" arrivals until 1896, while agitation for curtailing or shutting off immigration began in earnest in the 1880s.

But the voices of those who noted similarities between the "old" and "new" immigration and desired to deal with the immigration issue as part of the vexing problem of an unregulated industrial order were seldom heeded. Ethnocentric studies, including the widely quoted *Reports of the United States Immigration Commission,* published in 1910, encouraged the publication of many other books, articles, pamphlets, and cartoons of a sharply partisan nature. Like slavery, the immigration issue touched so many sensitive interests — economic, political, social, cultural, religious, racial, nationalist, emotional — that most writers concerned with it either tried to prove the inferiority of the "new" immigrants or exaggerated their positive qualities or "contributions" to American life.[17] The appearance of this highly partisan literature dealing with immigration issues led the sociologist C. Wright Mills to assert in his 1959 study, *The Sociological Imagination,* that the chief stimulus for the fledgling science of sociology in the United States had been provided by the immigration problem.

Even those who believed in the ultimate absorption of the "new" immigrants or their children generally assumed that a stable American society was also a homogeneous society. Only a small group, of whom John Dewey and Horace Kallen are best known, argued that cultural diversity was compatible with American democracy.

The "Red" hunts and "Americanization" drives of World War I embittered many immigrants and their children.[18] Feeling themselves rejected and suspected, they became more conscious of being members of a nationality or ethnic group in the United States, often more than they had felt in the old home.

Some groups organized defense organizations to engage in anti-defamation activities, including the promotion of historical studies designed to demonstrate the loyalty of each group and its "contributions" to American life. Others, their developing ethnic and nationalistic sensitivity heightened by the war, turned to minority political nationalist movements.

Between 1921 and 1941, a new generation of historians — themselves children of immigrants — turned to immigration history.[19] Not content to see the immigrants merely as a problem, they studied them for their significance for the larger trends in American history. Since the retirement of Carl Wittke, Theodore C. Blegen, and George M. Stephenson in the 1950s and 1960s — Marcus Lee Hansen died in 1938 — Profes-

[17] Jeremiah W. Jenks and W. Jett Lauck, *The Immigration Problem* (1917) is largely a reprint of the "Abstract of the Reports of the U.S. Immigration Commission."
[18] William Preston, Jr., *Aliens and Dissenters: Federal Suppression of Radicals, 1903–1933* (1963).
[19] O. Fritiof Ander, "Four Historians of Immigration" in Ander, ed., *In the Trek of the Immigrants, Essays Presented to Carl Wittke* (1964). Edward N. Saveth, *American Historians and European Immigrants, 1875–1925* (1948). Marcus L. Hansen, *The Immigrant in American History* (1940) and *The Atlantic Migration, 1607–1860* (1940). Carl Wittke, *We Who Built America* (1939 rev. ed., 1964).

sor Oscar Handlin of Harvard has become a commanding influence in the writing and study of immigrant history. Blending sociological and historical techniques, his books and articles and those of his students present the larger patterns of the immigrants' story without neglecting the immigrants' own psychic tensions and adjustment patterns. Broadened interest in immigration studies has also shifted emphasis from America-centered interpretations to the sending countries, particularly Europe, and to migration as a consequence of population growth and industrialization.[20]

Furthermore, ethnic and immigrant studies receive renewed attention because of heightened interest in the problems of the city and the Negro's attempt to construct a "usable" past for himself.[21] Investigators of discrimination and prejudice, rejecting theories arising from any single point of view, reexamine the full spectrum of race, religion, and national origins in search of causes of group conflicts and of institutional arrangements for the perpetuation and strengthening of ethnic identity and minority culture in a democratic society.[22]

Historians and sociologists agree that the melting pot has not produced a pressure-cooked, homogeneous population. Even the children and grandchildren retain some differences, suggesting such analogies as a "triple melting pot" or a salad bowl.[23] Life in the large urban areas — and most Americans will live there soon if present demographic trends continue — stripped children of immigrants of many of their parents' habits and values, yet recreated the ethnic group as "a new social form."[24] Candidates for political office do not overlook the possibility that ethnic voting is still vital.[25] In short, the cycle of self-definition, partial withdrawal, and, ultimately, almost complete acculturation to dominant life styles with retention of subculture loyalties and values that has been — and to some extent still is — the experience of many "new" immigrants and their descendents, has not stopped.[26] We are still, as the French observer Crevecoeur noted, a "promiscuous breed,"

[20] Carlton C. Qualey, "Immigration as a World Phenomenon," in Henry S. Commager (ed.), *Immigration and American History* (1961). Frank Thistlethwaite, "Migration from Europe Overseas in the Nineteenth and Twentieth Centuries," In Herbert Moller (ed.), *Population Movements in European History* (1964). Charles Price (ed.), *Australian Immigration, A Bibliography and Digest* (The Australian National University, 1966). Brinley Thomas (ed.), *The Economics of International Migration* (1958). See also the latter's article "Migration" in *The International Encyclopedia of the Social Sciences* (1968).

[21] J. Iverne Dowie, "The American Negro: An Old Immigrant on a New Frontier," in Ander, *In the Trek of the Immigrants*. Oscar Handlin, *The Newcomers: Negroes and Puerto Ricans in a Changing Metropolis* (1959). Richard Bardolph, *The Negro Vanguard* (1959).

[22] Milton M. Gordon, *Assimilation in American Life* (1964) reviews theories of assimilation and constructs a convincing "model" of subcommunity life in the U.S.A. today. See also Marshall Sklare and Joseph Greenblum, "The Lakeville Studies": I, *Jewish Identity on the Suburban Frontier: A Study of Group Survival in the Open Society;* and II, *The Edge of Friendliness: A Study of Jewish-Gentile Relations,* by Benjamin B. Ringer (1967).

[23] Carl N. Degler, *Out of Our Past* (1959); Will Herberg, *Protestant-Catholic-Jew* (1955).

[24] Nathan Glazer and Daniel Patrick Moynihan, *Beyond the Melting Pot: The Negroes, Puerto-Ricans, Jews, Italians and Irish of New York City* (1963).

[25] Louis L. Gerson, *The Hyphenates in Recent American Politics and Diplomacy* (1964); Lawrence H. Fuchs (ed.), *American Ethnic Politics* (1968).

[26] John J. Appel, "American Negro and Immigrant Experience: Similarities and Differences." *American Quarterly,* XVIII (Spring 1966), 95–103. Reprinted in Leonard Dinnerstein and Frederic C. Jaher (eds.), *The Aliens, A History of Ethnic Minorities in America* (1970).

but we have not become *one* out of many — oblivious of all ethnic, racial, or religious differences and preferences.

Once again, as between 1882 and 1924 when the "new" immigration provided the impetus, Americans are forced to ask themselves whether groups and individuals from different ethnic, racial, and (less important today, it seems) religious backgrounds can live, work, and play together in our cities in amity. Or at least, whether respect and tolerance for each other's traditions and values are possible in a country often referred to as "a nation of nations." We are, in sum, reopening the debate (see document 11) over the nature of American nationality: Whether the United States can be truly pluralistic or will remain at bottom the preserve of white, Anglo-Saxon, "Aryan" Protestants.

Since the eighteenth century, the conception of the United States as an evolving society, a blend of ethnic groups, religions, races, and cultures, has been a vital element of American thought. It gave rise to the metaphors of America as the "asylum of the oppressed" and the "melting pot of nations."[27]

Another tradition, not as strongly developed as the first until the latter half of the nineteenth century, appeared soon after the creation of the national government. Less optimistic, less ecumenical, this ideology stressed differences between original settlers and "immigrants" and did not celebrate religious, racial, and ethnic crossbreeding.[28]

While the first ideology often paid tribute to the Anglo-Saxon origins of American government and customs, it lacked a biological emphasis and envisioned a great, new, mixed American "race."[29] The second conception of American nationality stressed the English basis of American institutions. In the third quarter of the nineteenth century, it also adopted heredity and race as chief determinants of national character and destiny.

This narrower conception of American nationality, compounded of notions of racial superiority, exclusiveness, suspicion of urban values, anti-Semitism, anti-Catholicism, and xenophobia, dominated the debates over immigration restriction and regulation from 1882 to 1924. Its supporters thought they were defending cherished patterns of living and the *status quo* against the invasion of foreign ideologies imported by men with sharply different social, cultural, and religious standards.

Our courts have held, since World War II, that discrimination against fellow citizens based on race, color, and religion is illegal. But quotas or exclusions based on racial, ethnic, or religious grounds for the regulation of immigration and emigration are common in other independent nations. The repudiation of the national origins quotas by the passage of the United States Immigration Act of 1965 repaired,

[27] Philip Gleason, "Melting Pot: Symbol of Fusion or Confusion?" *American Quarterly*, XVI (Spring 1964), 20–46.

[28] John Higham, "Emma Lazarus' *The New Colossus*," in Daniel J. Boorstin (ed.), *An American Primer* (1968).

[29] Thomas F. Gossett, *Race: The History of an Idea in America* (Schocken, 1965).

in the words of President Lyndon B. Johnson, "a deep and painful flaw in the fabric of American justice" which had violated the principle that a man ought to be valued and rewarded "on the basis of his merit alone." Yet critics quickly charged after the act had taken full effect in 1968 that it substituted justification by skill for justification by skin and encouraged the perverse flow of skilled labor and professional and scientific manpower, known as the "brain drain," from still developing to already developed countries. The new preference system, others complained, favored those whom the national origins quota system had excluded! The president of a group calling itself the American Irish Immigration Society told a *New York Times* man in March, 1968, "The Irish can never stand satisfied until the disgraceful blot of the present United States Immigration law is erased."

The movement to slow down and regulate immigration, seen from the vantage point of the 1970s, appears as a culmination of fundamental nineteenth-century trends in the nation's maturation and consolidation. The historian John Higham has described one of these basic changes in American culture as its transformation "from boundlessness to consolidation."[30] Set in motion sometime during the 1850s, this trend manifested itself by intense feelings of alarm over the chaotic growth of industry and cities and attendant concern over the problems of law enforcement, sanitation, education, and health care. There emerged a sense that the American people must define what was American, what alien. Many older Americans were uneasy, even fearful over what appeared to be the breakdown of ethnic homogeneity and the loss of old values.

Professor Higham's broad thesis accommodates the facts revealed by the study of the new immigration. It explains why university-educated experts in population and race studies, status-conscious scions of old families, and xenophobic small-towners who supported the American Protective Association and the Ku Klux Klan, agreed ultimately on the necessity and virtue of a homogeneous, even intolerant society. Unlike those liberals who by the 1900s had begun to accept the necessity for regulation of immigration but insisted on the continued ability of American society to assimilate the newcomers, those favoring their exclusion on racist and nativist grounds saw themselves as the true defenders of traditional ideals of the United States as the most perfect society on earth, its customs and values fixed, to be protected from alien assault and perversion.

For the historian of the new immigration, all answers are by no means "in." For instance, he would like to know whether there is a relationship between the growing political conservatism of most American workers, the immigrants' belief in economic opportunity, and the rejection by many white American labor groups of identification with

[30] John Higham, *From Boundlessness to Consolidation: The Transformation of American Culture, 1848–1860* (Ann Arbor: William L. Clements Library, 1969), p. 26.

other economic-interest groups like Negro Americans. Did black Americans have to wait forty years after the closing of the gates to mass immigration before their demands for equal treatment as men, citizens, and workers received a hearing? Has mass European immigration been replaced by a new pattern involving Negroes, Puerto Ricans, Mexicans, and poor southern whites, who today predominate in the unskilled, dirty, badly paid occupations and form segregated societies?[31] Has competition between immigrant and native, immigrant and immigrant speeded up the destruction of traditions of pride in craft and love of place which linger in more stratified, less mobile societies? Or are these developments the result of advancing technology in all societies? Is the view of a more stable, less competitive American way of life before the age of the new immigration a nostalgic, retrospective vision of times and places that never existed?

Historians would also like to know why, forty-four years after the adoption of clearly discriminatory immigration quotas, the reasoning which supported their enactment seems no longer acceptable to the majority of the American people. What factors have influenced the changed outlook as reflected by opinion polls and legislation pertaining to race, religion, and ethnicity: Additional years of formal schooling for many Americans, with greater exposure of the college trained among them to the social sciences and their relativistic conceptions of ethnicity, race, and culture? Increased sympathy for and understanding of minority groups of all kinds — sexual, social, ethnic, and racial? A widespread realization that racial hatred and conceptions of racial superiority have in our time led to unprecedented brutalities and mass murder? Have advances in communications and transportation technology weakened ethnic loyalties and prejudices and fostered the growth of a blander, more tolerant, more homogeneous mass culture? Are more Americans self-conscious about the "image" of the United States as a "nation of nations" and the international champion of democratic cultural, racial, and ethnic pluralism? Have adroit educational and promotional activities of various ethnic, racial, and religious anti-defamation and defense organizations begun to bear fruit in changed attitudes and behavior?

History supplies few straightforward answers to such questions. Sociologists and psychologists are busy as never before administering questionnaires and programming computers to chart racial and ethnic loyalties and animosities. Historians must be satisfied with possible explanations rather than quantified proofs. This anthology will serve its purpose if it confronts the reader with basic issues of the new immigration as they were perceived by contemporaries, stimulates him to apply ideas suggested in its pages to crucial trends and events of our times, and encourages him to read more in immigrant history and sociology.

[31] Seymour Martin Lipset and Reinhard Bendix, *Social Mobility in Industrial Society* (1966), pp. 104–6.

PART I

ARRIVAL AND ADJUSTMENTS

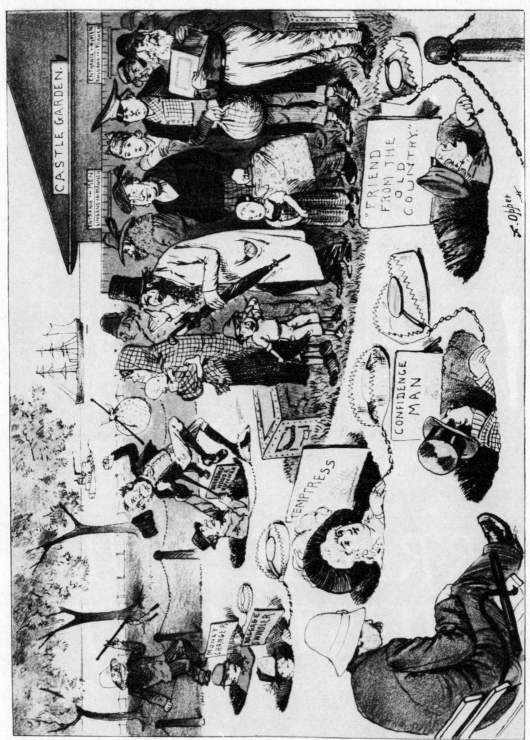

Castle Garden Emigrant Catchers. Frederick Opper, who drew this cartoon for *Puck*, later became one of the fathers of the comic strip. Such ethnic stereotypes were common in the late nineteenth century. Although Opper was sympathetic to the plight of the new immigrant, his portraits are nonetheless condescending and paternalistic.

1

LOOKING BACK-WARDS: AN OLD IMMIGRANT WATCHES THE ARRIVAL OF THE NEW

The first federal immigration station in the United States was built on tiny Ellis Island in New York Bay to replace the state-operated Castle Garden, a former entertainment center at the tip of Manhattan Island where the immigrants had been received for many years.

When Danish-born Jacob A. Riis (1849–1914) described the differences and similarities between immigrants who arrived with him in 1870 and the national types he saw debarking at Ellis Island thirty-three years later, he was already known as an able crusading journalist and "muckraking" reformer. He did not entirely transcend the contemporary stereotypes picturing Negroes as happy and carefree, Jews as miserly, and Italians as emotional. But his autobiography, *The Making of an American* (1901), revealed the then by no means widely held opinion that culture and environment, not race and heredity, were primary forces conditioning all immigrants. In the following article Riis asks questions repeatedly posed in contemporary writings about the new immigrants. Could these newcomers, of different "blood," with non-Anglo-Saxon values and traditions, and standards of living below those of most American workers, assimilate as readily as the Germans, Englishmen, and Scandinavians who had made up the bulk of the old immigration? Would these newcomers push the growing heterogeneity of American life to the point where native morals and democratic values were endangered? That is, would they "melt" into American society or remain in ethnic ghettoes, aliens in tongue and spirit, undigested lumps among our people?

In 1903, many Americans shared the apprehensions revealed by these questions. But not all who did so had Riis' faith in the power of American institutions, particularly the public school, to enable the new immigrants to escape from foul tenements and starvation wages and to become full participants in the duties and privileges of American life and citizenship.

For an illustration of the *padrone* system mentioned by Riis, see selection 5, from *The Biography of a Bootblack* by Rocco Corresca, pages 56–64.

IN THE GATEWAY OF NATIONS

Jacob A. Riis

How it all came back to me; that Sunday in early June when I stood, a lonely immigrant lad, at the steamer's rail and looked out upon the New World of my dreams; upon the life that teemed ashore and afloat, and was all so strange; upon the miles of streets that led nowhere I knew of; upon the sunlit harbor, and the gay excursion-boats that went to and fro with their careless crowds; upon the green hills of Brooklyn; upon the majestic sweep of the lordly river. I thought that I had never seen anything so beautiful, and I think so now, after more than thirty years, when I come into New York's harbor on a steamer. But now I am coming home; then all the memories lay behind. I squared my shoulders against what was coming. I was ready and eager. But for a passing moment, there at the rail, I would have given it all for one familiar face, one voice I knew.

How it all came back as I stood on the deck of the ferry-boat plowing its way from the Battery Park to Ellis Island. They were there, my fellow-travelers of old: the men with their strange burdens of feather beds, cooking-pots, and things unknowable, but mighty

FROM *The Century Magazine*, LXV (March, 1903), pp. 674–82.

of bulk in bags of bed-ticking much the worse for wear. There was the very fellow with the knapsack that had never left him once on the way over, not even when he slept. Then he used it as a pillow. It was when he ate that we got fleeting glimpses of its interminable coils of sausage, its uncanny depths of pumpernickel and cheese that eked out the steamer's fare. I saw him last in Pittsburg, still with his sack. What long-forgotten memories that crowd stirred! The women were there, with their gaudy head-dresses and big gold ear-rings. But their hair was raven black instead of yellow, and on the young girl's cheek there was a richer hue than the pink and white I knew. The men, too, looked like swarthy gnomes compared with the stalwart Swede or German of my day. They were the same, and yet not the same. I glanced out over the bay, and behold! all things were changed. For the wide stretch of squat houses pierced by the single spire of Trinity Church there had come a sky-line of towering battlements, in the shelter of which nestled Castle Garden, once more a popular pleasure resort. My eye rested upon one copper-roofed palace, and I recalled with a smile my first errand ashore to a barber's shop in the old Washington Inn, that stood where it is built. I went to get a bath and to have my hair cut, and they charged me two dollars in gold for it, with gold at a big premium; which charge, when I objected to it, was adjudged fair by a man who said he was a notary — an office I was given to understand was equal in dignity to that of a justice of peace or of the Supreme Court. And when, still unawed, I appealed to the policeman outside, that functionary heard me through, dangling his club from his thumb, and delivered himself of a weary "G'wan, now!" that ended it. There was no more.

"For the loikes o' them!" I turned sharply to the voice at my elbow, and caught the ghost of a grimace on the face of the old apple-woman who sat disdainfully dealing out bananas to the "Dagos" and "sheenies" of her untamed prejudices, sole survival in that crowd of the day that was past. No, not quite the only one. I was another. She recognized it with a look and a nod.

A curiously changing procession has passed through Uncle Sam's gateway since I stood at the steamer's rail that June morning in the long ago. Then the tide of Teutonic immigration that peopled the great Northwest was still rising. The last herd of buffaloes had not yet gone over the divide before the white-tented prairie-schooner's advance; the battle of the Little Big Horn was yet unfought. A circle drawn on the map of Europe around the countries smitten with the America-unrest would, even a dozen years later than that, have had Paris for its center. "To-day," said Assistant Commissioner of Immigration McSweeney, speaking before the National Geographic Society last winter, "a circle of the same size, including the sources of the present immigration to the United States, would have its center in Constantinople." And he pointed out that as steamboat transportation developed on the Danube the center would be more firmly fixed in the East, where whole populations, notably in the Balkan States, are catching the infection or having it thrust upon them. Secretary Hay's recent note to the powers in defense of the Rumanian Jews told part of that story. Even the Italian, whose country sent us half a million immigrants in the last four years, may then have to yield first place to the hill men with whom kidnapping is an established industry. I mean no disrespect to their Sicilian brother bandit. With him it is a fine art.

While the statesman ponders the perils of unrestricted immigration, and debates with organized labor whom to shut out and how, the procession moves serenely on. Ellis Island is the nations' gateway to the promised land. There is not another such to be found anywhere. In a single day it has handled seven thousand immigrants. "Handled" is the word; nothing short of it will do.

"How much you got?" shouts the inspector at the head of the long file moving up from the quay between iron rails, and, remembering, in the same breath shrieks out, "Quanto moneta?" with a gesture that brings up from the depths of Pietro's pocket a pitiful handful of paper money. Before he has it half out, the interpreter has him by the wrist, and with a quick movement shakes the bills out upon the desk as a dice-thrower "chucks" the ivories.

Ten, twenty, forty lire. He shakes his head. Not much, but — he glances at the ship's manifest — is he going to friends?

"Si, si! signor," says Pietro, eagerly; his brother of the vineyard — oh, a fine vineyard! And he holds up a bundle of grapesticks in evidence. He has brought them all the way from the village at home to set them out in his brother's field.

"Ugh," grunts the inspector as he stuffs the money back in the man's pocket, shoves him on, and yells, "Wie viel geld?" at a hapless German next in line. "They won't grow. They never do. Bring 'em just the same." By which time the German has joined Pietro in his bewilderment en route for something or somewhere, shoved on by guards, and the inspector wrestles with a "case" who is trying to sneak in on false pretenses. No go; he is hauled off by an officer and ticketed "S. I.," printed large on a conspicuous card. It means that he is held for the Board of Special Inquiry, which will sift his story. Before they reach the door there is an outcry and a scuffle. The tide has turned against the Italian and the steamship company. He was detected throwing the card, back up, under the heater, hoping to escape in the crowd. He will have to go back. An eagle eye, with a memory that never lets go, has spotted him as once before deported. King Victor Emmanuel has achieved a reluctant subject; Uncle Sam has lost a citizen. Which is the better off?

A stalwart Montenegrin comes next, lugging his gun of many an ancient feud, and proves his title clear. Neither the feud nor the blunderbuss is dangerous under the American sun; they will both seem grotesque before he has been here a month. A Syrian from Mount Lebanon holds up the line while the inspector fires questions at him which it is not given to the uninitiated ear to make out. Goodness knows where they get it all. There seems to be no language or dialect under the sun that does not lie handy to the tongue of these men at the desk. There are twelve of them. One would never dream there were twelve such linguists in the country till he hears them and sees them; for half their talk is done with their hands and shoulders and with the official steel pen that transfixes an object of suspicion like a merciless spear, upon the point of which it writhes in vain. The Syrian wriggles off by good luck, and to-morrow will be peddling "holy earth from Jerusalem," purloined on his way through the Battery, at half a dollar a clod. He represents the purely commercial element of our immigration, and represents it well — or ill, as you take it. He cares neither for land and cattle, nor for freedom to worship or work, but for cash in the way of trade. And he gets it. Hence more come every year.

Looking down upon the crowd in the gateway, jostling, bewildered, and voluble in a thousand tongues — so at least it sounds, — it seems like a hopeless mass of confusion. As a matter of fact, it is all order and perfect system, begun while the steamer was yet far out at sea. By the time the lighters are tied up at the Ellis Island wharf their human cargo is numbered and lettered in groups that correspond with like entries in the manifest, and so are marshaled upon and over the bridge that leads straight into the United States to the man with the pen who asks questions. When the crowd is great and pressing, they camp by squads in little stalls bearing their proprietary stamp, as it were, finding one another and being found when astray by the mystic letter that brings together in the close companionship of a common peril — the pen, one stroke which can shut the gate against them — men and women who in another hour go their way, very likely never to meet or hear of one another again on earth. The sense of the impending trial sits visibly upon the waiting crowd. Here and there a masterful spirit strides boldly on; the mass huddle close, with more or less anxious look. Five minutes after it is over, eating their dinner in the big waiting-room, they present an entirely different appearance. Signs and numbers have disappeared. The groups are recasting themselves on lines of nationality and personal preference. Care is cast to the winds. A look of serene contentment sits upon the face that gropes among the hieroglyphics on the lunch-counter bulletin-board for the things that pertain to him and his:

Röget Fisk

Kielbara

Szynka Gotowana

"Ugh!" says my companion, home-bred on fried meat, "I wouldn't eat it." No more would I if it tastes as it reads; but then, there is no telling. That lunch-counter is not half bad. From the kosher sausage to the big red apples that stare at one — at the children especially — wherever one goes, it is really very appetizing. The *röget fisk* I know about; it is good.

The women guard the baggage in their seats while *pater familias* takes a look around. Half of them munch their New World sandwich with an I-care-not-what-comes-next-the-worst-is-over air; the other half scribble elaborately with stubby pencils on postal cards that are all star-spangled and striped with white and red. It is their announcement to those waiting at home that they have passed the gate and are within.

Behind carefully guarded doors wait the "outs," the detained immigrants, for the word that will let down the bars or fix them in place immovably. The guard is for a double purpose: that no one shall leave or enter the detention — "pen" it used to be called; but the new regime under President Roosevelt's commission has set its face sternly against the term. The law of kindness rules on Ellis Island; a note posted conspicuously invites every employee who cannot fall in with it to get out as speedily as he may. So now it is the detention-"room" into which no outsider with unfathomed intentions may enter. Here are the old, the stricken, waiting for friends able to keep them; the pitiful little colony of women without the shield of a man's name in the hour of their greatest need; the young and pretty and thoughtless, for whom one sends up a silent prayer of thanksgiving at the thought of the mob at that other gate, yonder in Battery Park, beyond which Uncle Sam's strong hand reaches not to guide or guard. And the hopelessly bewildered are there, often enough exasperated at the restraint, which they cannot understand. The law of kindness is put to a severe strain here by ignorance and stubbornness. In it all they seem, some of them, to be able to make out only that their personal liberty, their "rights," are interfered with. How quickly they sprout in the gateway! This German girl who is going to her uncle flatly refuses to send him word that she is here. She has been taught to look out for sharpers and to guard her little store well, and detects in the telegraph toll a scheme to rob her of one of her cherished silver marks. To all reasoning she turns a deaf and defiant ear: he will find her. The important thing is that she is here. That her uncle is in Newark makes no impression on her. Is it not all America?

A name is cried at the door, and there is a rush. Angelo, whose destination, repeated with joyful volubility in every key and accent, puzzled the officials for a time, is going. His hour of deliverance has come. "Pringvilliamas" yielded to patient scrutiny at last. It was "Springfield, Mass.," and impatient friends are waiting for Angelo up there. His countryman, who is going to his brother-in-law, but has "forgotten his American name," takes leave of him wistfully. He is penniless, and near enough the "age limit of adaptability" to be an object of doubt and deliberation.

In laying down that limit, as in the case of the other that fixes the amount of money in hand to prove the immigrant's title to enter, the island is a law unto itself. Under the folds of the big flag which drapes the tribunal of the Board of Special Inquiry, claims from every land under the sun are weighed and adjusted. It is ever a matter of individual consideration. A man without a cent, but with a pair of strong hands and with a head that sits firmly on rugged shoulders, might be better material for citizenship in every way than Mr. Moneybags with no other recommendation; and to shut out an aged father and mother for whom the children are able and willing to care would be inhuman. The gist of the thing was put clearly in President Roosevelt's message in the reference to a certain economic standard of fitness for citizenship that must govern, and does govern, the keepers of the gate. Into it enter not only the man's years and his pocket-book, but the whole man, and he himself virtually decides the case. Not many, I fancy, are sent back without good cause. The law of kindness is strained, if anything, in favor of the immigrant to the doubtful advantage of Uncle Sam, on the presumption, I suppose, that he can stand it.

But at the locked door of the rejected, those whom the Board has heard and shut out, the process stops short. At least, it did when I was there. I stopped it. It was when the attendant pointed out an ex-bandit, a black and surly fellow with the strength of a wild boar, who was wanted on the other side for sticking a knife into a man. The knife they had taken from him here was the central exhibit in a shuddering array of such which the doorkeeper kept in his corner. That morning the bandit had "soaked" a countryman of his, waiting to be deported for the debility of old age. I could not help it. "I hope you — " I began, and stopped short, remembering the "notice" on the wall. But the man at the door understood. "I did," he nodded. "I soaked him a couple." And I felt better. I confess it, and I will not go back to the island, if Commissioner Williams will not let me, for breaking his law.

But I think he will, for within the hour I saw him himself "soak" a Flemish peasant twice his size for beating and abusing a child. The man turned and towered above the commissioner with angry looks, but the ordinarily quiet little man presented so suddenly a fierce and warlike aspect that, though neither understood a word of what the other said, the case was made clear to the brute on the instant, and he slunk away. Commissioner Williams's law of kindness is all right. It is based upon the correct observation that not one in a thousand of those who land at Ellis Island needs harsh treatment, but advice and help — which does not prevent the thousandth case from receiving its full due.

Two negroes from Santa Lucia are there to keep the stranded Italian company. Mount Pelée sent them hither, only to be bounced back from an inhospitable shore. In truth, one wintry blast would doubtless convince them it were so indeed; their look and lounging attitude betray all too clearly the careless children of the South. Gipsies from nowhere in particular are here with gold in heavy belts, but no character to speak of or to speak for them. They eye the throng making for the ferry with listless unconcern. It makes, in the end, little difference to them where they are, so long as there is a chance for a horse trade, or a horse, anyway. There is none here, and they are impatient only to get away somewhere. Meanwhile they live at the expense of the steamship company that brought them. They all do. It is the penalty for differing with the commission and the Board of Special Inquiry — that and taking them back whence they came without charge.

The railroad ferries come and take their daily host straight from

Ellis Island to the train, ticketed now with the name of the route that is to deliver them at their new homes, West and East. And the Battery boat comes every hour for its share. Then the many-hued procession — the women are hooded, one and all, in their gayest shawls for the entry — is led down on a long pathway divided in the middle by a wire-screen, from behind which come shrieks of recognition from fathers, brothers, uncles, and aunts that are gathered there in the holiday togs of Mulberry or Division street. The contrast is sharp — an artist would say all in favor of the newcomers. But they would be the last to agree with him. In another week the rainbow colors will have been laid aside, and the landscape will be the poorer for it. On the boat they meet their friends, and the long journey is over, the new life begun. Those who have no friends run the gantlet of the boarding house runners, and take their chances with the new freedom, unless the missionary of "the society" of their people holds out a helping hand. For at the barge-office gate Uncle Sam lets go. Through it they must walk alone.

However, in the background waits the universal friend, the padrone. Enactments, prosecutions, have not availed to eliminate him. He will yield only to the logic of the very situation he created. The process is observable among the Italians to-day: where many have gone and taken root, others follow, guided by their friends and no longer dependent upon the padrone. As these centers of attraction are multiplying all over the country, his grip is loosened upon the crowds he labored so hard to bring here for his own advantage. Observant Jews have adopted in recent days the plan of planting out their people who come here, singly or by families, and the farther apart the better, with the professed purpose of diverting as much of the inrush as may be from the city, and thus heading off the congestion of the labor market that perplexes philanthropy in Ludlow street and swells the profits of the padrone on the other side of the Bowery. Something of the problem will be solved in that way, though not in a year, or in ten. But what of those who come after? There is still a long way from the Bosporus to China, where the bars are up. Scarce a Greek comes here, man or boy, who is not under contract. A hundred dollars a year is the price, so it is said by those who know, though the padrone's cunning has put the legal proof beyond their reach. And the Armenian and Syrian hucksters are "worked" by some peddling trust that traffics in human labor as do other merchants in food-stuffs and coal and oil. So the thing, as it runs down, everlastingly winds itself up again. It has not yet run down far enough to cause anybody alarm. Three Mediterranean steamers and one from Antwerp, as I write, brought 4700 steerage passengers into port in one day, of whom only 1700 were bound for the West. The rest stayed in New York. The padrone will be able to add yet another tenement, purchased with his profits, to his holdings. In 1891, of 138,608 Italians who landed on Ellis Island, 67,231 registered their final destination as Mulberry street, and Little Italy in Harlem.

Many an emigrant vessel's keel has plowed the sea since the first brought white men greedy for gold. Some have come for conscience sake, some seeking political asylum. Long after the beginning of the last century, ship-loads were sold into virtual slavery to pay their passage money. Treated like cattle, dying by thousands on the voyage, and thrown into the sea with less compunction or ceremony than if they had been so much ballast, still they came. "If crosses and tombstones could be erected on the seas, as in the Western deserts," said Assistant Commissioner McSweeney in the speech before referred to, "the routes of the emigrant vessel from Europe to America would look like crowded cemeteries." They were not made welcome. The sharpers robbed them. Patriots were fearful. The best leaders of American thought mistrusted the outcome of it. The very municipal government of New York expressed apprehension at the handful, less than ten thousand, that came over in 1819–20. Still they came. The Know-nothings had their day, and that passed away. The country prospered and grew great, and the new citizens prospered and grew with it. Evil days came, and they were scorned no longer; for they were found on the side of right, of an undivided Union, of financial honor, stanch and unyielding. To them America had "spelled opportunity." They paid back what they had received, with interest. They saved the country they had made their own. They were of our blood. These are not; they have other traditions, not necessarily poorer. What people has a prouder story to tell than the Italian? Who is more marvelous than the Jew? But their traditions are not ours. Where will they stand when the strain comes?

I was concerned only with the kaleidoscope of the gateway, and I promised myself not to discuss politics, economics, or morals. But this is very certain: so long as the school-house stands over against the sweat-shop, clean and bright as the flag that flies over it, we need have no fear of the answer. However perplexed the to-day, the to-morrow is ours. We have the making of it. When we no longer count it worth the cost, better shut the gate on Ellis Island. We cannot be too quick about it — for their sake. The opportunity they seek here will have passed then, never to return.

2
TENEMENT HOUSE CONDITIONS

During the last two decades of the nineteenth century many American college students signed up for courses about charity organization, better housing, settlement houses, and other plans to solve the problems of growing cities. For instance, Harvard offered a course in the Ethics of Social Reform (called "drainage, drunkenness and divorce" by the students) which inspired some young men and women to work for reform on the local level by living in the slums among immigrants and Negroes.

Many young practical idealists stayed only a year or two, in the manner of Peace Corps and Vista volunteers today. Some devoted a lifetime to settlement work. Among the best known of this group are probably Jane Addams, Mary McDowell, Robert Woods, Graham Taylor, and Lillian Wald.

Lillian Wald (1867–1940), who read the paper which is reprinted here to a New York convention of the National Council of Jewish Women in November 1896, was a pioneer in public health nursing. The visiting nurse service she began in an apartment on the Lower East Side of New York in 1893 eventually grew into the notable Henry Street Settlement. She served on many welfare commissions, helped in the creation of the United States Children's Bureau, and crusaded for women suffrage. Both Lillian Wald and Jane Addams left autobiographical writings about their experiences. Miss Addams' *Forty Years at Hull-House* and Miss Wald's *The House on Henry Street* and *Windows on Henry Street* may suggest to some readers that perhaps the urban poor and the slums of the late nineteenth century and of today have much in common.

Furthermore, Miss Wald addressed herself to one of the central philosophical and moral issues of her times — and ours. How to explain the lot of the poor, the slum dweller, the less privileged, the apparent failure? Some Americans, remembered as Social Darwinists, applied the doctrines of struggle and survival of the fittest to social and economic issues. The fit rose to the top; the poor, dirty, and ignorant were the inevitable losers in the game of life. In contrast, Miss Wald chose the metaphor of "mutualism," a biologist's term for organisms living together in harmony and to each other's advantage, to describe her vision of a just and humane society. Phillips Brooks (1835–1893), from whose writings she borrowed the term, was a New England Episcopal clergyman well known for sermons that encouraged the faithful to reconcile the Darwinian hypothesis with the teachings of Christianity.

CROWDED DISTRICTS OF LARGE CITIES

Lillian Wald

In bringing a report of the crowded districts of great cities to you to-day, I am aware that whatever I could say to impress you would be from the personal experiences and conclusions obtained by some years' residence in such a quarter of one city only, or the less valuable observations made as visitor and stranger to like districts in other cities. But before we enter into particular descriptions or the ethics of their existence anywhere, I would remind you of the real insight that may be obtained by all, not only of the congested regions of great cities, but of the causes and results of their existence.

Such important education is to be found in the clear reading of official reports, vital statistics, labor reports and annuals, tenement-house reports, police records, school reports, charity organization and institution year-books — such literature as may be had for the asking, yet is, in many ways, the important social, history-making literature of our times. Then, more interesting, perhaps, are the evidences that may be found in stories and magazine articles, by the residents of social settlements and missions, the thoughts of visiting philosophers, who, eager to know the crowds, have camped for a time in these back-yards of our great cities, and

FROM *Proceedings of the First Convention of the National Council of Jewish Women, held at New York, November 15–19, 1896* (Philadelphia, 1897).

have given the fruit of their meditations to others. There are the deeper works of students of sociology, who have looked upon these crowded districts as human laboratories, coldly, or inspired by a higher than scientific interest, a human one, to know the people, the men and the women, the children and the conditions that make "masses" and "districts" and "East Sides," have brought their experiences to scholarly consideration. Knowing that these things are, they must next see why, and perhaps have thus furnished what has been likened to the ophthalmoscope, the instrument that made it possible to see into the eye, and thus revealing the disease, gave the physician the opportunity of curing it. Furnished with such an ophthalmoscope, the physician of social wrongs may heal and take from modern civilization its most baneful growth.

Such reading as this suggests might be called "dry," mere skeletons of figures to be recognized only by people "interested in that sort of thing," literature not to be found in any but the specialist's library. But it is not dry; and even if so, it is a literature that concerns us all, more than any news compiled, and if awaiting readers now, will some day *force* the attention of the whole world. But read each figure a human being; read that every wretched unlighted tenement described is a *home* for people, men and women, old and young, with the strength and the weaknesses, the good and the bad, the appetites and wants common to all. Read, in descriptions of sweat-shops, factories, and long-hour work-days, the difficulty, the impossibility of well-ordered living under the conditions outlined. Understanding reading of these things must bring a sense of fairness outraged, the disquieting conviction that something is wrong somewhere, and turning to your own contrasting life, you will feel a responsibility of the *how* and the *why* and the *wherefore*. Say to yourself, "If there is a wrong in our midst, what can *I* do? What is *my* responsibility? Who is to blame? Do *I* owe reparation?"

All this is a plea for the intelligent reading of the things that pertain to the people of the crowded districts of *all* cities, that something more may be given to the subject than the few moments in a convention's program; that the suggestion may be made, and the thought carried home that more carefully-prepared witnesses are yours to be called up at all times and for the asking.

Agreeing that a common condition must be produced by a common cause, in order to understand its life anywhere, we need only confine ourselves to a study of the crowded district that is familiar to the witness you have called up to-day. As it is a crowded district of our metropolis, it belongs to all the country, and therefore is yours. It presents, only in a greater degree due to an unfortunate geographical condition, the state of people anywhere who are poor, and unlearned, and clannish, and strange. Though a sweeping classification is an easy way of tabulating, it is unjust to say of our neighbors, the greater number of whom are Russian or Polish Jews, that they are the least clean, and most unlovely and ungrateful, and terms put more harshly. This is a generalization to be denied, excepting to put out that an equal degree of ignorance and an equal depth of poverty will create the same conditions of filth and unattractiveness, whether found among Russians, Italians, or Irish. It is more often a cause of astonishment to us to find polished brass and scrubbed floors under difficult circumstances than to find inexcusable uncleanliness; and the lessons of patience and affection and courtesy are constantly presented to us by them.

Let us take for definite allusion three wards of New York, those in my immediate neighborhood, the seventh, tenth, and eleventh, populated, according to the last census, by 190,388 people, covering 504 acres — something over 377 people to each acre — including in these figures, however, one division of 32 acres, — Second, Columbia, Rivington, and Clinton Streets (between Avenues B and D south of Second Street) — with 986.4 persons to every acre of the 32, representing the most crowded community on the face of the earth.

Now, I do not know what these figures may bring up to your vision; to one who has seen the portion of the city referred to, in summer and winter, by day and by night, they bring up a dark picture of this small part of an English-speaking city, peopled by nearly 200,000, the greater number of whom speak an unknown tongue; foreigners with foreign standards of living, often having been forced to leave their homes; coming here with the inheritances of mistrust and a low standard of living; coming, though, with high hopes of a new start, in a country where education is possible to all, where the poorest may be respected, and where democracy sways; coming here likewise with lower aspirations, or no aspiration at all; brought here in the expectation of profiting by the wealth and generosity of the country, without a thought of contributing to it. These parasites are a small number in the very large tenement-house population of New York, which is eight-fifteenths of the whole.

If to dwell upon the newly-arrived would divert our discussion to that of the restriction of emigration, let us rather consider what those who are here already actually experience: what opportunities the children of the poorly-paid and unskilled laborers have; what effect it may have upon the circulation of the body politic, to infuse into its arteries the life-current of people who live day after day under conditions disadvantageous to growth, civic, physical, and moral.

The crowding you may realize; the language of the street is a jargon; the signs over the places of business are frequently in Hebrew with misspelled English translations, occasionally furnishing grim humor to the foreigner, for here *you* are the foreigner yourself, in your own home. Your eye is met by such business notices as: "Marriages legally performed inside," and a competitor offers to perform the same service cheaper than any one else, and in most approved style; and by the hand organ, with or without a monkey — the greatest delight of the street — and the prettiest dancing of the prettiest, most neglected looking children that can be seen anywhere. The houses are dilapidated, filth-infected, and dark: old houses, once the homes of the wealthy and fastidious, converted to present uses by a process of decay, and maintained at the smallest expense possible to bring the largest returns possible; rear tenements, built upon what was left of the city lots of front houses; houses facing the street, utilizing the space that was once a garden; tall new tenements built upon single city lots 25 x 100 feet, with four families to a floor, each single lot house tenanted by 20 to 24 different families, with saloon and one store generally in the basement. This variety of tenement-house, the familiar "double-decker," occupying 86 to 90 per cent of the lot's depth, is in many ways worse than the old remodeled residence, its air-shafts and basement furnishing contaminated air and frequent fires to its one hundred to one hundred and fifty inhabitants. The houses are not fire-proof, though provided with fire-escapes; and almost constant use of kerosene, the darkness, the many children, the occupations in the houses, are causes of frequent fires. The Fire Department records show that in this third of the population of New York, the fires are more than one-half the whole number, and deaths and accidents are very frequent.

There are two so-called "model tenements" in the region we are describing, and in one part of this area, several houses occupied by single families, and at least two streets wide and favorably situated; but there are blocks almost entirely covered by buildings, one (brought up before the Tenement-House Commission of 1894) covering 93 per cent of the total area, and a total area of 34 blocks showing over 78 per cent built upon.

The very small space between the houses, sometimes only 18 inches, is utilized for the drying of clothes and as a receptacle for refuse of all kinds. The narrow street-space is a jostling, shoving, push-cart market for the selling of over-ripe fruit, fish, vegetables, etc. The halls of the houses are so dark that groping is the method of movement in them, and the little girl described hers when she lost something and said: "Oh! I'll find it at night when the gas is lighted." The nurses never overcome the fear of trampling on the children in the hall or on the street, a sound warning them when to tread carefully, or sometimes out of the darkness a tiny hand on the railing shocking suddenly with the sense of accident averted. It is not uncommon to go in daytime into the closet-room with candle in hand, in order to be able to see the patient at all; nor is it uncommon to go at night and see 10 or 11 people occupying two small rooms — people who have been working all day, freed for the night's rest, stretched on the floor, one next to the other, dividing the pillows, different sexes, not always of the same family, for there are "boarders," who pay a small sum for shelter, among their own, the family glad of the help toward paying the rent. The price of rooms in the most wretched basement in the rear-tenements is so high in comparison with the wage earned that it is for those who have employment based on something like regular incomes about one-fourth of the whole. But it must be remembered that few trades give employment all the year round. We hear more often than any other plaint that of the uncertainty of having a roof: the failure comes so often, and with it the "dispossess paper," that the sight of the household effects on the side-walk following its presentment is too common to collect a crowd, where crowds collect quickly.

During the hot months of July and August is the time to observe a crowded district at its worst. The vermin and the heat drive the people to the streets, which are crowded with these unfortunates the greater part of the night. Mothers sit on the curbstone with nursing babies, and the cool of the door-stone is coveted for a pillow: or, the refreshment of sleep on the roof or in the courts between the houses is sought, unless, indeed, the odors of the closets there are worse than the vermin or the heat within.

On the other hand, within these tenements are sometimes found the most scrupulously kept rooms; plants by the windows, happiness, and a real home; courtesy, devotion, and charity, such as one may seek for among the elect of the earth, and reverence; sufficient evidence of the original nobility of character, which can remain high despite all discouragements.

But the more frequent picture is that of the overcrowded rooms, denying the privacy and sacredness of home-life. Outside the house there is almost no park or playground for the children — nothing but the sidewalks and streets. Games for the boys are of necessity reduced to "leap-frog," "craps," or tossing pennies.

School-time comes, and the population increases so rapidly that, with the best intentions, it seems impossible to provide place, and with a less keen sense of responsibility, the worst occurs. An unlettered, indifferent parent, exhorted and then informed that education is compulsory, finally does exert himself to claim the place for his children in the school, to learn that compulsory education acts and truant officers are superfluous matters, since there is no place in the school for his children. There is considerable discrepancy in the figures giving the number of children out of school at present. To avoid inaccuracy, I will only state that there are many thousands — 400 in one school alone of the region I am making special reference to to-day.

The law says that the child must be in school until fourteen, that he or she may not be employed under that age; and as nothing more than the parent's testimony is required to give the child to the shops, the temptation to perjury is apparent.

We come now to the sweat-shops, labor in which is the principal occupation of our neighbors. Where a "union" has been established and is strong, the work-day may be ten hours; where the trade is unorganized (and that is more likely to be among the unskilled, therefore the poor, therefore the least educated) the work-day is more often fourteen hours. Have you heard of the diseases most prevalent among people who work in contaminated air, and then go home to sleep under the same conditions? In the Nurses' Settlement consumption is spoken of as the "tailors' disease."

Have you watched the drive, drive, drive of men and women at the machines, over cigar or cigarette making? Have you peeped down into the cellars, and seen the rags sorted, the shirts made, the washing done, shoes cobbled, cheese and bread made? Have you watched the making of the collars, passementerie, clothing, cloaks, and artificial flowers, the curling of feathers, the steaming of hats, the manufacture of neckties and boxes, the production of the whole long list of necessaries and luxuries for other people? Have you watched where the workers were laboring under the indifference or absenteeism of the employer? — working, working, working, until the pain in watching the ceaseless strain becomes unendurable and you cry out against the inhumanity of it all? Cry out because you can see how impossible it is for these men and women to have the leisure or the strength to rear their children into stalwart men and women, into citizens with intelligent reasoning of how to govern themselves or to choose their governors.

I bring up again for the thousandth time in excuse for uncleanliness or a low standard of social or moral ethics, when such exist, no education, crowded, dark rooms for a home, no time or opportunities for proper cleanliness, no opportunities for healthful pleasures; grinding work and small pay; no work, and then the necessaries of life a gift. "Charity covers a multitude of sins," but does not wipe them out. Anxiety lest ends might not meet, excludes even conversation in the home. All negatives are shifts to make ends meet; laws are evaded, breeding a contempt for law and order. Finally, there is the dumb discontent provoked into loud resentment; the distrust of class, creating leaders of their own who know what they have not, who can comprehend what they want. There can be no denial that the poor are poorer, that what is called "class feeling" has been intensified. This last election made many people see for the first time that there was what one side called revolt, that a "campaign of education" seemed necessary to save our institutions.

I am fully conscious of not bringing to you a complete picture of even the small section of one city; there is too much to be said. Many dark pictures have been omitted. There has been no reference to the peddlers who have no trade, only the instinct of trade, many of whom, however, are skilled workmen with no demand for their skill, obliged in dull seasons to do *anything*, and that means a basket, a box, or a push-cart, with some small outlay for stock; not that the occupation is desirable, but because that is all that is left, and work in the busy season has not paid enough to carry the family over.

Also should I like to dwell upon the affection and sobriety of our neighbors; the gratitude for courtesies, and the response to efforts for education among the children; the honest return of money loaned to them; the eagerness to show their patriotism, as instanced when the Russian brought his violin to us to show how well he had learned "our" national air, and forthwith played "After the ball is over" — he had come here three years ago, when that seemed the song of America — and the pride in having attained citizenship, when they do, framing and hanging the official testimony on the wall, though the vaccination certificate has been thus honored also.

I would not be reporting the crowded district of any city unless the many philanthropic efforts for relief of actual physical suffering were brought up. So numerous are these efforts in this city that it would appear as if no thought or plan of charity had been omitted, until the wise administration of charity and the study of the people who prefer to receive gratuitously instead of to work, has become a profession. We see from our East Side point of view the charities in operation, and their results, good or bad — good, if they are educational in any way (but this is a subject distinct in itself). You have not more than a suggestion of the features of life in a neighborhood. This avails nothing, however, if you do not seek for confirmation and elaboration of these suggestions; realize with me that a crowded district in its entirety is too great for single handling, too serious for dismissal in an afternoon paper.

I might appeal to your self-interests to recognize the close relationships between the crowded districts of great cities and the more fortunate regions; might prove that the danger of infected and unsanitary tenements are your direct affairs; tell of the things made in rooms where infectious diseases were or had been; — evidences of the dying consumptive working at cigarettes; of the filthy basement where the sick girl lay, and where candy was being made; of the felt slippers sewed in the room where scarlet-fever and diphtheria were; or of the servant-girl coming home to visit in similar circumstances and returning to the baby.

There is a higher, juster appeal that your own sense of responsibility will make to you. If the homes are poor, build others; not as charities, but as investments, satisfied with a four per cent return, in planning which have the comfort and education of the tenants in view. The testimony of people here and elsewhere who have had practical experience, proves that such investments pay in every way, and that almost all have given a satisfactory return upon the investment of money. Time and education, both of which are slow, are required to alter many things; but you can begin it for others and yourselves. You can help the labor difficulty by comprehending what a fair condition of labor is. If you have no "consumers' league" to receive your pledge, pledge its principles to yourself. If there is a strike, try to discover both sides of the question, not only the one vulgarly holding your butter, but the other's grievance also; not rejoicing in the workingman's failure without understanding (if that is possible) what was behind the discontent. Be fair enough to help that workingman in his way, if you can see that his way is right. Listen to the cries that come from crowded districts. Their people are patient, and are not demanding overmuch. The respectable workingman, the father of the children, is wanting work, and when he does work, sufficient pay for it, to be sure of a roof and life-sustaining food and some leisure, to know a world that is not only working and eating and sleeping. Don't you see how the lack of that must bring the begging letter, at first the shame-faced appeal for help that has not been earned, and then the indifference, and then the going-down and all the things debasing to manhood? It is *work* and *sufficient pay* for it that is the just demand. Last week a woman asked for some aid, and a few days later wrote that she would not require any, as God had sent her husband two days' work.

Do all that you can to make public sentiment for fair play in work and pay. Carry the thought of the workers with you when you are shopping. If the cry from the crowded district is for food, you will give that; but in relieving, give wisely and adequately, and see if the cause of that cry can be removed.

Last of all, you would be helping the labor and the unemployed question by making domestic service desirable, recognizing the need here also of stated hours, freedom, and occasional privacy. There is often as great a distance between drawing-room and kitchen as between up-town and down-town.

Let me retire as witness now and ending, bring Phillips Brooks' voice back to you for inspiration and right understanding of our mutual obligations: "The universal blunder of this world is in thinking that there are certain persons put into the world to govern, and certain others to obey. Everybody is in this world to govern, and everybody to obey. Men are coming to see that beyond and above this individualism there is something higher — Mutualism. Don't you see that in this Mutualism the world becomes an entirely different thing? Men's dreams are after the perfect world of Mutualism; men will think of it in the midst of the deepest subjection to the false conditions under which they are now living. This is new life, where service is universal law."

3

EXPLOITATION OF WOMEN

A majority of immigrants were below thirty years of age, and the largest group of all between sixteen and twenty-one. Many of these newcomers were unaccompanied women, lacking protection and unable to speak, read, or write English. On the one hand, this large pool of single girls found needed employment in domestic service and provided American housewives with the essential household help native white girls were reluctant to undertake. On the other hand, the immigrant girl in need of immediate employment was a ready prey for those who tried to entice or force her into commercialized prostitution. Private employment agencies, then known as "labor intelligence offices," frequently exploited the immigrant girl forced to depend on their services and sometimes supplied personnel for houses of prostitution.

In the selection which follows a social worker and a court official analyze the relationship between increased immigration, an apparent rise in urban prostitution in which immigrant girls played a conspicuous part, and the role of private employment agencies for domestic labor in the spread of commercialized vice.

Frances A. Kellor (1873–1952) who wrote the following article and the rejoinder to a court probation officer's criticism of her indictment of employment bureaus as accomplices in prostitution rings, was a Fellow of the New York City College Settlement Association and Chief Investigator of New York State's first Bureau of Industries and Immigration from 1910 to 1913. In 1904, her *Out of Work* (revised edition, 1915), a study of employment agencies for immigrant girls, was followed by an investigation of agents luring Negro girls into the cities. This investigation, in turn, led to the founding of the National League for the Protection of Negro Women, one of the charter groups, in 1911, for the organization known today as the National Urban League. Likewise, the National Council of Jewish Women began in 1893 to devote efforts to the protection of immigrant girls. In 1910, the National Young Women's Christian Association founded its International Institute for Young Women to protect immigrant girls from criminal exploitation.

It should be remembered that many of our grandfathers did not approve of women who concerned themselves with the sordid, largely hidden, at least not publicly mentioned, aspects of social problems like prostitution. Furthermore, calls for an end to the exploitation of domestic labor were in some quarters regarded as interference with the "right to work" and with private enterprise. In sum, the issues of the protection of immigrant women, of finding a ready supply of cheap domestic labor before the days of labor-saving appliances, and of facing up to the existence of vice and crime in still quite puritanical but increasingly anonymous large cities puzzled and shocked many Americans, particularly when those who discussed them in public were "decent" middle- and upper-class women.

IMMIGRATION AND HOUSEHOLD LABOR

Frances A. Kellor

FROM "Immigration and Household Labor" and "The Intelligence Office as a Feeder for Vice." *Charities,* XII (February 6, 1904), pp. 151–2; (March 5, 1904), pp. 255–6.

Immigration, the intelligence office, and household labor are factors which almost any householder who employs servants knows, are very closely related. In any further restriction of immigration, the effect upon the home and the servant problem will have to be considered.

New York City has in the neighborhood of 300 intelligence offices which supply chiefly domestic servants; one-third of these depend almost entirely upon the foreign-born, or American-born children of foreign parents for their supply, while another third depend quite entirely upon "green" girls or new arrivals — girls who have never been in this country and know little or no English. There is at present enough of such a supply to give at least a fair and in many instances a very good remuneration to these offices.

The supply of servants in New York, owing to competition, more attractive features of other occupations, and social obscurity and limitations in time and privileges in household work, is far inferior to the demands. One thing is inevitable. Unless conditions are improved so they will correspond more nearly with other trades, the American home cannot depend upon American labor. Indeed, it does not now, for the only hope of a *continued* supply comes from the immigrant class. This is especially true for general housework, for only the less desirable girls and new arrivals will go willingly into this work, which is less skilled than that of the waitress, maid, cook, etc., is heavier work and not so well paid. This supply is especially desirable from the standpoint of the employer. Although the immigrant so frequently lacks training, she is strong, asks few privileges, is content with lower wages and long hours, and has no consciousness of a social stigma attaching to her work.

But between the householder and the immigrant stands the intelligence office, which is both a blessing and a curse. To understand this demand for immigrants for households, glance at the methods of some of these offices. They cannot begin to meet the demand normally, so they import girls. They have agents who induce the girls to come over here upon the most extravagant promises; they prepay their passage, and they enter into collusion with boarding-houses to supply them with girls. Upon inquiries during the summer at agencies we were told "the proprietor is abroad getting a supply of girls for the winter." The immigration authorities refuse to release girls directly to these agencies, but they will give them to responsible relatives and friends, so the office has an army of enlisters who pose as such and secure the girls.

Even though such offices in an untold measure rob and defraud and extort money from these poor immigrants, they are still public servants, for they do bring the employer into contact with the employé, and because they know the language, customs, and habits.

But some offices are not wholly for the employers' interest. A conservative estimate shows that in New York alone they send some 10,000 or more a year into prostitution, thus depriving households of valuable help, for many go blindly and unwillingly. Their hold upon girls who know only their language is such that, once placed, they leave at the request of the office and are placed over again, thus increasing the fees of the office. They pilfer and rob homes and bring their plunder to the office to be disposed of, because the office treats them well and pays them. The office initiates them in deceit, lying, and fraud, so that when the home gets them they are no longer simple peasant girls, ready to work and honest, but instilled with all sorts of impossible ideas. One poor Jewish girl left place after place because an office which had imported her, told her the streets were "lined with gold," and she still hoped to find it.

These offices run lodging-houses and are often in tenements. When the girls come from the dirty, unsanitary, crowded, immoral conditions in which they have been kept until the office gets ready to place them, they may go into homes diseased and germ-laden and moral lepers. Employers who patronize better offices turn aside, feeling it is not their problem. It is their problem, for after awhile the girl learns the language, gets experience, and if she does not get into a disreputable house she gets into a better office and the employer gets, a "rounder" — intemperate, dishonest, inefficient, and impertinent — whose first step was the intelligence office which trained her.

This is only a pen picture of the vast system which honeycombs employment of immigrant women in household labor in New York.

The Irish, German and English immigrants no longer arrive in such great numbers, for these have no such elaborate systems. The statistics of female steerage passengers show that for 1903 there were: Swedes, 16,220; Austro-Hungarians, 58,027; Russians, 43,158, and of Germans only 15,225, Irish, 19,334, and English, 10,626. The offices which control these first three classes are those which have in largest measure such methods as have been given.

Anxious householders ask are there no remedies for such a condition, for they realize that this great source — the only source of supply for general housework girls — cannot be cut off and diverted. Yes, there are remedies — there is the free employment agency, but so long as it cannot speak the language of these immigrants, and has such a small appropriation that it cannot employ competent agents, it cannot compete with "native" offices. Then there are immigrant homes, doing a vast amount of good. These have missionaries at Ellis Island and they save and train many girls, but they do not cooperate with each other but are, rather, rivals. Even when these homes take girls in, the agencies employ spies or send out runners, who try to get hold of them.

What is needed is co-operation. An organization acting as a clearing-house which by efficient business methods can wrest this supply from these disreputable offices and place them in good positions. It must understand their methods and worst them by equally efficient but honest ones. Single-handed, these immigrant homes have been struggling with the problem for years, but the writer believes only an efficient business organization on a clearing-house plan, ready to give unsparingly in co-operation with all honest agencies and equally ready to expose every dastardly fraud and diversion of labor into ruinous channels, would meet the need. These offices combine, they exchange girls, they co-operate with boarding-houses and relatives where these immigrants lodge, they actually pay boarding-houses fifty cents or one dollar each for every girl they send; they work shipping companies to furnish transportation and then get this back with interest from the girls when they get them positions. These methods must be thoroughly understood, and only a combination understanding them can meet the combine which is operating them.

[*Correspondence relating to the article follows.*]

TO THE EDITOR OF CHARITIES:

I have read with interest Miss Kellor's article on "Immigration and Household Labor" in your February's magazine, and only regret that a large and important subject has been handled briefly. There are one or two points in especial on which it is desirable that the public should have fuller information. Miss Kellor states that "a conservative estimate shows that in New York alone they (certain intelligence offices) send some ten thousand or more (immigrant servant girls) a year into prostitution." It would be valuable, nay, one may say, it is urgent, that the sources of this appalling statement should be given. To follow the placement by employment bureaus of 10,000 girls each year for several years is so huge a task that any one who has done it should have full credit, and should not hide her light under a bushel by merely mentioning the estimate and giving no further particulars. It is not to be supposed that the offices guilty of this traffic give themselves away, and hunting down illegal practices in the careful and individual way that is the only justification for authoritative statement is a piece of work for Teutonic indefatigability.

Have those offices which are schools for crime and feeders of vice been reported to the district Attorney's office? That seems a more immediate public duty than the establishment of a clearing-house for domestic servants. The evidence that warrants an indictment so serious as that in Miss Kellor's article, certainly imposes a request for official investigation.

ADA ELIOT,
Probation Officer, Court of Special Sessions

TO THE EDITOR OF CHARITIES:

In reply to Miss Eliot's questions, the writer would say that her facts were gained in the following ways: First, every intelligence office in New York City was visited in the capacity of employer and employé, so that we know the tone of every office. From this we selected about fifty which seemed questionable. There were others, but we could not take them up. To these fifty, men were sent in the guise of representatives of disreputable houses. In this way they became acquainted with the office men, talked to them, spent money freely, and were treated as any other such patrons. Thirty of these offices in this way admitted that they furnished girls for such purposes, said they had regular contracts and gave their "usual fee." Money was actually paid these offices to ascertain their good faith in the matter. Among these offices, these men found some that were disorderly houses, others that were Raines Law hotels, and still others that had their own places in the country or elsewhere. Not only this, but we had men in the guise of "runners" and visitors at Ellis Island to fathom the methods of the importation, and from every immigrant home we gathered experience and facts of people who for many years have been fighting these conditions single-handed. Through our own advertising and special agents, we learned of the extent to which negro girls are imported from the South and green country girls brought into the city. Not only from the girls whom we met in offices and with whom we associated as employers have we heard these facts, but the threads have been gathered up in workhouses, reformatories, and rescue places for women. So close a bond did we find between offices and questionable houses that we learned that such houses are the financial backers of such offices, and pay the costs of any prosecution against the office. So absolute is the negligence in New York City that in only *three* of the many offices where we asked for girls for men's club-houses were we asked any questions. When there is such utter indifference and girls are daily sent out of the city with absolute strangers to the office, both men and women, no one can estimate the extent of this practice. When we went into offices where they would not sell girls for questionable houses, but accepted gifts from street walkers in return for allowing them to mingle with the working-girls, and we saw the silk-gowned, powdered, painted women taking the bare-headed peasant girls out to walk or to lunch, and then disappearing — then, again, we could not estimate the extent. When offices maintain expensive systems of runners, and men of such a stamp for runners, who gather in women from such a multitude of places that one doubts if any ignorant girl is safe — we say again the extent cannot be estimated. It is not a question of 1,000 or 10,000 girls which this investigation has demonstrated, but the fact that there are within this city so many agencies and they have such a fine network of systems that the doors of the former are always open, and the lines of the latter always ready to close about the homeless, friendless, penniless girl out of work — a time when she can least resist temptation, and especially when it is attractively presented.

These are some of the methods and some of the facts, and there are others which the writer deems too sacred to give to any but those who are willing to take up a further study and attempt to meet conditions. To such, our records and affidavits are open and if they do not substantiate our estimate, they at least render it exceedingly difficult to disprove it.

Why has the district attorney's office not these facts? Some of them will be found there, for two convictions were obtained last fall, and some licenses revoked. But New York has no adequate law under which we can prosecute these offices. Offices bribe, cajole, threaten, nag, and lead girls into these places by presenting the attractive side, but their defense is that the girl consented or wanted to go. When we urge an agency and lodging-house in the midst of these offices, it is because we know from personal observation and experience the skill with which they entrap girls and evade the responsibility, and know that some one must stand ready always to rescue girls from them. Not punishment after the girl has been lead astray, but prevention of their nefarious work, must be the means of forcing them into honest methods or out of business. When this city has a law which adequately protects these girls from the frauds and immorality of these offices, the complaints will be sent to their proper place. Much of our information, while establishing beyond a doubt the truth of our assertions, is not legal evidence, and was not gathered with that in view. We deemed the word of our man sufficient when he brought us a receipt for money paid for a girl for such a house, but legal evidence requires corroboration. Any attempt to make our evidence legal under the present law would be a waste of money.

We have not believed that with all this evidence in hand it was necessary to follow each case. When an office informs us that it has sent — girls to such a house and received — fees, we have not thought it necessary to follow that case, for we had no reason to doubt its word. We are willing, in the face of any other information as accurate as ours, to reduce our estimate and our regret is as great as the reader's that so large a one seems inevitable. We have no theories to prove and no hobbies to ride, and our judgment has been as dispassionate as the facts before us permitted.

FRANCES A. KELLOR,
*Fellow College Settlements
Association*

4

VICTIMS OF
FRAUD
AND DECEIT

How many Americans knew what it was to arrive in a strange country, with little or no knowledge of its language and customs — how to buy a railroad ticket, apply for a job, send a letter — daily habits the native takes for granted?

The federal government only admitted the immigrant; thereafter he was expected to find his own place in society. Few states provided special services to aid the newcomer's adjustment. Private philanthropic organizations rendered some services but were unable to cope with all the problems of new arrivals. Once settled in a predominantly ethnic section of a large city, the newly arrived immigrant was practically isolated from the native.

And because he was often helpless and ignorant of American ways, he became the victim of deceit and trickery. He was overcharged, underpaid, defrauded, exploited.

Gino C. Speranza (1872–1927), the American-born son of Italian immigrants, served for many years as legal advisor to Italian Consuls General in the United States, became a member of the New York State Immigration Commission, and of various other public committees and agencies. Despite his sympathetic understanding of the newly arrived immigrant's condition revealed in this article, Speranza in the 1920s joined that small but vocal group of immigrants and children of immigrants who, apparently from a compulsive need to prove their patriotism, joined the chorus of those who trumpeted the supremacy of Nordic, "Aryan" stocks and espoused "racial self-effacement" of new immigrants and their descendants in the name of Americanization.

Speranza's sound recommendations for protecting the immigrant from exploitation and fraud, written in 1910, should be compared with

Thaddeus Sleszynsky's call for enlisting the aid of the second generation of immigrants in the assimilative process, selection 10, pages
102–8.

HANDICAPS IN AMERICA

*Gino C.
Speranza*

When the subject of "immigration" comes up for discussion, either
in casual talk at table, or in the more serious magazine articles,
the discussion is almost invariably confined to the question, "Should
the admission of foreigners be restricted or not."

The immigrant is called "a problem" by those who stop to
think of him at all, and if his presence in this country is deemed
tolerable, it is only in his capacity of workman — a negotiable asset
on the troubled balance sheet of capital and labor. Rarely is he
thought of as a possible citizen, whose children, with the passing
of a few years, will be an inherent part of the strength, or weakness,
honor or dishonor of the nation.

Whose business is it to know how the stranger fares, what
influence he is giving out, what feeling he is acquiring toward the
new country, through the forces in it with which he is in contact —
often forces of malignity, greed, or indifference?

There is a singular gap in the chain of responsibility for the
immigrant, — for our alien population.

Congress, through the Bureau of Immigration, has the right to
say who shall be admitted to the country and to decide how many
may come in at any time. In the same governing body is vested
the right to send out of the country any foreigner who is shown
to be a striking menace or an undeniable burden, — the type of
immigrant who has brought into our current speech the memorable
phrase "undesirable citizen." Even though this power is in the
federal government, the state in some cases must find the delinquent
person and establish the charges against him.

With these purely technical and legislative relationships the
"responsibility" of the federal government ends; the real, human,
moral, mental, *actual* responsibility is upon the state; primarily and

FROM *The Survey* (January 1,
1910), pp. 465–72.

overwhelmingly upon the state of New York. A few facts and figures from the census and the reports of investigators, will show the extent of this responsibility.

In 1908 there were about a half million aliens within the state boundaries, who had been here less than five years.

Three-fifths of all immigrants to this country are set down on the New York docks, and in a recent investigation one-sixth of the arriving army expressed the intention of remaining in New York.

The census of 1905 showed many significant figures regarding the aliens then within the state, e.g. 1,004,320 had been here for periods of from one year upwards. In ten counties seven per cent of the population were aliens; in four counties over six per cent, and in seven counties five per cent.

So different from our native population, in race, customs, habit of thought and way of living — this mass of "foreigners," fed into the state from the federal government's hopper at Ellis Island, must be assimilated by the state. It is within this boundary that the greater numbers of the alien people make their homes, settle their families, find work, seek recreation and become a vital part, with their human influence, for better or worse, of the neighborhood, town or city which has become their harbor.

To fail to reckon with this power in its play on industrial, social and political conditions now existing in the state, would mean to omit from consideration a potent influence in all these phases of the life of the state.

It may be urged that this mass of people shares the protection and opportunities for industry, education, comfort and pleasure, which is available to any dweller within the province of organized government. This is true, speaking loosely; but a careful diagnosis of the case of the immigrant shows that for him, in the greater part of his relationship with the community, it is not true.

He cannot avail himself of benefits that are beyond his reach, nor of protection that is outside his knowledge. The wires of communication are down — between "the state" and the immigrant with his needs at the other end of the line.

The character of the contemporary and newest industries in our country calls for physical strength; bodily labor. To whom do we look to dig the ditches for our great waterways, to trench and drill for the treasures of our mines, and to labor with the strength of oxen in the midst of blast furnaces where the native products are being made into world supplies? A few cold figures — "statistics concerning immigrants" — show a great part of the answer.

In 1907, seventy-two per cent of all immigrants were men — eighty-nine per cent were above the age of fourteen and the nationalities that made up almost all the lists were the sturdy ones: Italians, Russians, Poles, and Hungarians. Between these peoples and our native-born there is the silent gap of an alien speech; strange customs, — unmeaning to the new-found neighbor but in many instances the mystic ritual of life to him who practices it; and toward government, the peasant's sense, sometimes the serf's fear, as against the American citizen's freedom in "the free city of his birth."

The forces at work for assimilation are not of a character which will best serve the state, or protect and develop the energy, power and spirit of the immigrant. They are in the hands of those who have been aliens themselves. There are Jewish, Hungarian, Austrian immigrant homes — but no American homes — for the coming Americans.

It may be well to remind our readers just here that we are in no sense entering a plea for a class of dependents or deficients in natural power or faculty; quite the contrary, for in the great majority of cases the newcomers take care of themselves with remarkable success in the face of great difficulties.

Some of these difficulties are inevitable — as the difference in language; but most of them, and unquestionably the greatest are superimposed by the greed and inhumanity of persons whose prey the immigrant has become — the petty and grand offenders who range in size and power from the shrewd thug on the dock, who extorts the stranger's few dollars on pretense of service to be rendered, to the big steamship company which locks him in the filthy hold of a boat and transports him, from New York to Fall River, for example, in conditions of distress and hardship unbelievable.

That the conditions are different for the foreigner and the American of the same general status is only too apparent to any one who has followed the trail of both. We speak from the actual cases which have come to the knowledge of the State Immigration Commission of 1908 and 1909. In the first place the American has cost the country several hundred dollars (and rightly so) before he has arrived at the age and capacity of a producer in the field of labor. The other with his full grown strength (all we seem to want of him) is handed over ready made by the older civilizations.

The American entering a new town or city arrives at a railway station, and in the language common to all, can inquire his way to a lodging, judge of or bargain for a fair charge for the same, and can rebuff and deal with any intrusion or molestation that may come his way.

The immigrant arrives at the Battery. He is immediately and violently besieged on all sides by tricksters and thieves in the persons of porters, hackmen, "runners" for employment agencies, many of whom speak his language. They profess friendliness and advise him about his lodgings, employment, transportation to his destination and the many things in which he needs help. Licensed city porters wear badges and pretend thereby to be city officials, and get large fees for taking the mute stranger and his bundles to a lodging or agency. A case is known of an immigrant to whom five dollars was charged for a five-cent elevated ticket, which was represented to be a "railroad ticket."

The loss of such amounts of money is a serious matter to a man without employment and the road to dependence, and deportation may be short if work is not immediately obtained.

The American laborer traveling from one place to another rides in the usual typical day-coach, pays a through fare to his destination, knows when and where to get off, and shares all the privileges of service, short of drawing room cars or special sleepers. If there is no dining car the train makes a short stop for lunch. The same is true of boat travel.

In an investigation of traveling conditions made by Commissioner Watchorn, and which the New York State Commission of Immigration found in 1909 had not been materially changed, it was shown that on some lines first-class rates were charged to immigrants for inferior cars; that smokers were used, containing no separate toilet facilities for men and women and no wash rooms. These coaches were crowded with men, women and children. No adequate stops were made to obtain food and no milk could be obtained *en route* for the babies. Lunch boxes can be bought at Ellis Island but there are no bottles or other receptacles to be had in which milk can be taken away. The mothers do not know the length of the journey they are to take from Ellis Island to their destination, nor how or where to get milk to take with them. In some instances much delay is experienced in sending off immigrant trains, and journeys are made across the state and even to Chicago on local trains. No choice of service or road is given to the travelers, who are made to use the worst cars and often to take a very indirect and long journey over a road to which they are assigned by general agreement among the representatives of the nine big companies, who have a system of "balancing the passenger business."

The situation on the docks and in the boats both of the coastwise steamers and of the night Hudson river boats is similar. Conditions vary: some better, some worse.

The steerage quarters on the boats are sometimes in the hold and the hatchway is locked after the immigrants are put inside. In some of these quarters there are no sleeping accommodations though the journey is invariably made at night. On one boat no provision whatever is made for sleeping. The passengers sleep among the freight bundles. In the boats where bunks are provided they are dirty and overcrowded. The difference in fare is rarely more than twenty-five or fifty cents between the quarters in the freight section of the boat and the general passenger quarters. For this difference the American gets fresh air, freedom, a promenade deck, saloon, music and access to the restaurant. The passengers in the hold are not allowed to buy food on most of the boats, and on one trip an investigator saw a porter charge five cents for every drink of water taken. Even when they are able to pay, aliens are not informed of, nor encouraged to use first-class accommodations.

It often happens that immigrants, ready and waiting at docks to return to their native countries, are prevented from sailing because the steerage quarters in the boat for which they hold tickets are already overcrowded. In this predicament and in the frequent accidents of lost tickets and lost baggage there is no one to help except in the cases in which immigrant societies (private and philanthropic concerns) keep a man or two on the docks. These men render such services as they can and obtain protection for their countrymen. On many docks no provision for help is made, and the foreigner must shift for himself amidst the impatience of officials and steamship employes who speak only English. The extent of confusion in the outgoing traffic can be judged by the fact that in 1908, 714,828 aliens returned to their foreign homes mostly through the port of New York.

The hardships encountered in transportation are but a rough introduction to the road the alien has ahead of him. For instance, how does he find work? If he has enough to buy the chance to work, he applies to an employment agent. Often the employment agent has been instrumental in bringing him to this country, and he is taken with his baggage, directly to the agent from the steamer. Many of the agents are *padroni* who apparently take the place of a friend or relative of the American looking for work. But the unchecked opportunities for the indulgence of greed have made the *padrone* one of the most unfortunate elements in the life of the alien. The exorbitant fees charged for putting him at work and the large and continuous profits obtained for supplying him with the necessities of life are the source of a spectacular revenue to the *padrone,* his countryman, who has preceded him in residence here, but a few years. Through this *padrone* system the alien may be sent to unsanitary labor camps, the life of which is pictured elsewhere. He may also be sent as a strike-breaker or sent without his knowledge into industries wherein his wages do not enable him to maintain a decent standard of living.

If he escapes the *padrone* and goes to an immigrant agency on his own initiative, he often encounters unforeseen abuses. An Italian carpenter came to the commission a while ago (he had seen a notice of it in a newspaper) to apply for help in the following case:

He had left his tools in his trunk at an agency while he went out to look for work. On his return he found that the agency had been sold "with all its contents" including quantities of baggage belonging to immigrants. The purchaser, who continued in the employment business at the house, refused to give the Italian his tools, and he had not been able to take up his work for two months before he came to the commission. The commissioner's representative talked the matter over with the new owner of the agency (who spoke no English) and persuaded her to give up the tools to their owner.

When the immigrant has found work and a lodging place and the prospect is looking better to him, his next thought is to communicate with his family or friends in the old country; to share his savings and perhaps to bring his family here. The typical method of setting about this process puts him into a labyrinth of difficulties and dangers of which he has never dreamed. In the same circumstances the American writes his own letter and gets his money order or registers his letter, or writes his family to come and goes to the train to meet them. The foreigner can do nothing so simple as this. There has sprung up to meet his peculiar situation "the immigrant bank", a flourishing and extensive enterprise. In 1908 records were obtained of more than five hundred such banks in New York City, and eighty-eight in other cities of the first and second class.

According to the testimony of one large banking house in New York, it had one thousand correspondents scattered throughout the state. Their business was to solicit the savings of immigrants. Fifty-six bonded bankers transmitted over sixteen million dollars in 1907. This represented but twenty-five per cent of the total amount transmitted. The greater part of this money is in amounts of a few dollars each. The deposit business done by these banks is also very large. In 1907 two and one-half million dollars was received on deposit, and in 1908 one and three-quarter millions. Much of the money sent to the people at home by the immigrant does not reach them.

There is no guarantee whatever to the immigrant that his savings will reach his family, and in cases of fraud the banker pleads delay and unavoidable loss in transmitting, and waives all responsibility. The money passes through many hands: the correspondent, the banker, often the express office, and the foreign representative who may mail the remittance from the port on the other side to the town or home of the waiting relatives. In case of loss how can the alien isolated in the labor camp, or isolated among his fellows, prove that the money did not arrive while his witness is across the ocean?

There is no regulation of these banks by the State Banking Department. Every bank under the Banking Department in 1907 which suspended business paid its depositors in full. Twenty-five immigrant banks which failed had money of immigrants amounting to a million and one-half dollars ($1,459,295.01). In 1909 the commission found that the assets of these banks amounted to but $295,331.13 and but $500 had been repaid by the bonding companies, though each banker was bonded for $15,000. 12,279 claimants lost their money through these banks. The size of the average claim was fifty-five dollars, but a great number of the claims were around twenty dollars. Any one familiar with the pay and the work of the day laborer on public works in our tunnels and ditches, and in places of danger, can best realize what these losses mean to the workman and to the family across the water, depending on the earnings and their safe transmission.

The immigrant bank is a curious institution. It not only undertakes to care for the savings of the immigrant but it acts as a social center and place of appeal in many emergencies. The banker maintains a post-office where mail can be called for or from which it can be forwarded. It sells steamship tickets and is the office of the notary public who prepares legal documents, performs legal services and helps the foreigner obtain citizenship papers.

One of the most profitable mediums of revenue to the vampires of immigrant ignorance is the sale of worthless steamship tickets. As soon as the immigrant has taken a foothold here and begins to plan to bring his family or brother or sister or parents to his new-found home, he becomes fair game for the bogus ticket seller.

The steamship companies have authorized agents in the foreign quarters of the city who are empowered to conduct a legitimate ticket selling business, but around these centers, both within their knowledge and outside it, many other agents and peddlers have sprung up who reap a livelihood from the sale of worthless pieces of paper purporting to be steamship tickets.

One of the authorized agents, a man of long experience in the business, who had offices in Manhattan, Brooklyn and the Bronx does a business amounting to over three hundred thousand dollars a year. He testified in a recent investigation that "there are about fifteen authorized agents on the East Side, and eight not authorized but doing business in offices and getting their tickets from authorized agents; that there are probably from five to six thousand, and certainly three thousand runners or peddlers in New York City, who sell tickets outside of offices."

The steamship companies have a technical rule in regard to furnishing tickets to peddlers, but it is not only not enforced but the traffic of the peddlers is secretly encouraged by the steamship companies. Another authorized agent testified that twenty per cent of his business consisted of the sale of tickets to peddlers. These peddlers sell steamship tickets from pushcarts, in tenements, and in small groceries and other shops.

A typical case of a defrauded man is given in the following testimony:

> I agreed to purchase from the firm of A and B two steamship tickets for passage from Antwerp to New York for the sum of ninety dollars and to pay twenty dollars down and two dollars each week until the ninety dollars should be paid. I paid the twenty dollars and received an order which I sent to my sister and her husband in Russia. Upon receipt of this they started at once for Antwerp. When they presented the order they were told that it was no good. My sister and her husband were stranded and were obliged to beg. As soon as they wrote me these facts I went to the agents and they demanded an additional ten dollars to have the original order stopped and agreed to give me another order. This second order I sent to my sister and it likewise was no good. As soon as I learned this I went again to the office of the agent but it was closed. They had moved away and I have never been able to find them since, nor have I been able to get back the sum of sixty-eight dollars which I had paid them on the orders for the first two tickets, or the additional ten dollars which I gave.

Another avenue of fraudulent practice is the notaries' office. The foreign notary has a peculiar leverage on his countryman, or one whose language he speaks, from the circumstance that in foreign countries the office of a notary is one of honor and importance. The holder of the office is a man of character and education and standing in the community. With this tradition in his mind the foreigner trustfully goes to the representative of this calling in the new country and confides his affairs to him. One notary who is also a real estate agent in Brooklyn drafted a bill of sale of a clothing store and antedated the document for the purpose of avoiding the payment of notes which had been protested. For this service he charged five dollars and the cost of filing the document. It is a common custom for these notaries to ask whether bills of sale are *bona fide* or are made to prevent creditors from collecting money due them. If the latter purpose is admitted a higher fee is charged for the document. The superintendent of labor complained against one notary for issuing fraudulent permits enabling children to work who are not legally qualified.

The list of offenses is long and many of them are ingenious in character and illustrate only too graphically that in their self-interest the notary public, the employment agent, and the immigrant banker are strong forces against the assimilation of the alien by the new country.

The banker does not want him to invest his money here as that would remove it from his own profitable custody, both from savings accounts and from passing through his hands to the foreign relatives. The employment agent is not interested in his buying a little farm; that might take him out of the ranks of the frequently unemployed who need his offices. The notary public is not enthusiastic that he should learn English, as that would equip him to attend to matters which the notary must now transact for him.

Some kind of clearing house or utility center is indispensable and the alien is naturally attracted to these professedly friendly countrymen rather than to impersonal corporations, however legitimate in character.

As conducted now, every function of the immigrant bank, the employment agency and the notary's office is open to abuse. There is no supervision; no one is disinterestedly concerned about the alien and in his ignorance he responds to overtures of professed friendliness, believing that it is all part of the wonder of the new country.

Here then is a suggestion of the alien's handicap: exploitation at docks and on trains and boats; traveling conditions which imperil safety and health; oppression at the hands of the *padroni;* isolation from family life and comforts; frauds on the part of the banker, notary, and steamship agent, and misrepresentation at the hands of interpreters and fraudulent lawyers when he violates the laws he does not know or understand.

The voices of a few "fervid spokesmen of the inarticulate and unassimilated" are being raised in petition that "the wires of communication" be put up without delay. It is true that the aliens are in a gravely different case from the native-born; that they form a great group of persons to be reckoned with; that the state has no record of them, and that its educational and assimilative powers do not reach them.

5

ONE WHO MADE GOOD

 The term *padrone* is an Italian word signifying proprietor, boss, master, or a person who has either legal or moral powers over others. The United States Immigration Commission, investigating the padrone system in the United States in 1910, said ignorance of the English language and of conditions of labor in the United States had compelled Italian immigrants to depend entirely upon labor contractors of their own nationality who were familiar with language and labor conditions here. Eventually, the term "padrone labor" came to be applied to all workmen who were exploited by their leaders. The Commission found that "as more progressive colonies were established the evil diminished rapidly."

Rocco's story touches on several significant aspects of Italian-American immigrant experience: The Italian immigrant's desire, sometimes realized, sometimes forgotten or modified, to return to his old home after working in America for a period. The preponderance of males among Italian immigrants and their employment in the least skilled trades — heavy labor, the rag-gathering trade, bootblacking. The custom of entrusting some children from very large, very poor families to a *padrone,* who paid their fare and maintained them in return for the children's labor. The rivalry between Irish and Italian immigrants for housing and jobs was so intense that, although both groups were largely Roman Catholic in religion, the Irish voted overwhelmingly Democratic and the Italians largely Republican in those localities where they lived and competed with each other.

According to Hamilton Holt, ex-settlement house worker and editor of *The Independent* in which Rocco's story appeared, it was "presented almost as he told it" to a representative of the magazine, with "some suppressions and changes of language" but no change of meaning. At the time of the interview Rocco was already known as "Joe" to many people. He said his last name, Corresca, was given him when he went aboard the ship that brought him here. It was entered on the books, and he kept it for official purposes.

THE BIOGRAPHY OF A BOOTBLACK

Rocco Corresca

When I was a very small boy I lived in Italy in a large house with many other small boys, who were all dressed alike and were taken care of by some nuns. It was a good place, situated on the side of the mountain, where grapes were growing and melons and oranges and plums.

They taught us our letters and how to pray and say the catechism, and we worked in the fields during the middle of the day. We always had enough to eat and good beds to sleep in at night, and sometimes there were feast days, when we marched about wearing flowers.

Those were good times and they lasted till I was nearly eight years of age. Then an old man came and said he was my grandfather. He showed some papers and cried over me and said that the money had come at last and now he could take me to his beautiful home. He seemed very glad to see me and after they looked at his papers he took me away and we went to the big city — Naples. He kept talking about his beautiful house, but when we got there it was a dark cellar that he lived in and I did not like it at all. Very rich people were on the first floor. They had carriages and servants and music and plenty of good things to eat, but we were down below in the cellar and had nothing. There were four other boys in the cellar and the old man said they were all my brothers. All were larger than I and they beat me at first till one day Francisco said that they should not beat me any more, and then Paulo, who was the largest of all, fought him till Francisco threw a knife and gave him a cut. Then Paulo, too, got a knife and said that he would

FROM *The Independent,* LIV (December 4, 1902), pp. 2863-70.

kill Francisco, but the old man knocked them both down with a stick and took their knives away and gave them beatings.

Each morning we boys all went out to beg and we begged all day near the churches and at night near the theatres, running to the carriages and opening the doors and then getting in the way of the people so that they had to give us money or walk over us. The old man often watched us and at night he took all the money, except when we could hide something.

We played tricks on the people, for when we saw some coming that we thought were rich I began to cry and covered my face and stood on one foot, and the others gathered around me and said:

"Don't cry! Don't cry!"

Then the ladies would stop and ask: "What is he crying about? What is the matter, little boy?"

Francisco or Paulo would answer: "He is very sad because his mother is dead and they have laid her in the grave."

Then the ladies would give me money and the others would take most of it from me.

The old man told us to follow the Americans and the English people, as they were all rich, and if we annoyed them enough they would give us plenty of money. He taught us that if a young man was walking with a young woman he would always give us silver because he would be ashamed to let the young woman see him give us less. There was also a great church where sick people were cured by the saints, and when they came out they were so glad that they gave us money.

Begging was not bad in the summer time because we went all over the streets and there was plenty to see, and if we got much money we could spend some buying things to eat. The old man knew we did that. He used to feel us and smell us to see if we had eaten anything, and he often beat us for eating when we had not eaten.

Early in the morning we had breakfast of black bread rubbed over with garlic or with a herring to give it a flavor. The old man would eat the garlic or the herring himself, but he would rub our bread with it, which he said was as good. He told us that boys should not be greedy and that it was good to fast and that all the saints had fasted. He had a figure of a saint in one corner of the cellar and prayed night and morning that the saint would help him to get money. He made us pray, too, for he said that it was good luck to be religious.

We used to sleep on the floor, but often we could not sleep

much because men came in very late at night and played cards with the old man. He sold them wine from a barrel that stood on one end of the table that was there, and if they drank much he won their money. One night he won so much that he was glad and promised the saint some candles for his altar in the church. But that was to get more money. Two nights after that the same men who had lost the money came back and said that they wanted to play again. They were very friendly and laughing, but they won all the money and the old man said they were cheating. So they beat him and went away. When he got up again he took a stick and knocked down the saint's figure and said that he would give no more candles.

I was with the old man for three years. I don't believe that he was my grandfather, tho he must have known something about me because he had those papers.

It was very hard in the winter time for we had no shoes and we shivered a great deal. The old man said that we were no good, that we were ruining him, that we did not bring in enough money. He told me that I was fat and that people would not give money to fat beggars. He beat me, too, because I didn't like to steal, as I had heard it was wrong.

"Ah!" said he, "that is what they taught you at that place, is it? To disobey your grandfather that fought with Garibaldi! That is a fine religion!"

The others all stole as well as begged, but I didn't like it and Francisco didn't like it either.

Then the old man said to me: "If you don't want to be a thief you can be a cripple. That is an easy life and they make a great deal of money."

I was frightened then, and that night I heard him talking to one of the men that came to see him. He asked how much he would charge to make me a good cripple like those that crawl about the church. They had a dispute, but at last they agreed and the man said that I should be made so that people would shudder and give me plenty of money.

I was much frightened, but I did not make a sound and in the morning I went out to beg with Francisco. I said to him: "I am going to run away. I don't believe 'Tony is my grandfather. I don't believe that he fought for Garibaldi, and I don't want to be a cripple, no matter how much money the people may give."

"Where will you go?" Francisco asked me.

"I don't know," I said; "somewhere."

He thought awhile and then he said: "I will go, too."

So we ran away out of the city and begged from the country people as we went along. We came to a village down by the sea and a long way from Naples and there we found some fishermen and they took us aboard their boat. We were with them five years, and tho it was a very hard life we liked it well because there was always plenty to eat. Fish do not keep long and those that we did not sell we ate.

The chief fisherman, whose name was Ciguciano, had a daughter, Teresa, who was very beautiful, and tho she was two years younger than I, she could cook and keep house quite well. She was a kind, good girl and he was a good man. When we told him about the old man who told us he was our grandfather, the fisherman said he was an old rascal who should be in prison for life. Teresa cried much when she heard that he was going to make me a cripple. Ciguciano said that all the old man had taught us was wrong — that it was bad to beg, to steal and to tell lies. He called in the priest and the priest said the same thing and was very angry at the old man in Naples, and he taught us to read and write in the evenings. He also taught us our duties to the church and said that the saints were good and would only help men to do good things, and that it was a wonder that lightning from heaven had not struck the old man dead when he knocked down the saint's figure.

We grew large and strong with the fisherman and he told us that we were getting too big for him, that he could not afford to pay us the money that we were worth. He was a fine, honest man — one in a thousand.

Now and then I had heard things about America — that it was a far off country where everybody was rich and that Italians went there and made plenty of money, so that they could return to Italy and live in pleasure ever after. One day I met a young man who pulled out a handful of gold and told me he had made that in America in a few days.

I said I should like to go there, and he told me that if I went he would take care of me and see that I was safe. I told Francisco and he wanted to go, too. So we said good-by to our good friends. Teresa cried and kissed us both and the priest came and shook our hands and told us to be good men, and that no matter where we went God and his saints were always near us and that if we lived well we should all meet again in heaven. We cried, too, for it was our home, that place. Ciguciano gave us money and slapped us on the back and said that we should be great. But he felt bad, too, at seeing us go away after all that time.

The young man took us to a big ship and got us work away down where the fires are. We had to carry coal to the place where it could be thrown on the fires. Francisco and I were very sick from the great heat at first and lay on the coal for a long time, but they threw water on us and made us get up. We could not stand on our feet well, for everything was going around and we had no strength. We said that we wished we had stayed in Italy no matter how much gold there was in America. We could not eat for three days and could not do much work. Then we got better and sometimes we went up above and looked about. There was no land anywhere and we were much surprised. How could the people tell where to go when there was no land to steer by?

We were so long on the water that we began to think we should never get to America or that, perhaps, there was not any such place, but at last we saw land and came up to New York.

We were glad to get over without giving money, but I have heard since that we should have been paid for our work among the coal and that the young man who had sent us got money for it. We were all landed on an island and the bosses there said that Francisco and I must go back because we had not enough money, but a man named Bartolo came up and told them that we were brothers and he was our uncle and would take care of us. He brought two other men who swore that they knew us in Italy and that Bartolo was our uncle. I had never seen any of them before, but even then Bartolo might be my uncle, so I did not say anything. The bosses of the island let us go out with Bartolo after he had made the oath.

We came to Brooklyn to a wooden house in Adams Street that was full of Italians from Naples. Bartolo had a room on the third floor and there were fifteen men in the room, all boarding with Bartolo. He did the cooking on a stove in the middle of the room and there were beds all around the sides, one bed above another. It was very hot in the room, but we were soon asleep, for we were very tired.

The next morning, early, Bartolo told us to go out and pick rags and get bottles. He gave us bags and hooks and showed us the ash barrels. On the streets where the fine houses are the people are very careless and put out good things, like mattresses and umbrellas, clothes, hats and boots. We brought all these to Bartolo and he made them new again and sold them on the sidewalk; but mostly we brought rags and bones. The rags we had to wash in the back yard and then we hung them to dry on lines under the ceiling in our room. The bones we kept under the beds till Bartolo could find a man to buy them.

Most of the men in our room worked at digging the sewer. Bartolo got them the work and they paid him about one quarter of their wages. Then he charged them for board and he bought the clothes for them, too. So they got little money after all.

Bartolo was always saying that the rent of the room was so high that he could not make anything, but he was really making plenty. He was what they call a padrone and is now a very rich man. The men that were living with him had just come to the country and could not speak English. They had all been sent by the young man we met in Italy. Bartolo told us all that we must work for him and that if we did not the police would come and put us in prison.

He gave us very little money, and our clothes were some of those that were found on the street. Still we had enough to eat and we had meat quite often, which we never had in Italy. Bartolo got it from the butcher — the meat that he could not sell to the other people — but it was quite good meat. Bartolo cooked it in the pan while we all sat on our beds in the evening. Then he cut it into small bits and passed the pan around, saying:

"See what I do for you and yet you are not glad. I am too kind a man, that is why I am so poor."

We were with Bartolo nearly a year, but some of our countrymen who had been in the place a long time said that Bartolo had no right to us and we could get work for a dollar and a half a day, which, when you make it *lire* (reckoned in the Italian currency) is very much. So we went away one day to Newark and got work on the street. Bartolo came after us and made a great noise, but the boss said that if he did not go away soon the police would have him. Then he went, saying that there was no justice in this country.

We paid a man five dollars each for getting us the work and we were with that boss for six months. He was Irish, but a good man and he gave us our money every Saturday night. We lived much better than with Bartolo, and when the work was done we each had nearly $200 saved. Plenty of the men spoke English and they taught us, and we taught them to read and write. That was at night, for we had a lamp in our room, and there were only five other men who lived in that room with us.

We got up at half-past five o'clock every morning and made coffee on the stove and had a breakfast of bread and cheese, onions, garlic and red herrings. We went to work at seven o'clock and in the middle of the day we had soup and bread in a place where we got it for two cents a plate. In the evenings we had a good dinner with meat of some kind and potatoes. We got from the butcher the meat that other people would not buy because they said it was old, but they don't know what is good. We paid four or five cents a pound for it and it was the best, tho I have heard of people paying sixteen cents a pound.

When the Newark boss told us that there was no more work Francisco and I talked about what we would do and we went back to Brooklyn to a saloon near Hamilton Ferry, where we got a job cleaning it out and slept in a little room upstairs. There was a bootblack named Michael on the corner and when I had time I helped him and learned the business. Francisco cooked the lunch in the saloon and he, too, worked for the bootblack and we were soon able to make the best polish.

Then we thought we would go into business and we got a basement on Hamilton avenue, near the Ferry, and put four chairs in it. We paid $75 for the chairs and all the other things. We had tables and looking glasses there and curtains. We took the papers that have the pictures in and made the place high toned. Outside we had a big sign that said:

THE BEST SHINE FOR TEN CENTS

Men that did not want to pay ten cents could get a good shine for five cents, but it was not an oil shine. We had two boys helping us and paid each of them fifty cents a day. The rent of the place was $20 a month, so the expenses were very great, but we made money from the beginning. We slept in the basement, but got our meals in the saloon till we could put a stove in our place, and then Francisco cooked for us all. That would not do, tho, because some of our customers said that they did not like to smell garlic and onions and red herrings. I thought that was strange, but we had to do what the customers said. So we got the woman who lived upstairs to give us our meals and paid her $1.50 a week each. She gave the boys soup in the middle of the day — five cents for two plates.

We remembered the priest, the friend of Ciguciano, and what

he had said to us about religion, and as soon as we came to the country we began to go to the Italian church. The priest we found here was a good man, but he asked the people for money for the church. The Italians did not like to give because they said it looked like buying religion. The priest says it is different here from Italy because all the churches there are what they call endowed, while here all they have is what the people give. Of course I and Francisco understand that, but the Italians who cannot read and write shake their hands and say that it is wrong for a priest to want money.

We had said that when we saved $1,000 each we would go back to Italy and buy a farm, but now that the time is coming we are so busy and making so much money that we think that we will stay. We have opened another parlor near South Ferry, in New York. We have to pay $30 a month rent, but the business is very good. The boys in this place charge sixty cents a day because there is so much work.

At first we did not know much of this country, but by and by we learned. There are here plenty of Protestants who are heretics, but they have a religion, too. Many of the finest churches are Protestant, but they have no saints and no altars, which seems strange.

These people are without a king such as ours in Italy. It is what they call a Republic, as Garibaldi wanted, and every year in the fall the people vote. They wanted us to vote last fall, but we did not. A man came and said that he would get us made Americans for fifty cents and then we could get two dollars for our votes. I talked to some of our people and they told me that we should have to put a paper in a box telling who we wanted to govern us.

I went with five men to the court and when they asked me how long I had been in the country I told them two years. Afterward my countrymen said I was a fool and would never learn politics. "You should have said you were five years here and then we would swear to it," was what they told me.

There are two kinds of people that vote here, Republicans and Democrats. I went to a Republican meeting and the man said that the Republicans want a Republic and the Democrats are against it. He said that Democrats are for a king whose name is Bryan and who is an Irishman. There are some good Irishmen, but many of them insult Italians. They call us Dagoes. So I will be a Republican.

I like this country now and I don't see why we should have a king. Garibaldi didn't want a king and he was the greatest man that ever lived.

I and Francisco are to be Americans in three years. The court gave us papers and said we must wait and we must be able to read some things and tell who the ruler of the country is.

There are plenty of rich Italians here, men who a few years ago had nothing and now have so much money that they could not count all their dollars in a week. The richest ones go away from the other Italians and live with the Americans.

We have joined a club and have much pleasure in the evenings. The club has rooms down in Sackett Street and we meet many people and are learning new things all the time. We were very ignorant when we came here, but now we have learned much.

On Sundays we get a horse and carriage from the grocer and go down to Coney Island. We go to the theatres often and other evenings we go to the houses of our friends and play cards.

I am nineteen years of age now and have $700 saved. Francisco is twenty-one and has about $900. We shall open some more parlors soon. I know an Italian who was a bootblack ten years ago and now bosses bootblacks all over the city, who has so much money that if it was turned into gold it would weigh more than himself.

Francisco and I have a room to ourselves now and some people call us "swells." Ciguciano said that we should be great men. Francisco bought a gold watch with a gold chain as thick as his thumb. He is a very handsome fellow and I think he likes a young lady that he met at a picnic out at Ridgewood.

I often think of Ciguciano and Teresa. He is a good man, one in a thousand, and she was very beautiful. May be I shall write to them about coming to this country.

PART II

BUILDING A NEW LIFE

As he is when he arrives in America.

As we find him six months later.

The Evolution of the Anarchist. This cartoon reflects the growing suspicion, dating from the late 1880s, of the "new" immigrant as a threat to American institutions.

6

GROUP LIFE IN AN ETHNIC COLONY

For many immigrants, the move to the New World meant a wrenching personal experience. Oscar Handlin has argued in his *The Uprooted* (1951) that the peasants who migrated to the United States from the 1840s to the 1920s came from villages where mutual assistance and solidarity were a way of life. The move to a new land and to cities generally inhospitable to familiar values, customs, and institutions meant, in Handlin's view, a serious disruption of accustomed ways of living, working, and worshipping.

Other historians have questioned the applicability of Professor Handlin's generalizations to *all* those who came from peasant backgrounds. (References to Handlin's work and that of his chief critic are given in the bibliographical essay.)

For most immigrant groups the uprooting experience of migration was eventually followed by the reorganization of the migrants' personal lives and the restructuring of the old institutions and the creation of new ones. The following article by Antonio Mangano, a Baptist minister engaged in Protestant missionary efforts among Italians in the United States, describes such institutional arrangements in New York City around the turn of the century. Like other foreign-born spokesmen for the immigrant, he tried to show that America uplifted and transformed the newcomer.

Mangano also describes the Italian immigrant's tendency to identify with his village rather than his country, to regard himself not so much as an Italian as a Calabrian or Abruzzi. Because the church bell-tower, or *campanile,* was the focal point of small Italian villages, this attachment to hometown or region instead of national territory has been called

Campanilismo. It was known among other groups such as Irish, Germans, and Jews as well. The latter two in particular organized *Landsmanschaften* for social and charitable purposes long before they became conscious of belonging to a common nationality.

The immigrant colony or community, seen as tightly organized by outsiders, was therefore seldom ever united in outlook, thought, or action. No single bond, not even common religion, united Italians and other ethnic or national groups who lived in urban ethnic enclaves. This internal division gave rise to many ambitious plans for achieving unity, all failures in the end. It also helped to maintain ethnic consciousness because the multiplicity of formal and informal groupings, each with its officers and closely knit membership, involved thousands who devoted considerable energies to the network of ethnic groups which clamored for the allegiance of immigrants and their children. The Germans even invented a word for this never-ending activity: *Vereinsmeierei!*

THE ASSOCIATED LIFE OF THE ITALIANS IN NEW YORK CITY

Antonio Mangano

It is generally supposed by those unfamiliar with actual conditions, that the Italian colony of the Borough of Manhattan is a well-organized and compact body of people, having a common life and being subject to the absolute control and leadership of some one person or group of persons. To the reader of popular articles describing Italian life and customs, in these days so frequently appearing in newspapers and magazines; to the enthusiastic and romantic slum visitor, who walks through Mulberry street, and possibly peeps into the dark and dismal hallway of some dilapidated tenement and feels that he knows just how Italians live and act; to the theoretical sociologist, to whom all Italians look alike and in whose estimation all Italians are alike, think alike, and act alike — to such persons the mere mention of the Italian colony inevitably suggests unity of

FROM *Charities,* XII (May 7, 1904), pp. 476–82.

thought and action as well as of mode of life on the part of all who belong to that colony. And yet nothing is farther from the real truth.

Although many of the people of the Italian colony could not tell what the word *republic* means, and while none of them prior to coming to America have ever breathed the atmosphere created by republican institutions, it must be said that the love of freedom and the spirit of independence are elements inherent in the Italian character. Countless battlefields, made sacred during many centuries by the blood of those who rather than be subject to tyranny or foreign dominion offered their lives, as well as their substance, as a sacrifice, are unmistakable witnesses to the love of Italians for freedom and for liberty. When the Italian lands upon our shores and catches the spirit of the independence which prevails here, his own nature finds itself in a congenial atmosphere and begins to expand along those lines. Under the social and economic conditions in his own country, he could not assert himself; he was timid; he did not dare say his soul was his own for fear of being deprived of the means of subsistence. Here a very different state of affairs prevails. He somehow catches the idea that if he works faithfully and behaves himself, he need fear no man. This means an appeal to his manhood.

No one will deny that development along this line is good and wholesome. But, unfortunately, the good is accompanied by a shadow of evil. The spirit of independence seems to go to seed. The members of the Italian colony have a certain element in their general make-up which has rendered it virtually impossible for them to act unitedly and harmoniously. Each man feels that he is a law unto himself; each small group of men are a law unto themselves. They appreciate most keenly that it is their right and privilege to do as they see fit — providing they do not interfere with other people's rights — but they lose sight of this other great fact equally important, that personal rights and privileges should be modified by consideration for the welfare of the community — the only condition under which men can live together in any proper and mutually helpful relation.

But, now, if we are asked whether any plausible reason can be advanced as to why the Italians seem to lack natural capacity for a large co-operation, we would answer that they have for centuries lived in the midst of an environment which has tended to develop in them a spirit of division and sectional feeling. Prior to the formation of the present Italian kingdom, the country was divided into numerous dukedoms and principalities among which there was constant rivalry and bitter feeling, if not open warfare. As a natural consequence, the people not only have lacked sympathy for those outside of their particular principality or dukedom, but even have nursed a strong feeling of hostility toward them. Added to this, there is the spirit which prevails to-day in many parts of Italy — a clearly marked rivalry between two towns or two cities within the same province. Doubtless such contention has its good effect in inducing rival towns to put forth every effort for their improvement; but on the other hand, division and dissension are unconsciously fostered under the guise of a false patriotism.

The New York colony is composed of persons coming from nearly every nook and corner of the old peninsula. It is by no means strange, then, that they should bring with them local prejudices and narrow sympathies; it is not to be wondered that they feel that highest duty consists in being loyal to the handful who come from their immediate section and in manifesting opposition toward those who come from other localities. Thus it comes to pass that while a man may be known as an Italian, he is far better known as a Napoletano, Calabrese, Veneziano, Abbruzese, or Siciliano. This means that the Italian colony is divided into almost as many groups as there are sections of Italy represented.

There are, however, many signs which unmistakably point to a decided change for the better in the near future. There are certain forces at work which have for their ultimate object the development of a larger spirit of co-operation, which will enable the Italians as a whole to unite for the attainment of specific objects. The main purpose of this article, therefore, is to point out the chief Italian institutions which indicate the lines along which Italian organized effort is directed, and to describe briefly their operations.

Among the agencies which have for their ideal united Italian action, there are none more potent than the Italian Chamber of Commerce. This organization, founded in 1887 with but a few members, to-day embraces in its membership of 201 a majority of the Italian business men in Greater New York. The objects for which it was established may best be stated by translating a few articles from its constitution and by-laws:

[1]   a. To promote, develop and protect commercial relations between Italy and the United States.

      b. To facilitate and protect orderly interests, both commercial and industrial, which the Italians residing in the United States of America may have with other countries, and especially with Italy.

[2] a. To act as interpreter to the Italian government, to public or private officials, foreign or domestic, in regard to all matters concerning the development of Italian commercial interests in the United States.

b. To study the existing commercial and industrial reports between Italy and the United States; indicate the causes which hinder the development and suggest remedies.

c. To transmit to the Italian government all such information which may be of value in matters commercial and industrial between the mother country and the United States.

d. To compile a general annual directory of all Italian merchants in New York city and in the principal centres of the American union.

e. In general, to lend its good offices in the settlement of any difficulties which might arise between Italians, or between Italians and other nationalities.

In addition, the chamber occupies itself with a number of other things which are not specifically stated in the constitution. It aims at increasing Italian exports to this country and American exports to Italy; it acts as a medium in suggesting to dealers, both Americans and Italians, where they can secure the particular goods desired.

But to my mind, while I would not for a moment detract from the commercial functions of the chamber, its greatest good is achieved along another line — one which is destined eventually to lead the Italians to drop sectional feeling and rejoice in the glory of a common nationality. That the Neapolitan, the Sicilian, the Roman, can all join this organization and have as the one object the advancement of Italian interests, is a step in the right direction and toward another end which is eminently wholesome and greatly to be desired.

The Columbus Hospital is situated on Twentieth street between Second and Third avenues. Organized in 1892 and incorporated in 1895, it has been from its beginning under the direct supervision of the missionary Sisters of the Sacred Heart. Were it possible for the hospital to secure increased accommodations and better facilities, it would be of far greater service to those in whose interests it is dedicated. The following paragraph is taken from the last annual report: ''During the year, 1,098 patients were admitted, and of this number only sixty-three paid full board. When we consider that the hospital is devoid of endowment, annuity, or permanent fund for its maintenance, depending entirely upon the energies of the sisters and the voluntary contributions of those who have its well-being at heart, it becomes a problem which those unacquainted with the management would find difficulty in solving."

Columbus Hospital is generally known as an Italian institution, yet of the twenty-one physicians on its medical and surgical staff not one is an Italian, but the sisters who carry it on are all native Italians, and ninety-five per cent of the patients treated are of that race.

The Society for the Protection of Italian Immigrants was founded three years ago, and since then has, without a shadow of a doubt, rendered more practical assistance to the thousands flocking to our shores than any other institution working in the interest of Italians.

Speaking of the conditions in which Italians find themselves on arrival, Eliot Norton, president of the society, says in his annual report: "These immigrants are landed at Ellis Island, where they are examined by United States officials. From there some go into the interior of the country and some remain in New York. Almost all of them are very ignorant, very childlike, and wholly unfamiliar with the ways, customs and language of this country. Hence it is obvious that they need friendly assistance from the moment of debarcation at Ellis Island. Those who go into the interior of the country need to be helped in getting on the right train, without losing their way or money; while those coming to New York city need guidance to their destination and, while going there, protection from sharps, crooks and dishonest runners, and thereafter to have advice and employment."

The society is constantly enlarging its activities. It has had the hearty co-operation of Commissioner Williams and of the police department. Its officials are stationed at Ellis Island and act as interpreters for the newcomers. With such immigrants as have friends either on Ellis Island or on the New York side, awaiting them, the society does not concern itself. Its attention is fully occupied in attending to those who have no friends and who have not the remotest idea as to the place for which they are bound. These are taken directly to its office at 17 Pearl street, and later turned over to its guards or runners. For this service the immigrant is charged a nominal fee. During the first two years and a half, 7,293 friendless immigrants were conducted to their destinations, in or about New York city, at an average cost of thirty-two cents apiece, as against an average expenditure of from $3.00 to $4.00, which immigrants formerly were forced to pay by sharpers.

Closely associated with the work of the Society for the Protection of Italian Immigrants is the Italian Benevolent Institute. Within the past two years it has taken on new life. The work was encouraged by gifts from many quarters, the most noteworthy one being from His Majesty the King of Italy, which amounted to 20,000 lire. One of its encouraging features is the fact that it is maintained almost exclusively by Italians.

The institute has its headquarters in a double house, 165-7 West Houston street, which is intended as a place of refuge for the destitute. It often happens that newcomers, bound for interior points, land in New York without a cent in their pockets, expecting to find at the post-office or some bank the sum necessary to carry them to their destination; it also often happens that the money expected does not arrive in time. To such persons as these the Benevolent Institute opens its doors. Then, too, there are immigrants who come with the intention of settling in New York. Such persons may have $8 or $10, but unless they find work at once they too are compelled to seek aid from some source. Further, New York has become, in a sense, a central market for Italian labor, and of those who go to distant points in search of work some fail to find it, and return to the city.

Attention has already been called to the fact that the Italian is lacking in the spirit of unity, and of association in a large sense. The last few years, however, have witnessed a few noteworthy victories in the interest of larger sympathy — mainly through the efforts of a few leading spirits who have been prominent in the affairs of the colony. If one can prophesy, in the light of tendencies already at work, the day is coming when the Italian colony will recognize its responsibilities, and throwing aside petty jealousies, will launch out upon such a policy as will best enhance the interests of the Italians as a whole.

If we were asked, therefore, whether there is any bond which unites the Italian colony as a whole, we must answer no. Even the Roman Church cannot be considered such a unifying factor in the attitude of indifference taken toward its claims.

It must be observed, however, that the Italian manifests a strong tendency toward organization with small groups for social ends and for the purpose of mutual aid. There are in Manhattan alone over one hundred and fifty Italian societies of one sort or another. "The moral disunity of the old peninsula is transplanted here."

The Italian does not lack the instinct of charity or mutual helpfulness; but at present he lacks the instinct in a broad sense.

He would take the bread from his own mouth in order to help his fellow townsman; there is nothing he will not do for his *paesano;* but it must not be expected from this that he will manifest such an attitude toward *all Italians.* Notwithstanding, were it not for this strong feeling, even though limited to small groups, we should have many more calls upon public charity on the part of the Italians than we now do.

In matters of amusement and recreation, the Italian stands in great contrast with his American cousin who too often goes to extremes and excesses. When the Italian goes off for an afternoon's or evening's outing, he does not demand horse racing, cock fights, vulgar exhibitions or other forms of violent excitement. He finds boundless pleasure in comparatively simple things. Gathered about a table sipping coffee or wine, listening to some music, a stroll up and down the street, a game of cards in a saloon or in some friend's house — these are the chief amusements of the masses. Italian temperance along this line might well teach the American a wholesome lesson.

The Italian does not lack the instinct of charity or mutual of plays which appeal to him. The one distinctly Italian theatre, *Teatro Drammatico Nazionale,* which furnishes nightly performances in New York, is situated on the Bowery in the heart of the Italian population, and is fairly well supported. But there are numerous small places throughout the colony, mainly in connection with saloons, where light comedies and bits of tragedy are given. There is also the little marionette theatre in an upper room on Elizabeth street, with its doughty knights and plaintive spokesman, and the clash of arms in its battles royal to the crooning of a violin.

It is music, however, which appeals most strongly to the Italian character. He is not carried away with our slam-bang-band music, nor do you hear him whistling and humming the so-called popular songs of the day. Negro melodies are pleasing to him because of their combined elements of sweetness and sadness. But it is the opera which lifts him to the third heaven. The favorite operas of Verdi, Puccini and Mascagni, always draw large Italian audiences at the Metropolitan, especially so if the leading artists are Italians, and often such is the case. With the love of music is joined a sentiment of patriotism. I have in mind a young barber — and he one of a class who earns less than ten dollars a week — who rarely, if ever, misses one of the great Italian operas. During the season — it is a common experience to hear shoeblacks, and even day laborers, discussing the merits of this or that singer, and giving their reasons why this or that opera pleases them.

Italians from every nook and corner of the tenements largely make up the great crowds which listen to the park concerts at Mulberry Bend.

It is the custom of each of the small group societies to give an annual festival, and it is in connection with such festal occasions that the Italian manifests his love for show and pomp, uniforms, banners, music, elaborate discourses. Eating and drinking are the chief features, and order generally prevails.

On religious holidays the greatest and most extravagant celebrations take place. They, as a rule, occur in midsummer, when prodigal decoration, street illuminations — such as one sees so frequently in Italy, fireworks, processions, etc. — are indulged in. No inducement could tempt the Italian to miss these festivals. At such a one held three years ago in "Little Italy," in honor of one of the saints, it was claimed that no less than fifteen thousand men paraded up and down the streets each day, bearing banners on which were pinned offerings of money. In the three days, the contributions were said to have amounted to something over $20,000.

If the Italian is anything he is convivial. Nothing gives him more pleasure than to meet with his friends. In this strong desire within him for companionship may be found a cause of the herding of Italians together in certain "quarters" and of his reluctance to seek employment on farms where he would have far better opportunity for rearing his children.

As one passes through the Italian quarter and observes the number of windows displaying the sign "Banca Italiana," he is naturally led to think that the Italians do nothing but deposit money. I am told on very good authority that in Greater New York the number of so-called "banks" — distinctively Italian — is beyond three hundred. It should be said, however, that ninety per cent of these banks are nothing more or less than forwarding agencies. They are constantly springing up to meet the needs of this or that group of persons, coming from a particular town or village. For example, here is a group of people from Cosenza. They want a place where they can have their letters directed. They need some one who can assist them in the matter of sending home money now and then. They look for information regarding new fields of labor which are developing. It is in response to these needs that the larger part of these so-called banks have been brought into existence. They are generally attached to a saloon, grocery store, or cigar store — sometimes to a cobbler shop. The "banker" is always a fellow townsman of the particular group that does business with him, and this for the simple reason that the *paesano* is trusted more, no matter how solid, financially, another bank may be.

The one real substantial Italian bank, incorporated in 1896 under the laws of the state of New York, is the Italian Savings Bank, situated on the corner of Mulberry and Spring streets. It has to-day on deposit $1,059,369.19. Its report shows open accounts to the number of 7,000, and books up to date to the number of 10,844. The moneys deposited in this bank, as might be supposed, are generally in very small sums, but the figures show an average sum on deposit of about $170. The depositors as a rule are Italians, but persons of any nationality may open accounts if they wish.

This institution was started at a time when small Italian banks were failing, and when there was special antagonism to such institutions, both on the part of those who had lost money through the failure of the smaller banks and on the part of those of the small banks which continued to do business. But through determination and perseverance on the part of the officers under the lead of Cav. J. N. Francolini, who was chosen president, and who for two years gave his services free of charge, the institution was placed upon a firm foundation, and is to-day a credit to the colony.

Any discussion of the associated life of the Italians would be incomplete unless some mention were made of religious organizations. There are on Manhattan, 23 Roman Catholic churches which are entirely or in part devoted to the Italians. As one enters these churches, he is struck by a certain warmth and artistic display which are lacking in many of the other churches. The Italian has had centuries of training in the matter of artistic cathedral decorations and, taking into account the fact that so much of his life has been centered about the church, it is but natural that his places of worship should embody all that art and aesthetic natures can contribute. The church does work for Italians along the lines of parochial schools, and maintains a home in the lower part of the city for female immigrants.

In Manhattan, there are four regularly organized evangelical churches — maintained by the Presbyterian, Methodist, Protestant Episcopal and Baptist denominations. With the exception of the beautiful little Episcopal church on Broome street, the evangelical churches may be said to lack altogether the very elements which the Italian, in view of his past training, deems most essential to his environment for worship. And yet notwithstanding this, these churches are well attended. There are several other missions established for Italians, but results of their work cannot easily be seen, simply because they lack the organization necessary to hold together the people whom they reach in a more or less effective manner.

Probably the institution which has done more than any other for the Italian colony in an educational way is the school on Leonard street, devoted exclusively to Italians and maintained by the Children's Aid Society. This school, with its faithful body of teachers, has exerted a strong influence upon the Italian colony. The day sessions are conducted precisely along public school lines, mainly for children who do not enter the public schools for a variety of reasons. A night school is conducted in the same building, which aims primarily at giving instruction in the English language. There is an average attendance of men and boys at these classes of about three hundred. Besides this, there is a department of Italian instruction. A teacher who has this work in charge is supported by the Italian government. The building is also used for social purposes, and entertainments are held during the winter every Friday evening.

As an evidence of the esteem felt by Italians who have come under the influence of this school, a movement is now on foot among them to secure funds — $3,000 has already been raised — for the establishment of a similar school for the Italians in "Little Italy."

7
ENTERTAINMENT

The new mass magazines during the first decade of this century often described life in overcrowded immigrant quarters of our cities. Occasionally they reported how the new immigrants had organized their own cultural institutions, particularly newspapers and theatres. Among ethnic theatres in the United States probably none achieved greater popularity and vitality than the Yiddish stage in New York City. Moses Rischin's excellent study of New York's Jews from 1870 to 1914, *The Promised City*, calls the Yiddish theatre "educator, dream-maker, chief agent of charity, social center and recreation hub for the family." The German historian Karl Lamprecht recorded in his diary after a visit to the Grand Street Yiddish Theatre in 1904 how he had sensed there "what Greek drama meant while it retained its religious significance."

Hutchins Hapgood (1869–1944), a talented staff member of the *New York Commercial Advertiser,* devoted many hours to the exploration of the city's Lower East Side. In 1902, a collection of his magazine pieces dealing with the artistic, human, and literary aspects of immigrant life were assembled into what has become a minor classic, *The Spirit of the Ghetto.* Its illustrations were supplied by a friend of Hapgood's, Sir Jacob Epstein, the famous sculptor, then an unknown youth in the crowded ghetto.

THE FOREIGN STAGE IN NEW YORK

THE YIDDISH THEATRE

Hutchins Hapgood

In the three Yiddish theatres on the Bowery is expressed the world of the Ghetto — that New York City of Russian Jews, large, complex, with a full life and civilisation. In the midst of the frivolous Bowery, devoted to tinsel variety shows, "dive" music-halls, fake museums, trivial amusement booths of all sorts, cheap lodging-houses, ten-cent shops and Irish-American tough saloons, the theatres of the chosen people alone present the serious as well as the trivial interests of an entire community. Into these three buildings crowd the Jews of all the Ghetto classes — the sweat-shop woman with her baby, the day-labourer, the small Hester Street shopkeeper, the Russian-Jewish anarchist and socialist, the Ghetto rabbi and scholar, the poet, the journalist. The poor and ignorant are in the great majority, but the learned, the intellectual and the progressive are also represented, and here as elsewhere exert a more than numerically proportionate influence on the character of the theatrical productions, which, nevertheless, remain essentially popular. The socialists and the literati create the demand that forces into the mass of vaudeville, light opera, historical and melodramatic plays a more serious art element, a simple transcript from life or the theatric presentation of a Ghetto problem. But this more serious element is so saturated with the simple manners, humour and pathos of the life of the poor Jew, that it is seldom above the heartfelt understanding of the crowd.

The audiences vary in character from night to night rather more than in an uptown theatre. On the evenings of the first four week-days the theatre is let to a guild or club, many hundred of which exist among the working people of the East Side. Many are labour organisations representing the different trades, many are purely social, and others are in the nature of secret societies. Some of these clubs are formed on the basis of a common home in Russia. The people, for instance, who came from Vilna, a city in the old country,

From *The Bookman*, XI (June, 1900), pp. 348–58. Abridged by the editor.

have organised a Vilna Club in the Ghetto. Then, too, the anarchists have a society; there are many socialistic orders; the newspapers of the Ghetto have their constituency, which sometimes hires the theatre. Two or three hundred dollars is paid to the theatre by the guild, which then sells the tickets among the faithful for a good price. Every member of the society is forced to buy, whether he wants to see the play or not, and the money made over and above the expenses of hiring the theatre is for the benefit of the guild. These performances are therefore called "benefits." The widespread existence of such a custom is a striking indication of the growing sense of corporate interests among the labouring classes of the Jewish East Side. It is an expression of the socialistic spirit which is marked everywhere in the Ghetto.

On Friday, Saturday and Sunday nights the theatre is not let, for these are the Jewish holidays, and the house is always completely sold out, although prices range from twenty-five cents to a dollar. Friday night is, properly speaking, the gala occasion of the week. That is the legitimate Jewish holiday, the night before the Sabbath. Orthodox Jews, as well as others, may then amuse themselves. Saturday, although the day of worship, is also of holiday character in the Ghetto. This is due to the Christian influences, to which the Jews are more and more sensitive. Through economic necessity Jewish workingmen are compelled to work on Friday, and, like other workingmen, look upon Saturday night as a holiday, in spite of the frown of the orthodox. Into Sunday, too, they extend their freedom, and so in the Ghetto there are now three popularly recognised nights on which to go with all the world to the theatre.

On those nights the theatre presents a peculiarly picturesque sight. Poor workingmen and women with their babies of all ages fill the theatre. Great enthusiasm is manifested, sincere laughter and tears accompany the sincere acting on the stage. Pedlars of soda-water, candy, of fantastic gewgaws of many kinds mix freely with the audience between the acts. Conversation during the play is received wih strenuous hisses, but the falling of the curtain is the signal for groups of friends to get together and gossip about the play or the affairs of the week. Introductions are not necessary, and the Yiddish community can then be seen and approached with great freedom. On the stage curtain are advertisements of the wares of Hester Street or portraits of the "star" actors. On the programmes and circulars distributed in the audience are sometimes amusing announcements of coming attractions or lyric praise of the "stars."

Poetry is not infrequent, an example of which, literally translated, is:

> Labour, ye stars, as ye will,
> Ye cannot equal the artist;
> In the garden of art ye shall not flourish;
> Ye can never achieve his fame.
> Can you play *Hamlet* like him?
> The *Wild King,* or the *Huguenots?*
> Are you gifted with feeling
> As much as to imitate him like a shadow?
> Your fame rests on the pen;
> On the show-cards your flight is high;
> But on the stage every one can see
> How your greatness turns to ashes,
> Tomashevsky! Artist great!
> No praise is good enough for you;
> Every one remains your ardent friend.
> Of all the stars you remain the king.
> You seek no tricks, no false quibbles;
> One sees Truth itself playing.
> Your appearance is godly to us;
> Every movement is full of grace;
> Pleasing is your every gesture;
> Sugar-sweet your every turn;
> You remain the King of the Stage;
> Everything falls to your feet.

On the playboards outside the theatre, containing usually the portrait of a star, are also lyric and enthusiastic announcements. Thus, recently on the return of the great Adler, who had been ill, it was announced on the boards that "the splendid eagle has spread his wings again."

The Yiddish actors, as may be inferred from the verses quoted, take themselves with peculiar seriousness, justified by the enthusiasm, almost worship, with which they are regarded by the people. Many a poor Jew, man or girl, who makes no more than $10 a week in the sweatshop, will spend $5 of it on the theatre, which is practically the only amusement of the Ghetto Jew. He has not the loafing and sporting instincts of the poor Christian, and spends his money for the theatre rather than for drink. It is not only to see the play that the poor Jew goes to the theatre. It is to see his friends and the actors. With these latter he, and more frequently she, try in every way to make acquaintance, but commonly are compelled to adore at a distance. They love the songs that are heard on the stage, and for these the demand is so great that a certain bookshop on the East Side makes a specialty of publishing them.

The actor responds to this popular enthusiasm with sovereign contempt. He struts about in the cafes on Canal and Grand Streets, conscious of his greatness. He refers to the crowd as "Moses" with superior condescension or humorous vituperation. Like thieves, the actors have a jargon of their own, which is esoteric and jealously guarded. Their pride had recently given rise to an amusing strike at the People's Theatre. The actors of the three Yiddish companies in New York are normally paid on the share rather than the salary system. In the case of the company now at the People's Theatre, this system has proved very profitable for the past two years. The star actors, Jacob Adler and Boris Thomashevsky, and their wives, who are actresses — Mrs. Adler being the heavy realistic tragedienne and Mrs. Thomashevsky the star soubrette — have probably received on an average during that time as much as $125 a week for each couple. But they, with Mr. Edelstein, the business man, are lessees of the theatre, run the risk and pay the expenses, which are not small. The rent of the theatre is $20,000 a year, and weekly expenses, besides, amount to about $1100. The subordinate actors, who risk nothing, since they do not share the expenses, have made amounts during this favourable period ranging from $14 a week on the average for the poorest actors to $75 for those just beneath the "stars." But, in spite of what is exceedingly good pay in the Bowery, the actors of this theatre recently formed a union, and struck for wages instead of shares. This, however, was only an incidental feature. The real cause was that the management of the theatre, with the energetic Thomashevsky at the head, insisted that the actors should be prompt at rehearsals, and if they were not, indulged in unseemly epithets. The actors' pride was aroused, and the union was formed to insure their ease and dignity and to protect them from harsh words, particularly from those of Mr. Thomashevsky. The management imported actors from Chicago. Several of the actors here stood by them, notably Miss Weinblatt, a popular young ingénue, and Miss Gudinski, an actress of commanding presence. Miss Weinblatt forced her father, once an actor, now a farmer, into the service of the management. But the actors easily triumphed. Misses Gudinski and Weinblatt were forced to join the union, Mr. Weinblatt returned to his farm, the "scabs" were packed off to Philadelphia, and the wages system introduced. A delegation was sent to Philadelphia to throw cabbages at the new actors, who appeared in the Yiddish performances in that city. The triumphant actors now receive on the average probably $10 to $15 a week less than under the old system. Mr. Conrad, who began the disaffection, receives a salary of $29 a week, fully $10 less than he received for months before the strike. But the dignity of the Yiddish actor is now placed beyond assault. As one of them recently said: "We shall no longer be spat upon nor called 'dog.'"

The Yiddish actor is so supreme that until recently a regular system of hazing playwrights was in vogue. Joseph Latteiner and Professor M. Horowitz were long recognised as the only legitimate Ghetto playwrights. When a new writer came to the theatre with a manuscript, various were the pranks the actors would play. They would induce him to try, one after another, all the costumes in the house, in order to help him conceive the characters; or they would make him spout the play from the middle of the stage, they themselves retiring to the gallery, to see how it sounded. In the midst of his exertions they would slip away, and he would find himself shouting to the empty boards. Or, in the midst of a mock rehearsal, some actor would shout, "He is coming, the great Professor Horowitz, and he will eat you;" and they would rush from the theatre with the panic-stricken playwright following close at their heels.

The plays at these theatres vary in a general way with the varying audiences of which I have spoken above. The thinking socialists naturally select a less violent play than the comparatively illogical anarchists. Societies of relatively conservative Jews desire a historical play in which the religious Hebrew in relation to the persecuting Christian is put in pathetic and melodramatic situations. There are a very large number of "culture" pieces produced, which, roughly speaking, are plays in which the difference between the Jew of one generation and the next is dramatically portrayed. The pathos or tragedy involved in differences of faith and "point of view" between the old rabbi and his more enlightened children is expressed in many historical plays of the general character of *Uriel Acosta*, though in less lasting form. Such plays, however, are called "historical plunder" by that very up-to-date element of the intellectual Ghetto which is dominated by the Russian spirit of realism. It is the demand of these fierce realists that of late years has produced a supply of theatrical productions attempting to present a faithful picture of the actual conditions of life. Permeating all these classes of plays is the amusement instinct pure and simple. For the benefit of the crowd of ignorant people grotesque humour, popular songs, vaudeville tricks, are inserted everywhere.

Of these plays the realistic are of the most value, for they often give the actual Ghetto life with surprising strength and fidelity. This year has been their great season, and has developed a large crop of new playwrights, mainly journalists who write miscellaneous articles for the East Side newspapers. Jacob Gordin, who has been writing plays for several years, and who was the first realistic playwright, remains the strongest and most prominent in this kind of play. Professor Horowitz, who is now the lessee of the Windsor Theatre, situated on the Bowery, between Grand and Canal Streets, represents, along with Joseph Latteiner, the conservative and traditional aspects of the stage. He is an interesting man, fifty-six years of age, and has been connected with the Yiddish stage practically since its origin. His father was a teacher in a Hebrew school, and he himself is a man of uncommon learning. He has made a great study of the stage, has written one hundred and sixty-seven plays, and claims to be an authority on *dramaturgie*. The professor naturally regards himself and Latteiner as the "real" Yiddish playwrights. For many years after the first bands of actors reached the New York Ghetto these two men held undisputed sway. Latteiner leaned to "romantic," Horowitz to "culture," plays, and both used material which was mainly historical. The professor regards that as the bright period of the Ghetto stage. Since then there has been, in his opinion, a decadence which began with the translation of the classics into Yiddish. *Hamlet, Othello, King Lear*, and plays of Schiller, were put upon the stage and are still being performed. Sometimes they are almost literally translated, sometimes adapted until they are realistic representations of Jewish life. Gordin's *Yiddish King Lear*, for instance, represents Shakespeare's idea only in the most general way, and weaves about it a sordid story of Jewish character and life. Of *Hamlet* there are two versions, one adapted, in which Shakespeare's idea is reduced to a ludicrous shadow, the interest lying entirely in the presentation of Jewish customs; the other an almost literal translation. Professor Horowitz objects to the translation of the classics on the ground that the ignorant Yiddish public cannot understand them, because what learning they have is limited to distinctively Yiddish subjects and traditions.

Another important step in what the professor calls the degeneration of the stage was the introduction a few years ago of the American "pistol" play — meaning the fierce melodrama which has been for so long a characteristic of the English plays produced on the Bowery.

But what has contributed more than anything else to what the good man calls the present deplorable condition of the theatre was the advent of realism. "It was then," said the professor one day with calm indignation, "that the genuine Yiddish play was persecuted. Young writers came from Russia and swamped the Ghetto with scurrilous attacks on me and Latteiner. No number of the newspaper appeared that did not contain a scathing criticism. They did not object to the actors, who in reality were very bad, but it was the play they aimed at. These writers knew nothing about *dramaturgie*, but their heads were filled with senseless realism. Anything historical and distinctively Yiddish they thought bad. For a long time Latteiner and I were able to keep their realistic plays off the boards, but for the last few years there has been an open field for everybody. The result is that horrors under the mask of realism have been put upon the stage. This year is the worst of all — characters butchered on the stage, the coarsest language, the most revolting situations, without ideas, with no real material. It cannot last, however. Latteiner and I continue with our real Yiddish plays, and we shall yet regain entire possession of the field."

8
SCHOOLING

What should the public schools teach "minority"
youths? What should be the nature of the relation-
ship between the school, the home, and the community at large? Should the common schools teach
minority children something about their ethnic
background and the culture of their parents? What
kinds of teachers are needed to harmonize educa-
tion for citizenship with the special needs of culturally different and
usually poor children? What vocational preparation should be provided
for "minority" children by the public school curriculum? Should it be
the same for boys and girls?

Though a few key words have changed — "immigrant" has become
"minority" or "culturally deprived" or "black" — the questions sound
familiar today though they were posed in 1908 by Jane Addams before
a meeting of the National Education Association.

Then as now, the schools were admonished to do something about
high dropout rates among children of the poor and to improve the
vocational, civic, social, and cultural competence of hundreds of thousands of newcomers. Largely the children of parents who had migrated
from overseas, these pupils included substantial numbers of Negroes
and whites who were moving to the cities from farms, plantations, and
small towns.

In 1889 Jane Addams (1860–1935) and Ellen Gates Starr founded
Hull House in Chicago, one of the earliest social settlements in the
United States devoted to the betterment of civic and social life in the
slums. Winner, with Nicholas Murray Butler, of the 1931 Nobel Peace
Prize for her efforts to find moral substitutes for war, Miss Addams
was throughout her long life a tireless advocate of adult education for

the foreign-born, champion of child labor laws, and supporter of major welfare research undertakings.

John Rogers Commons (1862–1944), mentioned in the following selection, was an economist and reform-minded labor historian who taught at the University of Wisconsin. He served on various government commissions and published a ten-volume *Documentary History of Industrial Society* and a *History of Labor in the United States* which remain basic works in the academic study of labor history.

THE PUBLIC SCHOOL AND THE IMMIGRANT CHILD

Jane
Addams

I am always diffident when I come before a professional body of teachers, realizing as I do that it is very easy for those of us who look on to bring indictments against results; and realizing also that one of the most difficult situations you have to meet is the care and instruction of the immigrant child, especially as he is found where I see him, in the midst of crowded city conditions.

And yet in spite of the fact that the public school is the great savior of the immigrant district, and the one agency which inducts the children into the changed conditions of American life, there is a certain indictment which may justly be brought, in that the public school too often separates the child from his parents and widens that old gulf between fathers and sons which is never so cruel and so wide as it is between the immigrants who come to this country and their children who have gone to the public school and feel that they have there learned it all. The parents are thereafter subjected to certain judgment, the judgment of the young which is always harsh and in this instance founded upon the most superficial standard of Americanism. And yet there is a notion of culture which we would define as a knowledge of those things which have been long cherished by men, the things which men have loved because thru generations they have softened and interpreted life, and have endowed it with value and meaning. Could this standard have been given rather than the things which they see about them as the test

FROM *Proceedings and Addresses of the National Education Association, 1908* (Washington, D.C., 1908), pp. 99–102. Reprinted by permission of the National Education Association.

of so-called success, then we might feel that the public school has given at least the beginning of culture which the child ought to have. At present the Italian child goes back to its Italian home more or less disturbed and distracted by the contrast between the school and the home. If he throws off the control of the home because it does not represent the things which he has been taught to value he takes the first step toward the Juvenile Court and all the other operations of the law, because he has prematurely asserted himself long before he is ready to take care of his own affairs.

We find in the carefully prepared figures which Mr. Commons and other sociologists have published that while the number of arrests of immigrants is smaller than the arrests of native born Americans, the number of arrests among children of immigrants is twice as large as the number of arrests among the children of native born Americans. It would seem that in spite of the enormous advantages which the public school gives to these children it in some way loosens them from the authority and control of their parents, and tends to send them, without a sufficient rudder and power of self-direction, into the perilous business of living. Can we not say, perhaps, that the schools ought to do more to connect these children with the best things of the past, to make them realize something of the beauty and charm of the language, the history, and the traditions which their parents represent. It is easy to cut them loose from their parents, it requires cultivation to tie them up in sympathy and understanding. The ignorant teacher cuts them off because he himself cannot understand the situation, the cultivated teacher fastens them because his own mind is open to the charm and beauty of that old-country life. In short, it is the business of the school to give to each child the beginnings of a culture so wide and deep and universal that he can interpret his own parents and countrymen by a standard which is world-wide and not provincial.

The second indictment which may be brought is the failure to place the children into proper relation toward the industry which they will later enter. Miss Arnold has told us that children go into industry for a very short time. I believe that the figures of the United States census show the term to be something like six years for the women in industry as over against twenty-four years for men, in regard to continuity of service. Yet you cannot disregard the six years of the girls nor the twenty-four years of the boys, because they are the immediate occupation into which they enter after they leave the school — even the girls are bound to go thru that period — that is, the average immigrant girls are — before they enter the second serious business of life and maintain homes of their own. Therefore, if they enter industry unintelligently, without some notion of what it means, they find themselves totally unprepared for their first experience with American life, they are thrown out without the proper guide or clue which the public school might and ought to have given to them. Our industry has become so international, that it ought to be easy to use the materials it offers for immigrant children. The very processes and general principles which industry represents give a chance to prepare these immigrant children in a way which the most elaborated curriculum could not present. Ordinary material does not give the same international suggestion as industrial material does.

Third, I do not believe that the children who have been cut off from their own parents are going to be those who, when they become parents themselves, will know how to hold the family together and to connect it with the state. I should begin to teach the girls to be good mothers by teaching them to be good daughters. Take a girl whose mother has come from South Italy. The mother cannot adjust herself to the changed condition of housekeeping, does not know how to wash and bake here, and do the other things which she has always done well in Italy, because she has suddenly been transported from a village to a tenement house. If that girl studies these household conditions in relation to the past and to the present needs of the family, she is undertaking the very best possible preparation for her future obligations to a household of her own. And to my mind she can undertake it in no better way. Her own children are mythical and far away, but the little brothers and sisters pull upon her affections and her loyalty, and she longs to have their needs recognized in the school so that the school may give her some help. Her mother complains that the baby is sick in America because she cannot milk her own goat; she insists if she had her own goat's milk the baby would be quite well and flourishing, as the children were in Italy. If that girl can be taught that the milk makes the baby ill because it is not clean and be provided with a simple test that she may know when milk is clean, it may take her into the study not only of the milk within the four walls of the tenement house, but into the inspection of the milk of her district. The milk, however, remains good educational material, it makes even more concrete the connection which you would be glad to use between the household and the affairs of the American city. Let her not follow the mother's example of complaining about changed conditions; let her rather make the adjustment for her mother's entire household. We cannot tell what adjustments the girl herself will be called upon to make ten years from now; but we can give her the clue and the aptitude to adjust the family with which she is identified to the constantly changing conditions of city life. Many of us feel that, splendid as the public schools are in their relation to the immigrant child, they do not understand all of the difficulties which surround that child — all of the moral and emotional perplexities which constantly harass him. The children long that the school teacher should know something about the lives their parents lead and should be able to reprove the hooting children who make fun of the Italian mother because she wears a kerchief on her head, not only because they are rude but also because they are stupid. We send young people to Europe to see Italy, but we do not utilize Italy when it lies about the schoolhouse. If the body of teachers in our great cities could take hold of the immigrant colonies, could bring out of them their handicrafts and occupations, their traditions, their folk songs and folk lore, the beautiful stories which every immigrant colony is ready to tell and translate; could get the children to bring these things into school as the material from which culture is made and the material upon which culture is based, they would discover that by comparison that which they give them now is a poor meretricious and vulgar thing. Give these children a chance to utilize the historic and industrial material which they see about them and they will begin to have a sense of ease in America, a first consciousness of being at home. I believe if these people are welcomed upon the basis of the resources which they represent and the contributions which they bring, it may come to pass that these schools which deal with immigrants will find that they have a wealth of cultural and industrial material which will make the schools in other neighborhoods positively envious. A girl living in a tenement household, helping along this tremendous adjustment, healing over this great moral upheaval which the parents have suffered and which leaves them bleeding and sensitive — such a girl has a richer experience and a finer material than any girl from a more fortunate household can have at the present moment.

I wish I had the power to place before you what it seems to me is the opportunity that the immigrant colonies present to the public school: the most endearing occupation of leading the little child, who will in turn lead his family, and bring them with him into the brotherhood for which they are longing. The immigrant child cannot make this demand upon the school because he does not know how to formulate it; it is for the teacher both to perceive it and to fulfil it.

9

THE COURTS

"The alarming increase of the number of alien criminals" became a favorite topic for newspaper editorials sometime after 1890 whenever a sensational crime was committed in the foreign section of a large city. During the first decade of the twentieth century, official statistics fell in line with popular sentiment. In his reports for 1908 and 1909, the Commissioner-General of Immigration noted an increase in the number of aliens in penal institutions from 1904 to 1908. The superintendent of the New York State prisons in his report for 1909 emphasized that "the crowded condition of our prisons is largely due to the influx of immigrants during the last few years" and recommended the "exclusion of this undesirable class of immigrants."

Many Americans therefore began to ask questions which do not sound at all strange today if we substitute "minority" for immigrants or aliens. Why were there so many immigrants in our jails? What was the nature, extent, and cause of immigrant criminality? Was it true that courts and police did not understand the alien and therefore magnified his conflicts with our laws? To what extent did the failure of law enforcement agencies to understand and deal effectively with immigrant lawbreakers intensify their resentment against a system of law and order they did not understand?

Questions like these had been discussed extensively in the popular magazines and newspapers for some thirty years when a wave of nationalist hysteria around 1915 began to carry along sizable numbers of Americans. Heretofore, the foreign-born had been suspected of furnishing too many lawbreakers and prison inmates. After our entry into World War I, the alien was also suspected of "un-American" activities in the service of foreign enemies.

An army of self-appointed superpatriots and watchdogs of one hundred percent Americanism broadened what was at first a drive against foreign-born suspected of sympathies for Germany and her allies into a crusade against Bolshevism from about 1917 to 1920. Many states passed laws banning the use of foreign languages for instruction in public and private primary schools. Government investigators, led by the ambitious Attorney General A. Mitchell Palmer, searched everywhere for disloyal "Reds." This search for enemies within generally focused upon the foreign-born — those with an accent, little or no English, or members of radical organizations.

The book review reprinted below appeared in *The Survey*, a weekly devoted to local and general philanthropy. The volume it describes was commissioned as part of a cooperative research project into methods of assimilating immigrants initiated in 1918 by the Carnegie Corporation. The books, which appeared in the 1920s, analyzed the difficulties encountered by aliens in the Americanization process. Kate Holladay Claghorn (1863–1938) whose *The Immigrant's Day in Court* dealt with the important topic of the immigrants' contact with American law and the courts, was educated at Bryn Mawr College and Yale, where she earned a Ph.D. degree. Well known as sociologist, author, and housing authority, Miss Claghorn worked for various governmental and private agencies dealing with juvenile delinquency and the tenement house issues, wrote numerous articles and several books, and was a staff member of the New York School of Social Work from 1912 to 1932.

PILOTING THE BOMB SQUAD

A BOOK ON THE IMMIGRANT AND THE LAW

Ruth Crawford

FROM *The Survey*, XLIX (January 1, 1923), pp. 461–2.

Some months ago a well known social worker said: "I have just checked at the Grand Central station a suitcase with enough dynamite to get me arrested." The dynamite is all in the ninth volume of the Carnegie Foundation Americanization Studies, shortly to appear: *The Immigrant's Day in Court* by Kate Holladay Claghorn, Harper's. It rests in the fearlessness with which Miss Claghorn presents in all their crudity the stupidity and exploitation which exist in that realm of our national and civil life that is designated to guarantee justice. It lies in the skill with which she uses the "case method" to pile up evidence bringing the reader through independent conviction to inevitable conclusions.

"It is the purpose of this study to follow the immigrant from the port of entry, through some of the troubles that call for the intervention of the law, to see to what extent the law reaches his troubles, how far the administration of law secures for him the substantial justice aimed at in any legal system, what is done by various agencies to adjust him to our laws and legal procedure, and what are his reactions in the way of satisfaction with the country and friendliness to it."

We are led, first, to a survey of the schemes whereby unsuspecting immigrants may be defrauded from the day when a ticket is bought in the old country at second-class rates for subsequent steerage accommodation, through the perils of the journey, the hurdles of our exclusion law, the expense of getting and holding a job, or the loss of months of savings at the hands of a "friend," to the latest style in immigrant exploitation; shrewd profiteering in the fluctuation of European currency. Money Troubles, the chapter is entitled — and they are the first troubles often that bring the immigrant into contact with American law. It is a shock to perceive that much of the reference material dates back to the report of the United States Immigration Commission and to the pre-war studies of the Massachusetts and New York Bureaus of Immigration — that these illustrations over a decade old still accurately portray conditions that obtain today; and this in spite of some legislation that has been put on the statute books of many states since 1910, such as workmen's compensation laws and laws regulating private banking.

Through misfortune of some such sort, the immigrant is frequently brought into contact with the law and the court almost immediately upon his arrival. Each such experience affords him a lesson in what is established as justice in this country and adds its weight toward establishing the degree to which his allegiance and respect for the country will rise.

Public opinion has been led to believe that the "burden of foreign criminality is unduly heavy, and attention is called to criminality rates apparently showing that the foreign-born resident of this country is far more prone to offend against the law than is the native born." On this point Miss Claghorn's training as a statistician provides her with more "dynamite." She shows the fallacy of comparing the foreign-born population, with its large proportion of young adult males and its low proportion of women and children, with the white population of native parentage. When the necessary corrections for sex and age have been made, the ratios for the two groups are about the same. Not only that, but an analysis of the causes of commitments brings Miss Claghorn to the following conclusion:

"From the statistics at best, with all possible corrections and allowances, we can get only a rough measurement of foreign criminality. Really to understand the immigrant as an offender we must go back of the statistics to concrete cases, follow the social history of the offender, and note the tangle of circumstances involved. In many of the cases of foreign criminality, we cannot discover a clear connection between the native qualities or the peculiar circumstances of the immigrant in this country and the fact of commitment for crime. In many others, however, we seem able to trace such a connection. Cases are found in which the immigrant who is innocent of the offense charged has been committed to prison for it as a result of his ignorance of our language and customs. In other cases the changed circumstances of life in the new country, the breaking down of old habits and old restraints, seem to occasion criminal conduct on the part of people who probably would have gone straight in their habitual surroundings.

"For example:

"In one instance a Pole deserted by his wife who had gone to live with another man, made three successive visits to the police station to enquire what he could do in the matter. The police gave him no satisfaction at any visit, and in despair of getting his wrong redressed in any legal way, he took matters into his own hands and shot his wife and her lover."

Other cases are cited which show that "conversion of normal humanity into a criminal class may be going on simply through failure to understand and deal with the peculiar elements involved." Such cases are strong arguments for the proposition:

"The judge who handles immigrant cases should understand the character, the situation and the racial peculiarities of the immigrant in order to adjust the treatment of the case in accordance with true principles of justice."

Introduction in rapid succession to the saloon keeper, the landlord and the banker to whom the immigrant may turn when in trouble to ask for legal advice show that even the approach of the foreign-born complainant to the court and the judge is fraught with peril:

"When this species of assistance comes to be asked frequently from the same friendly advisor, he may organize a method of supplying it and form the habit of recommending certain lawyers who will pay him in return for the patronage secured."

Thus arises the genus "runner." There are many varieties, the "ambulance chaser" who gets daily lists of accidents and descends upon the injured person or his family, importuning them to engage the services of this or that particular lawyer. There is the bail commissioner who frequents the police station at night and approaches the newly arrested immigrant, offering to release him on bail, and finally the eternal string of runners for the "immigrant lawyer" who, with the language at his command, usually convinces the poor immigrant that there is "no chance before the American court without the aid of a lawyer skilled in the special kind of tricks."

Of the immigrant's experience in the court itself Miss Claghorn writes at length, using to excellent advantage the first-hand information gathered by the field workers for this study in the Justice and Aldermanic courts of many of the smaller cities of Illinois, Ohio and Pennsylvania. The lack of educational qualification for the office of justice, the dependence upon fees for a livelihood, the election to office for short terms by local constituencies — all these are factors which warrant the dismal verbal pictures of the justices interviewed and the conclusion that not only are many of them notorious grafters but that they connive with the court constable who goes out and "makes arrests, with or without cause, for the sake of the resulting court fees which are shared by the justice."

In the larger cities where the justice courts have been done away with and a municipal or magistrates court has been established instead, the investigators found the situation improved. The Central Court of Boston, the Municipal Courts of Chicago, Cleveland, Philadelphia and Cincinnati, and the Magistrates' Courts of New York City are in a different class. The removal of the fee system has done away with one great source of exploitation — "we do not find open swindling." The especial need of the foreign-born appears to center around the absence, often, of honest and trained court interpreters; and there is need for a wider use of discretionary power by the judge so that not only the essential element of justice, "equality before the law," be recognized but also the fact that "equal treatment of unequals leads to inequality." Miss Claghorn pleads:

"If we cannot require foreign birth or knowledge of foreign languages on the part of the judge and the probation officer, we can at least ask that the judge have added to his legal knowledge a certain broad sociological and psychological equipment, and at least some knowledge of the racial varieties with which he deals."

The reaction of the immigrant to the institutions in his new environment is colored by his old-world conceptions. The state of bewilderment which often results is apt to be disregarded or even used against him.

But the most important contribution of the volume is its chapter on the deportations of 1919 and 1920. Here, at length, with carefully annotated references, is an exhaustive statement concerning the activity of the Department of Labor and the Department of Justice in their hysterical search for anarchists, I. W. W.s, Communists and kindred radicals. Here we find the history of the "Red Special" which brought the first train-load of fifty-four persons ordered deported under the anarchy clause of the Immigration Law to Ellis Island in February, 1919; of the campaign in the Far West against the I. W. W.; of the difficulties of combating Habeas Corpus proceedings under the indefinitely framed provisions of our immigration law which made active agitation, not membership in a radical organization, cause for deportation; of the change in the law whereby Congress decided that membership should be sufficient reason for deportation. The next sweep of the Department of Justice resulted in a passenger list of 249 for the steamship *Buford*, popularly known as the Soviet Ark because a large majority of the deportees were Russians, picked up in raids on People's Houses — the name by which the cooperative home of Russian societies in a given community was usually known — houses where the unmarried Russian immigrant men gathered at night, "not because they were especially interested in any one society or activity, but simply to be where they could meet other Russians, speak the Russian language, find Russian books and newspapers to read if they were able to read, get someone to write letters for them if they were not able to write, drink tea served in the Russian style, play games to while away the long evenings after work was over, and to have an opportunity to study." Soon after the sailing of the *Buford*, there were raids in thirty-three cities and towns against members of the Communist Labor Party. More raids followed in Detroit and in New York City and vicinity. The details of the raids, together with the verbal testimony of men seized, affidavits of the unwarranted cruelty of the police agents, of frequent seizure without warrant, and of the keeping of men in jail or at an immigration station for months, should provide food for serious thought on the part of every American interested in the process of evolving a nation of loyal citizens. Miss Claghorn says:

"As a result of the year's campaign, how far did the government actually clear the country of elements considered dangerous? The estimates of the number of 'dangerous radicals' made by the government agents both at the beginning and in the course of the campaign were alarmingly large. A record of the activities of the Department of Justice, presented by the attorney general at the hearings of June 1 and 2, 1920, estimated the number of radicals as follows: I. W. W., 300,000; Communists, 40,000; Communist Labor Party, 10,000; Union of Russian Workers, 4,000; and two small anarchist groups of Spaniards and Italians.

"Then when we note that the entire number actually deported for anarchy for the fiscal year ending June 30, 1920, the year covering the raids, was only 314, and for the fiscal year of 1921, the year in which most of the cases were disposed of, was only 446, it is seen how ineffective, even from the government's point of view, was the long and expensive and terrifying campaign against the Reds."

As regards the effect on the hundreds of aliens who were arrested, after being beaten and dragged about, and held "incommunicado" before being given a trial at which, in some cases, there was no interpreter although the accused could not speak English, the feelings of one Mike Bratko, "a bus boy at a restaurant on Fourteenth Street," are probably general. Mike had dropped into the People's House on Seventeenth Street, "to ask about a Russian entertainment," when he was arrested. He used to drop in there occasionally, he said, but any one could go to the People's House, they did not have to be members. He went to meetings occasionally but did not understand their teachings — he was not literate enough. He denied that he was an anarchist, and said he did not believe in violence. He was also asked whether he believed in God, which was certainly beside the point. He would like to go back to Russia, he said, because, "since my arrival in this country I found an unfriendly attitude toward me, by the people of this country. They call me Polak, they say I cannot have everything they have, and I am treated in a manner that I feel I would do better in returning to my native country where my relatives are. I cannot make a living here. Whatever factory I go to, when they hear I am a Russian, I am discriminated against. I am opposed to violence, but they use violence against me in beating me up, so I do not care to remain in this country." There was nothing against this man except the claim that anarchist literature had been found in his room, but it took three hearings at three different dates to secure his release under surveillance.

The "means of adjustment," discussed in the concluding chapter, apparently to Miss Claghorn rest chiefly with the legal aid societies in the various cities and with certain private social agencies which in the course of their service to immigrants are called upon to give legal advice or to see that their client gets legal redress in one form or another.

Miss Claghorn has pointed the way in her quotation from an address of Charles E. Hughes before the New York Bar Association, in which he said:

"We are fond of speaking of Americanization. If our Bar Association could create a sentiment which would demand that in all our cities the police courts and minor civil courts should fairly represent the republic as the embodiment of the spirit of justice, our problem of Americanization would be more than half solved. . . . The security of the republic will be found in the treatment of the poor and the ignorant."

Whether the fuse is lighted depends upon the citizens who create public opinion and determine whether the attitude of the foreign-born to the law shall be one of resentment or of confidence in its fairness.

10
MARGINAL MEN

Historians generally have studied and written about the first generation of new Americans, the men and women who got off the boat. Sociologists have been attracted more by the lot of the second and third generations, the children and grandchildren of immigrants. The sociologist Robert E. Park was one of the first to describe the son of immigrants who is torn between the conflicting demands of two cultural traditions. Park conceived of him as "condemned to live in two societies and in two, not merely different but antagonistic cultures." An individual who lives in two worlds, yet belongs truly to none — a "marginal man," Park called him.

While sociologists usually treat marginality as a social handicap, for some children of immigrants this kind of "in-between-ness" has meant an opportunity to become mediators between two cultures. Ethnic leaders and politicians depending on ethnic votes have capitalized on their position between two cultural worlds. The sociologist's view of marginality is summed up in James W. Vander Zanden, *American Minority Relations, The Sociology of Race and Ethnic Groups* (New York, The Ronald Press Company, 1966). Oscar Handlin's *Children of the Uprooted* (New York, George Braziller, Inc., 1966) surveys the making of Americans as revealed in writings of members of the second generation, the children of immigrants. The following appeal for giving children of immigrants a chance to assume a leadership in the assimilative process was written by the executive secretary of the Erie, Pennsylvania, County Anti-Tuberculosis Society.

THE SECOND GENERATION OF IMMIGRANTS IN THE ASSIMILATIVE PROCESS

Thaddeus
Sleszynski

The second generation of immigrants is considered by most writers and students as one group, thoroughly American. Because these young people are born in America, because they understand and speak English, their assimilation is taken for granted. Closer observation and analysis, however, reveal the fact that this is not altogether true. There are several more or less distinct groups among these people, depending on the different attitudes and reactions they may have to the highly organized life of the foreign communities which has in some way influenced the lives of nearly all of them.

These foreign colonies, which are to be found in every industrial center in the United States, are an outgrowth of the attempt made by the immigrants to adjust themselves to the strange conditions in a new land. A common language and in nearly every case a common faith are the foundations on which these communities are built. As they exist today they furnish the elements for satisfying all the social, economic and spiritual needs of their members. With many of the racial groups the parish is the center of all the community activities. In it are centered the religious and social activities, the dramatic clubs, the singing societies and the mutual benefit associations. Besides the parish halls there are other common meeting places, such as lodge halls erected and used almost exclusively by the immigrants of one nationality. Amusement places where the people can enjoy vaudeville and dialogue in their own language are found in every foreign colony. Whether published there or not, some foreign language newspaper circulates in the community. Through it is sifted all the news of the outside world. Practically all business is transacted in the common language, and the community has its own doctors and lawyers.

If the colonies are large enough, they are sure to be represented by politicians who are members of the dominant race. Since these men are usually interested in delivering the votes, they encourage their fellow countrymen to become citizens, often to the extent of organizing classes in English and citizenship. Consequently, whatever

FROM *The Annals of the American Academy of Political and Social Science*, XCIII (January, 1921), pp. 156–61. Reprinted by permission of the American Academy of Political and Social Science.

ideals of American citizenship the members of the community hold are acquired largely through these men. In many of the parochial schools the foreign language is given equal prominence with the English. Thus, in addition to hearing the foreign language spoken at home, the children learn it in school and come to use it even on the playground. It is more necessary to know the foreign language than to know English in order to make one's way about in some of these neighborhoods. Moreover, in most instances, these more or less isolated foreign colonies are more closely in touch with one another than with the city of which they form a geographical part. The contact with the larger community is maintained through a few leaders, usually politicians, who are in touch with American institutions. Many of these are already of the second generation. It is no doubt necessary for the immigrants who are ignorant of American ways of life to work out community problems along racial lines. There is no other way in which they can do it. In many of the older communities where large numbers of the people speak and read English this practice is no longer necessary. Nevertheless it is perpetuated to the advantage of a few and carried on even by the second and third generations.

There is much of art and beauty among our foreign folk that should be preserved for future generations. Their music and folk songs have a rhythm and a beauty all their own. We have nothing in America quite like the dances which they all danced together at the village festivals in Europe. There is an appreciation of opera and good music among the common people found only among Americans of education and training. More of their books deserve to be translated into English for the profit and enjoyment of all. There is a hospitality and a spirit of neighborliness among our foreign born which we of this day have somehow lost. There is a feeling of pride in their work felt by artisans who have had their training in the small towns of Europe that is not often found among American workmen. All these things and many more should be passed on to become the heritage of future generations. Plainly, whatever of this heritage is preserved must be done so through the second and third generations. The question that arises is, are they doing this or are they merely perpetuating racial solidarity?

Because the young people of the second generation mingle more or less with Americans, gain a knowledge of American traditions and institutions and speak English fluently, they come under influences that have not touched their parents. As a result, there is an inevitable reaction on their part to the standards, interests and attitudes found in the foreign colony. This reaction is different with different individuals. In general they may be divided into five groups. One group of these young people largely conforms to the dominant tendencies of the foreign colony and remains a part of it. A second group entirely loses its contact with the foreign colony. A third group, though in no way participating in the life of the colony, is claimed because of unusual achievements. A fourth group, though it has been absorbed by the larger community, plays an important part in the organized life of the foreign community. The last group keeps in touch with the foreign colony and appreciates probably more than the others the desirable elements that should be preserved, but at the same time it is making a conscious effort to remove the barriers that separate the immigrant colony from the larger community.

GROUP CONFORMING TO STANDARDS OF FOREIGN COLONY

The members of the first group are handicapped more than any of the others, in fact more than any group of young people in America. Practically all of them come from homes where there are large families and no leisure. Most of them are compelled to leave school at an early age because of the economic conditions of their parents. In many cities where one-quarter to one-third of the children in the elementary schools is of foreign parentage, only a small percentage is found in the high schools and less than two per cent in our colleges. When they are old enough to work they must have a job. If through great sacrifice on the part of hard-working parents they receive the minimum education for one of the professions, they start out burdened with debts to pay or relatives to support. So they must devote all of their time to making ends meet. Because of their lack of leisure, but few of them are well acquainted with the music, art and literature of their own nationality. At the same time, they have only a superficial knowledge of the best in American life.

These young people remain always definite factors in the life of the immigrant community in which they were born. In most instances they speak the foreign language and read the foreign language newspaper. Their social life is limited to the foreign colony, and they usually marry in their own group. Most of them are employed as unskilled workmen in our various industries, but some of them learn a trade or take the places of the older men in business

and become the small shop-keepers of the neighborhood. Some of
them become lawyers and doctors and a few become the political
and religious leaders for their community. The members of this group
no doubt exercise an Americanizing influence, but their tendency
is to follow the line of least resistance and conform to the accepted
standards of the community. They form a group that, though born
in America, is not entirely of America.

THOSE SEPARATED FROM FOREIGN COLONY

In the second group may be placed those young people born in
America of foreign parentage who either lose their contact with the
foreign colony or perhaps have never had any. They may have the
same educational and economic handicaps as the first group. Some
of them are born outside the foreign colony, never learn to speak
the foreign language and never come in contact with any people
of like parentage. Others become separated from friends and relatives
through permanent employment and residence in a place where there
is no community of their particular nationality. Since there is no
opportunity to speak or read the foreign language, it is often forgotten. Many of these young people, seeing the difference between
their social life in the colony and the less limited one of their
American friends, come to despise everything connected with the
foreign colony. They often deliberately leave home, change their
names and by so doing renounce their nationality. Association with
people who look down upon foreigners brings about similar results.
Some of the members of this group lose everything of their foreign
heritage and acquire only that which is cheapest in American life.
On the other hand, others are thoroughly American and hold their
own in American society.

THOSE CLAIMED BY THE FOREIGN COLONIES

The third group, doubtless the smallest of all, includes those who
have no social or economic interests in an immigrant community.
They are the artists, writers and musicians to whom the members
of their own nationality point with pride as being of the same race
with themselves. They belong entirely to the larger community.

Nevertheless, they do not deny their nationality or change their names, but are proud of their heritage, and interpret for the rest of the world the music, art and philosophy of their own race. They are not only keeping alive the best of their own traditions, but they are also making a great contribution to America.

LEADERS OF BOTH FOREIGN BORN AND AMERICANS

The fourth group includes those who because of unusual opportunity or ability have succeeded in winning a place in the larger community as well as in the immigrant colony. They usually acquire a good education, and by dint of hard work and persistent effort gain positions of leadership among both foreign born and Americans. They often do not live in the foreign colony, but at the same time they keep in touch with it because of financial or political interests there. They speak the foreign language fluently and are more or less acquainted with the culture and traditions of their own nationality. At the same time they know the best in American life. Among them are bankers, business men, lawyers and doctors. They serve not only the members of their own racial group but the larger community as well. Many of them are public-spirited citizens who are entrusted with high public offices by the larger community. In this capacity they render valuable service and gain the respect and recognition of all. They are becoming the real leaders in our immigrant communities and are in a position to serve as the interpreters of their people to America and of America to their people. Unfortunately, instead of bringing the foreign colony closer to America, many of them capitalize its racial solidarity for their own private interests. As American citizens, with interests and experiences reaching far beyond the limits of the foreign colony, they do not approve of the standards set by the foreign-born leaders. There is no doubt that they exercise an Americanizing influence, but they are prone to feel out the sentiments of the majority before taking a stand on any issue involving the colony.

THOSE ACTIVE IN ASSIMILATION

The distinguishing characteristics of the last group are exemplified in a few social workers who speak foreign languages. Most of these young people are born in a foreign colony and few have had the advantages of a liberal education. Many of them have not even finished the high school. Because of their knowledge of foreign languages, social agencies have taken them out of their jobs in factories, department stores and offices to serve as clerks and stenographers as well as interpreters. Many of them continue to occupy these minor positions, others become efficient social workers, and a few succeed to executive positions. They are familiar not only with the language but also with the traditions, customs and peculiarities of their immigrant fathers. Most of them take an active part in the social and religious life of the foreign colonies, and at the same time they participate in the activities of the larger community. They thus have points of contact which the American social workers can never hope to gain.

Because these young people are working through the community agencies they have an opportunity to view the problems of their own people from the standpoint of the needs of the community as a whole. They are specializing in the solution of problems arising from maladjustments, and so they see more clearly than those in any of the other groups just what are the narrowing influences in our immigrant communities that should be removed. Moreover, they feel that it is their duty to remain in these communities and by working from within them to remove these influences. They appreciate that there is much that should be preserved and passed on as the heritage of future generations, that many activities must be continued along racial lines, and that the use of the foreign language is still necessary. But because they have gained a vision of the ultimate social goal, they see the next steps that are to be taken to bring the foreign colonies into closer relationship with the larger communities of which they are parts.

Inevitably, they clash with the present leaders. This clash of ideas as to methods and policies in working out the problems of our immigrant communities can be illustrated by an account of what took place in a club formed by the social workers who spoke the language of the most important racial group in one of our large cities. This club included, in addition to about twenty workers employed by American social agencies, a number of leaders interested in social work in the colony. These foreign leaders usually considered the problems of the colony from the standpoint of their people alone. The social workers considered them from the standpoint of the community as a whole. The foreign leaders were inclined to work out a solution separately, by action taken through their own organizations. The social workers believed the solution should be found through community agencies. Where the foreign leaders often regarded the community agencies as instruments to be used for the particular advantage of their people, the social workers naturally regarded them as the means whereby all the racial groups could be brought together. The foreign leaders usually expected the social workers to favor the members of the colony and to conceal from the agencies that employed them many of the existing evils. At the same time, they hesitated to take any stand against the members of the colony who were responsible for some of these evils. Because of these opposing tendencies, the club went to pieces after three years of useful existence. This same conflict is in evidence wherever these young people meet with the present leaders in the foreign colonies. Though this group is best fitted to hasten the process of assimilation its peculiar value has as yet not been generally recognized.

Each group has its place and its share in the assimilation of the foreign born. Without the first group, the organizations and institutions established by the immigrants would go to pieces before their period of usefulness is past. The second proves that complete assimilation is possible, but not always desirable. The third group emphasizes the cultural contribution which our immigrants can make to America. The fourth suggests what these people, through their inherent ability, can accomplish when their handicaps are removed. The last group shows that the process of assimilation can be worked out from within if those capable of leadership could be given the opportunity to prepare themselves for this responsibility.

11

CULTURAL PLURAL-ISM vs. ABSORPTION

 In 1914 the sociologist Edward A. Ross, a prolific writer, advocate of immigration restriction, and race-conscious social scientist, published his *The Old World in the New*. In a chapter typically entitled "American and Immigrant Blood" he wrote that ten to twenty percent of the new immigrants "are hirsute, low-browed, big-faced persons of obviously low mentality ... [who] clearly belong in skins, in wattled huts at the close of the Great Ice Age. These oxlike men are descendants of those *who always stayed behind*."

Ross' ideas concerning race and nationality are no longer accepted by most educated men and women. However, most American historians and sociologists agree that the "melting pot" did not obliterate all distinct traits of the ethnic, racial, and religious groups in it and reduce them to a bland, uniform mixture, or produce a new American type.

If the attempt to absorb the immigrants failed, then what did happen to them? The following article, the concluding part of a long review of Ross' *The Old World in the New* by Horace Kallen, a Harvard-educated philosopher, is perhaps the best-known statement of the cultural pluralism view of what ought to be happening to immigrant groups in the United States.

Though the cultural pluralism hypothesis is espoused today by representatives of various ethnic groups, including some Black Nationalists, there are also serious objections to it as an accurate *description* of ethnic group life in the United States. Proponents of cultural pluralism overlook the extreme mobility of Americans. They admit that ethnic life in the past depended upon the existence of ethnic districts which, except for Negroes, have largely disappeared for other groups. Self-help

109

societies, once so important in the life of subcultures, are less important in the welfare state. Many men today have first loyalties to their professions or specialized vocations rather than to ethnic and familial traditions. The general movement of our society, and of technological society in general, is away from tribal and group and ethnic exclusivity toward national uniformity. Language, dress, separate ethnic churches, the ethnic press, even gestures and ethnic food preferences are on the decline. The concentration of members of some ethnic groups in certain occupations is diminishing, while the rate of intermarriage, that other barometer of the extent of ethnic solidarity, is going up for all groups.

Conversely, technology, usually the foe of ethnic exclusiveness and solidarity, has opened up some unforeseen opportunities for the strengthening of ethnic traditions. Microfilm allows the reproduction and inexpensive distribution of scarce books, church, and birth records. Recordings spread folk music into homes and schools. Lower air fares and group flights enable many to take frequent trips to the "old country." Greater leisure and less demand for the work of the young allow some of them to spend a summer or a year abroad studying their grandparents' language, culture, and history. In several large cities television and radio stations cater to special ethnic groups. In short, while ethnic subcultures are apparently on the decline if measured by the usual indices like language maintenance, endogamy (marrying only within one's ethnic or social group), and residential segregation, subcultures continue to supplement an emergent national cultural "style." Whether subcultures are, therefore, in the long view of history, declining, holding their own in attenuated form, or gaining strength, each reader will have to decide for himself.

DEMOCRACY VERSUS THE MELTING POT

Horace M. Kallen

The array of forces for and against that like-mindedness which is the stuff and essence of nationality aligns itself as follows: *For* it make social imitation of the upper by the lower classes, the facility of communications, the national pastimes of baseball and motion-picture, the mobility of population, the cheapness of printing, and the public schools. *Against* it make the primary ethnic differences with which the population starts, its stratification over an enormous extent of country, its industrial and economic stratification. We are an English-speaking country, but in no intimate and inevitable way, as is New Zealand or Australia, or even Canada. English is to us what Latin was to the Roman provinces and to the middle ages — the language of the upper and dominant class, the vehicle and symbol of culture: for the mass of our population it is a sort of Esperanto or Ido, a *lingua franca* necessary less in the spiritual than the economic contacts of the daily life. This mass is composed of elementals, peasants — Mr. Ross speaks of their menacing American life with "peasantism" — the proletarian foundation material of all forms of civilization. Their self-consciousness as groups is comparatively weak. This is a factor which favors their "assimilation," for the more cultivated a group is, the more it is aware of its individuality, and the less willing it is to surrender that individuality. One need think only of the Puritans themselves, leaving Holland for fear of absorption into the Dutch population; of the Creoles and Pennsylvania Germans of this country, or of the Jews, anywhere. In his judgment of the assimilability of various stocks Mr. Ross neglects this important point altogether, probably because his attention is fixed on existing contrasts rather than potential similarities. Peasants, however, having nothing much to surrender in taking over a new culture, feel no necessary break, and find the transition easy. It is the shock of confrontation with other ethnic groups and the feeling of aliency that generates in them an intenser self-consciousness, which then militates against Americanization in spirit by reinforcing the two factors to which the spiritual expression of the proletarian has been largely confined. These factors are language and religion. Religion is, of course, no more a "universal" than language. The history of Christianity makes evident enough how religion is modified, even

FROM *The Nation*, C (February 25, 1915), pp. 217 – 20. Reprinted by permission of Liveright Publishing Corp., New York, from *Culture and Democracy in the United States* by Horace M. Kallen. Copyright Renewal 1952 by Horace M. Kallen.

inverted, by race, place, and time. It becomes a principle of separation, often the sole repository of the national spirit, almost always the conservator of the national language and of the tradition that is passed on with the language to succeeding generations. Among immigrants, hence, religion and language tend to be coordinate: a single expression of the spontaneous and instinctive mental life of the masses, and the primary inward factors making against assimilation. Mr. Ross, I note, tends to grow shrill over the competition of the parochial school with the public school, at the same time that he belittles the fact "that on Sundays Norwegian is preached in more churches in America than in Norway."

And Mr. Ross's anxiety would, I think, be more than justified were it not that religion in these cases always does more than it intends. For it conserves the inward aspect of nationality rather than mere religion, and tends to become the centre of exfoliation of a higher type of personality among the peasants in the natural terms of their own *natio*. This *natio*, reaching consciousness first in a reaction against America, then as an effect of the competition with Americanization, assumes spiritual forms other than religious: the parochial school, to hold its own with the public school, gets secularized while remaining national. *Natio* is what underlies the vehemence of the "Americanized" and the spiritual and political unrest of the Americans. It is the fundamental fact of American life to-day, and in the light of it Mr. Wilson's resentment of the "hyphenated" American is both righteous and pathetic. But a hyphen attaches, in things of the spirit, also to the "pure" English American. His cultural mastery tends to be retrospective rather than prospective. At the present time there is no dominant American mind. Our spirit is inarticulate, not a voice, but a chorus of many voices each singing a rather different tune. How to get order out of this cacophony is the question for all those who are concerned about those things which alone justify wealth and power, concerned about justice, the arts, literature, philosophy, science. What must, what *shall* this cacophony become — a unison or a harmony?

For decidedly the older America, whose voice and whose spirit was New England, is gone beyond recall. Americans still are the artists and thinkers of the land, but they work, each for himself, without common vision or ideals. The older tradition has passed from a life into a memory, and the newer one, so far as it has an Anglo-Saxon base, is holding its own beside more and more formidable rivals, the expression in appropriate form of the national inheritances of the various populations concentrated in the various

States of the Union, populations of whom their national self-consciousness is perhaps the chief spiritual asset. Think of the Creoles in the South and the French-Canadians in the North, clinging to French for so many generations and maintaining, however weakly, spiritual and social contacts with the mother-country; of the Germans, with their *Deutschthum*, their *Männerchöre, Turnvereine,* and *Schützenfeste*; of the universally separate Jews; of the intensely nationalistic Irish; of the Pennsylvania Germans; of the indomitable Poles, and even more indomitable Bohemians; of the 30,000 Belgians in Wisconsin, with their "Belgian" language, a mixture of Walloon and Flemish welded by reaction to a strange social environment. Except in such cases as the town of Lead, South Dakota, the great ethnic groups of proletarians, thrown upon themselves in a new environment, generate from among themselves the other social classes which Mr. Ross misses so sadly among them: their shopkeepers, their physicians, their attorneys, their journalists, and their national and political leaders, who form the links between them and the greater American society. They develop their own literature, or become conscious of that of the mother-country. As they grow more prosperous and "Americanized," as they become freed from the stigma of "foreigner," they develop group self-respect: the "wop" changes into a proud Italian, the "hunky" into an intensely nationalist Slav. They learn, or they recall, the spiritual heritage of their nationality. Their cultural abjectness gives way to cultural pride and the public schools, the libraries, and the clubs become beset with demands for texts in the national language and literature.

The Poles are an instance worth dwelling upon. Mr. Ross's summary of them is as striking as it is premonitory. There are over a million of them in the country, a backward people, prolific, brutal, priest-ridden — a menace to American institutions. Yet the urge that carries them in such numbers to America is not unlike that which carried the Pilgrim Fathers. Next to the Jews, whom their brethren in their Polish home are hounding to death, the unhappiest people in Europe, exploited by both their own upper classes and the Russian conqueror, they have resisted extinction at a great cost. They have clung to their religion because it was a mark of difference between them and their conquerors; because they love liberty, they have made their language of literary importance in Europe. Their aspiration, impersonal, disinterested, as it must be in America, to free Poland, to conserve the Polish spirit, is the most hopeful and American thing about them — the one thing that stands actually between them and brutalization through complete economic degradation. It lifts them higher than anything that, in fact, America offers them. The same thing is true for the Bohemians, 17,000 of them, workingmen in Chicago, paying a proportion of their wage to maintain schools in the Bohemian tongue and free thought; the same thing is true of many other groups.

How true it is may be observed from a comparison of the vernacular dailies and weeklies with the yellow American press which is concocted expressly for the great American masses. The content of the former, when the local news is deducted, is a mass of information, political, social, scientific; often translations into the vernacular of standard English writing, often original work of high literary quality. The latter, when the news is deducted, consists of the sporting page and the editorial page. Both pander rather than awaken, so that it is no wonder that in fact the intellectual and spiritual pabulum of the great masses consists of the vernacular papers in the national tongue. With them go also the vernacular drama, and the thousand and one other phenomena which make a distinctive culture, the outward expression of that fundamental like-mindedness wherein men are truly "free and equal." This, beginning for the dumb peasant masses in language and religion, emerges in the other forms of life and art and tends to make smaller or larger ethnic groups autonomous, self-sufficient, and reacting as spiritual units to the residuum of America.

What is the cultural outcome likely to be, under these conditions? Surely not the melting-pot. Rather something that has become more and more distinct in the changing State and city life of the last two decades, and which is most articulate and apparent among just those peoples whom Mr. Ross praises most — the Scandinavians, the Germans, the Irish, the Jews.

It is in the area where Scandinavians are most concentrated that Norwegian is preached on Sunday in more churches than in Norway. That area is Minnesota, not unlike Scandinavia in climate and character. There, if the newspapers are to be trusted, the "foreign language" taught in an increasingly larger number of high schools is Scandinavian. The Constitution of the State resembles in many respects the famous Norwegian Constitution of 1813. The largest city has been chosen as the "spiritual capital," if I may say so, the seat of the Scandinavian "house of life," which the Scandinavian Society in America is reported to be planning to build as a centre from which there is to spread through the land Scandinavian culture and ideals.

The eastern neighbor of Minnesota is Wisconsin, a region of great concentration of Germans. Is it merely a political accident that the centralization of State authority and control has been possible there to a degree heretofore unknown in this country? That the Socialist organization is the most powerful in the land, able under ordinary conditions to have elected the Mayor of a large city and a Congressman, and kept out of power only by coalition of the other parties? That German is the overwhelmingly predominant "foreign language" in the public schools and in the university? Or that the fragrance of *Deutschthum* pervades the life of the whole State? The earliest German immigrants to America were group conscious to a high degree. They brought with them a cultural tradition and political aspiration. They wanted to found a State. If a State is to be regarded as a mode of life of the mind, they have succeeded. Their language is the predominant "foreign" one throughout the Middle West. The teaching of it is required by law in many places, southern Ohio and Indianapolis, for example. Their national institutions, even to cooking, are as widespread as they are. They are organized into a great national society, the German-American Alliance, which is dedicated to the advancement of German culture and ideals. They encourage and make possible a close and more intimate contact with the fatherland. They endow Germanic museums, they encourage and provide for exchange professorships, erect monuments to German heroes, and disseminate translations of the German classics. And there are, of course, the very excellent German vernacular press, the German theatre, the German club, the German organization of life.

Similar are the Irish, living in strength in Massachusetts and New York. When they began to come to this country they were far less well off and far more passionately self-conscious than the Germans. For numbers of them America was and has remained just a centre from which to plot for the freedom of Ireland. For most it was an opportunity to escape both exploitation and starvation. The way they made, was made against both race and religious prejudice; in the course of it they lost much that was attractive as well as much that was unpleasant. But Americanization brought the mass of them also spiritual self-respect, and their growing prosperity both here and in Ireland is what lies behind the more inward phases of Irish Nationalism — the Gaelic movement, the Irish theatre, the Irish Art Society. I omit consideration of such organized bodies as the Ancient Order of Hibernians. All these movements alike indicate the conversion of the negative nationalism of the hatred of England to the positive nationalism of the loving care and development of the cultural values of the Celtic spirit. A significant phase of it is the voting of Irish history into the curriculum of the high schools of Boston. In sum, once the Irish body had been fed and erected, the Irish mind demanded and generated its own peculiar form of self-realization and satisfaction.

And, finally, the Jews. Their attitude towards America is different in a fundamental respect from that of other immigrant nationalities. They do not come to the United States from truly native lands, lands of their proper *natio* and culture. They come from lands of sojourn, where they have been for ages treated as foreigners, at most as semi-citizens, subject to disabilities and persecutions. They come with no political aspirations against the peace of other states such as move the Irish, the Poles, the Bohemians. They come with the intention to be completely incorporated into the body-politic of the state. They alone, as Mr. H. G. Wells notes, of all the immigrant peoples have made spontaneously conscious and organized efforts to prepare themselves and their brethren for the responsibilities of American citizenship. There is hardly a considerable municipality in the land, where Jews inhabit, that has not its Hebrew Institute, or its Educational Alliance, or its Young Men's Hebrew Association, or its Community House, especially dedicated to this task. They show the highest percentage of naturalization, according to Mr. Ross's tables, and he concedes that they have benefited politics. Yet of all self-conscious peoples they are the most self-conscious. Of all immigrants they have the oldest civilized tradition, they are longest accustomed to living under law, and are at the outset the most eager and the most successful in eliminating the external differences between themselves and their social environment. Even their religion is flexible and accommodating, as that of the Christian sectaries is not, for change involves no change in doctrine, only in mode of life.

Yet, once the wolf is driven from the door and the Jewish immigrant takes his place in our society a free man and an American, he tends to become all the more a Jew. The cultural unity of his race, history, and background is only continued by the new life under the new conditions. Mr. H. G. Wells calls the Jewish quarter in New York a city within a city, and with more justice than other quarters because, although it is far more in tune with Americanism than the other quarters, it is also far more autonomous in spirit and self-conscious in culture. It has its sectaries, its radicals, its artists, its literati; its press, its literature, its theatre, its Yiddish and its Hebrew, its Talmudical colleges and its Hebrew schools, its charities and its vanities, and its coordinating organization, the Kehilla, all more or less duplicated wherever Jews congregate in mass. Here not religion alone, but the whole world of radical thinking, carries the mother-tongue and the father-tongue, with all that they imply. Unlike the parochial schools, their separate schools, being national, do not displace the public schools; they supplement the public schools. The Jewish ardor for pure learning is notorious. And, again, as was the case with the Scandinavians, the Germans, the Irish, democracy applied to education has given the Jews their will that Hebrew shall be coordinate with French and German in the regent's examination. On a national scale of organization there is the American Jewish Committee, the Jewish Historical Society, the Jewish Publication Society. Rurally, there is the model Association of Jewish Farmers, with their cooperative organization for agriculture and for agricultural education. In sum, the most eagerly American of the immigrant groups are also the most autonomous and self-conscious in spirit and culture.

Immigrants appear to pass through four phases in the course of being Americanized. In the first phase they exhibit economic eagerness, the greed of the unfed. Since external differences are a handicap in the economic struggle, they "assimilate," seeking thus to facilitate the attainment of economic independence. Once the proletarian level of such independence is reached, the process of assimilation slows down and tends to come to a stop. The immigrant group is still a national group, modified, sometimes improved, by environmental influences, but otherwise a solitary spiritual unit, which is seeking to find its way out on its own social level. This search brings to light permanent group distinctions, and the immigrant, like the Anglo-Saxon American, is thrown back upon himself and his ancestry. Then a process of dissimilation begins. The arts, life, and ideals of the nationality become central and paramount; ethnic and national differences change in status from disadvantages to distinctions. All the while the immigrant has been using the English language and behaving like an American in matters economic and political and continues to do so. The institutions of the Republic have become the liberating cause and the background for the rise of the cultural consciousness and social autonomy of the immigrant Irishman, German, Scandinavian, Jew, Pole, or Bohemian. On the whole, Americanization has not repressed nationality. Americanization has liberated nationality.

Hence, what troubles Mr. Ross and so many other Anglo-Saxon Americans is not really inequality; what troubles them is *difference*. Only things that are alike in fact and not abstractly, and only men that are alike in origin and in spirit and not abstractly, can be truly "equal" and maintain that inward unanimity of action and outlook which make a national life. The writers of the Declaration of Independence and of the Constitution were not confronted by the practical fact of ethnic dissimilarity among the whites of the country. Their descendants are confronted by it. Its existence, acceptance, and development provide one of the inevitable consequences of the democratic principle on which our theory of government is based, and the result at the present writing is to many worthies very unpleasant. Democratism and the Federal principle have worked together with economic greed and ethnic snobbishness to people the land with all the nationalities of Europe, and to convert the early American nation into the present American state. For in effect we are in the process of becoming a true federal state, such a state as men hope for as the outcome of the European war, a great republic consisting of a federation or commonwealth of nationalities.

Given, in the economic order, the principle of *laissez-faire* applied to a capitalistic society, in contrast, with the manorial and guild systems of the past and the Socialist utopias of the future, the economic consequences are the same, whether in America, full of all Europe, or in England, full of the English, Scotch, and Welsh. Given, in the political order, the principle that all men are equal and that each, consequently, under the law at least, shall have the opportunity to make the most of himself, the control of the machinery of government by the plutocracy is a foregone conclusion. *Laissez-faire* and unprecedentedly bountiful natural resources have turned the mind of the state to wealth alone, and in the haste to accumulate wealth considerations of human quality have been neglected and forgotten, the action of government has been remedial rather than constructive, and Mr. Ross's "peasantism," i.e., the growth of an expropriated, degraded industrial class, dependent on the factory rather than on land, has been rapid and vexatious.

The problems which these conditions give rise to are important, but not primarily important. Although they have occupied the minds of all our political theorists, they are problems of means, of instruments, not of ends. They concern the conditions of life, not the *kind of life*, and there appears to have been a general assumption that only one kind of human life is possible in America. But the same democracy which underlies the evils of the economic order

underlies also the evils — and the promise — of the ethnic order.
Because no individual is merely an individual, the political autonomy
of the individual has meant and is beginning to realize in these
United States the spiritual autonomy of his group. The process is
as yet far from fruition. We are, in fact, at the parting of the ways.
A genuine social alternative is before us, either of which parts we
may realize if we will. In social construction the will is father to
the fact, for the fact is nothing more than the concord or conflict
of wills. What do we *will* to make of the United States — a unison,
singing the old Anglo-Saxon theme "America," the America of the
New England school, or a harmony, in which that theme shall be
dominant, perhaps, among others, but one among many, not the
only one?

The mind reverts helplessly to the historic attempts at unison
in Europe — the heroic failure of the pan-Hellenists, of the Romans,
the disintegration and the diversification of the Christian Church,
for a time the most successful unison in history; the present-day
failures of Germany and of Russia. Here, however, the whole social
situation is favorable, as it has never been at any time elsewhere — everything is favorable but the basic law of America itself,
and the spirit of American institutions. To achieve unison — it can
be achieved — would be to violate these. For the end determines
the means, and this end would involve no other means than those
used by Germany in Poland, in Schleswig-Holstein, and Alsace-Lor-
raine; by Russia in the Pale, in Poland, in Finland. Fundamentally
it would require the complete nationalization of education, the abolition of every form of parochial and private school, the abolition
of instruction in other tongues than English, and the concentration
of the teaching of history and literature upon the English tradition.
The other institutions of society would require treatment analogous
to that administered by Germany to her European acquisitions. And
all of this, even if meeting with no resistance, would not completely
guarantee the survival as a unison of the older Americanism. For
the programme would be applied to diverse ethnic types, and the
reconstruction that, with the best will, they might spontaneously
make of the tradition would more likely than not be a far cry from
the original. It is, already.

The notion that the programme might be realized by radical
and even enforced miscegenation, by the creation of the melting-pot
by law, and thus by the development of the new "American race,"
is, as Mr. Ross points out, as mystically optimistic as it is ignorant.
In historic times, so far as we know, no new ethnic types have

originated, and what we know of breeding gives us no assurance of the disappearance of the old types in favor of the new, only the addition of a new type, if it succeeds in surviving, to the already existing older ones. Biologically, life does not unify; biologically, life diversifies; and it is sheer ignorance to apply social analogies to biological processes. In any event, we know what the qualities and capacities of existing types are; we know how by education to do something towards the repression of what is evil in them and the conservation of what is good. The "American race" is a totally unknown thing; to presume that it will be better because (if we like to persist in the illusion that it is coming) it will be later, is no different from imagining that, because contemporary, Russia is better than ancient Greece. There is nothing more to be said to the pious stupidity that identifies recency with goodness. The unison to be achieved cannot be a unison of ethnic types. It must be, if it is to be at all, a unison of social and historic interests, established by the complete cutting-off of the ancestral memories of our populations, the enforced, exclusive use of the English language and English and American history in the schools and in the daily life.

The attainment of the other alternative, a harmony, also requires concerted public action. But the action would do no violence to our fundamental law and the spirit of our institutions, nor to the qualities of men. It would seek simply to eliminate the waste and the stupidity of our social organization, by way of freeing and strengthening the strong forces actually in operation. Starting with our existing ethnic and cultural groups, it would seek to provide conditions under which each may attain the perfection that is proper to its kind. The provision of such conditions is the primary intent of our fundamental law and the function of our institutions. And the various nationalities which compose our commonwealth must learn first of all this fact, which is perhaps, to most minds, the outstanding ideal content of "Americanism" — that democracy means self-realization through self-control, self-government, and that one is impossible without the other. For the application of this principle, which is realized in a harmony of societies, there are European analogies also. I omit Austria and Turkey, for the union of nationalities is there based more on inadequate force than on consent, and the form of their organization is alien to ours. I think of England and of Switzerland. England is a state of four nationalities — the English, Welsh, Scotch, and Irish (if one considers the Empire, of many more), and while English history is not unmarred by attempts at unison, both the home policy and the imperial policy have, since the Boer War, been realized more and more in the application of the principle of harmony: the strength of the kingdom and the empire have been posited more and more upon the voluntary and autonomous cooperation of the component nationalities. Switzerland is a state of three nationalities, a republic as the United States is, far more democratically governed, concentrated in an area not much different in size, I suspect, from New York City, with a population not far from it in total. Yet Switzerland has the most loyal citizens in Europe. Their language, literary and spiritual traditions are on the one side German, on another Italian, on a third side French. And in terms of social organization, of economic prosperity, of public education, of the general level of culture, Switzerland is the most successful democracy in the world. It conserves and encourages individuality.

The reason lies, I think, in the fact that in Switzerland the conception of "natural rights" operates, consciously or unconsciously, as a generalization from the unalterable data of human nature. What is inalienable in the life of mankind is its intrinsic positive quality — its psychophysical inheritance. Men may change their clothes, their politics, their wives, their religions, their philosophies, to a greater or lesser extent: they cannot change their grandfathers. Jews or Poles or Anglo-Saxons, in order to cease being Jews or Poles or Anglo-Saxons, would have to cease to be. The selfhood which is inalienable in them, and for the realization of which they require "inalienable" liberty, is ancestrally determined, and the happiness which they pursue has its form implied in ancestral endowment. This is what, actually, democracy in operation assumes. There are human capacities which it is the function of the state to liberate and to protect; and the failure of the state as a government means its abolition. Government, the state, under the democratic conception, is merely an instrument, not an end. That it is often an abused instrument, that it is often seized by the powers that prey, that it makes frequent mistakes and considers only secondary ends, surface needs, which vary from moment to moment, is, of course, obvious: hence our social and political chaos. But that it is an instrument, flexibly adjustable to changing life, changing opinion, and needs, our whole electoral organization and party system declare. And as intelligence and wisdom prevail over "politics" and special interests, as the steady and continuous pressure of the inalienable qualities and purposes of human groups more and more dominate the confusion of our common life, the outlines of a possible great and truly democratic commonwealth become discernible.

Its form is that of the Federal republic; its substance a democracy of nationalities, cooperating voluntarily and autonomously in the enterprise of self-realization through the perfection of men according to their kind. The common language of the commonwealth, the language of its great political tradition, is English, but each nationality expresses its emotional and voluntary life in its own language, in its own inevitable aesthetic and intellectual forms. The common life of the commonwealth is politico-economic, and serves as the foundation and background for the realization of the distinctive individuality of each *natio* that composes it. Thus "American civilization" may come to mean the perfection of the cooperative harmonies of "European civilization," the waste, the squalor, and the distress of Europe being eliminated — a multiplicity in a unity, an orchestration of mankind. As in an orchestra, every type of instrument has its specific timbre and tonality, founded in its substance and form; as every type has its appropriate theme and melody in the whole symphony, so in society each ethnic group is the natural instrument, its spirit and culture are its theme and melody, and the harmony and dissonances and discords of them all make the symphony of civilization, with this difference: a musical symphony is written before it is played; in the symphony of civilization the playing is the writing, so that there is nothing so fixed and inevitable about its progressions as in music, so that within the limits set by nature they may vary at will, and the range and variety of the harmonies may become wider and richer and more beautiful.

But the question is, do the dominant classes in America want such a society?

PART III

THE DEBATE OVER RESTRICTION

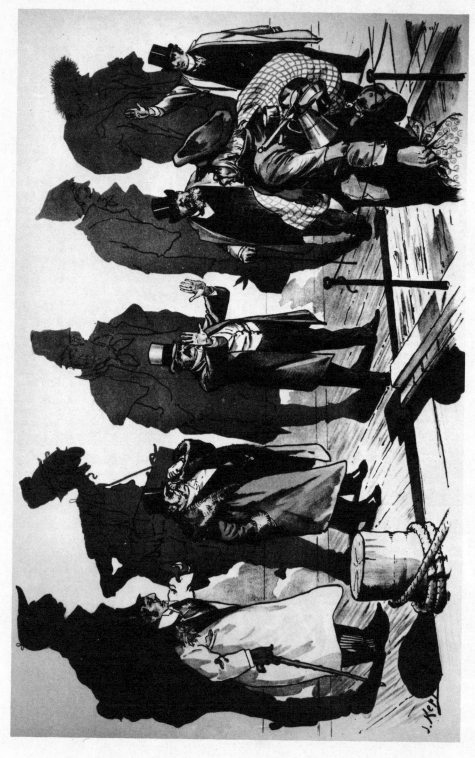

In this cartoon from the early 1890s, Joseph Keppler satirizes the "old" immigrants who want to close to the "new" immigrant the bridge over which they and their fathers arrived.

12
A SENATOR

 Henry Cabot Lodge (1850–1924) was an influential Massachusetts Republican leader, staunch Anglophile, and a nationalist for whom immigration restriction became something of a holy crusade as well as a practical political matter. A descendant of Puritans, he felt himself and his class doomed in his native land by invading, "inferior" people. As Representative and, from 1893 until 1924, Senator for his state, he could count on the votes of skilled workers whom he warned against the menace of wages depressed by competition from aliens with low standards of living.

For Lodge, the immigration question was basically a *racial* issue. The "new" immigrants became his special target. Their alleged inferiority he saw as ineradicable traits when compared with virtues he ascribed to the "German races." With respect to the Irish, whom no New England politician could afford to offend, his dislike of non-Teutonic peoples was judiciously retired into private life.

In collaboration with the Immigration Restriction League and other supporters of his views, Lodge promoted a bill requiring all European immigrants to show a knowledge of reading and writing for admission to the United States as the best available legal device for excluding undesirable nationalities. After passing both houses of Congress, the literacy test bill was vetoed in March 1897 by President Grover Cleveland. In his veto message, the President reminded the sponsors of the bill that "the time is quite within recent memory when the same thing was said of immigrants who, with their descendants . . . now [are] among our best citizens."

The verses quoted by Senator Lodge are the third stanza of a poem "Unguarded Gates," by Thomas Bailey Aldrich. It appeared originally in *The Atlantic Monthly* in 1892. Aldrich had described it to a friend as "a poem in which I mildly protest against America becoming the cesspool of Europe."

THE LITERACY TEST

*Henry Cabot
Lodge*

Mr. President, this bill is intended to amend the existing law so as to restrict still further immigration to the United States. Paupers, diseased persons, convicts, and contract laborers are now excluded. By this bill it is proposed to make a new class of excluded immigrants and add to those which have just been named the totally ignorant. The bill is of the simplest kind. The first section excludes from the country all immigrants who can not read and write either their own or some other language. The second section merely provides a simple test for determining whether the immigrant can read or write, and is added to the bill so as to define the duties of the immigrant inspectors, and to assure to all immigrants alike perfect justice and a fair test of their knowledge.

Two questions arise in connection with this bill. The first is as to the merits of this particular form of restriction; the second as to the general policy of restricting immigration at all. I desire to discuss briefly these two questions in the order in which I have stated them. The smaller question as to the merits of this particular bill comes first. The existing laws of the United States now exclude, as I have said, certain classes of immigrants who, it is universally agreed, would be most undesirable additions to our population. These exclusions have been enforced and the results have been beneficial, but the excluded classes are extremely limited and do not by any means cover all or even any considerable part of the immigrants whose presence here is undesirable or injurious, nor do they have any adequate effect in properly reducing the great body of immigration to this country. There can be no doubt that there is a very earnest desire on the part of the American people to restrict further, and much more extensively than has yet been done, foreign immigration to the United States. The question before

FROM *Congressional Record*, 1896, 54th Congress, 1st Session, XXVIII, pp. 2816–20. Abridged by the editor.

the committee was how this could best be done; that is, by what method the largest number of undesirable immigrants and the smallest possible number of desirable immigrants could be shut out.

Three methods of obtaining this further restriction have been widely discussed of late years and in various forms have been brought to the attention of Congress. The first was the imposition of a capitation tax on all immigrants. There can be no doubt as to the effectiveness of this method if the tax is made sufficiently heavy. But although exclusion by a tax would be thorough, it would be undiscriminating, and your committee did not feel that the time had yet come for its application. The second scheme was to restrict immigration by requiring consular certification of immigrants. This plan has been much advocated, and if it were possible to carry it out thoroughly and to add very largely to the number of our consuls in order to do so, it would no doubt be effective and beneficial. But the committee was satisfied that consular certification was, under existing circumstances, impractical; that the necessary machinery could not be provided; that it would lead to many serious questions with foreign governments, and that it could not be properly and justly enforced. It is not necessary to go further into the details which brought the committee to this conclusion. It is sufficient to say here that the opinion of the committee is shared, they believe, by all expert judges who have given the most careful attention to the question.

The third method was to exclude all immigrants who could neither read nor write, and this is the plan which was adopted by the committee and which is embodied in this bill. In their report the committee have shown by statistics, which have been collected and tabulated with great care, the emigrants who would be affected by this illiteracy test. It is not necessary for me here to do more than summarize the results of the committee's investigation, which have been set forth fully in their report. It is found, in the first place, that the illiteracy test will bear most heavily upon the Italians, Russians, Poles, Hungarians, Greeks, and Asiatics, and very lightly, or not at all, upon English-speaking emigrants or Germans, Scandinavians, and French.

In other words, the races most affected by the illiteracy test are those whose emigration to this country has begun within the last twenty years and swelled rapidly to enormous proportions, races with which the English-speaking people have never hitherto assimilated, and who are most alien to the great body of the people of the United States. On the other hand, immigrants from the United

Kingdom and of those races which are most closely related to the English-speaking people, and who with the English-speaking people themselves founded the American colonies and built up the United States, are affected but little by the proposed test. These races would not be prevented by this law from coming to this country in practically undiminished numbers. These kindred races also are those who alone go to the Western and Southern States, where immigrants are desired, and take up our unoccupied lands. The races which would suffer most seriously by exclusion under the proposed bill furnish the immigrants who do not go to the West or South, where immigration is needed, but who remain on the Atlantic Seaboard, where immigration is not needed and where their presence is most injurious and undesirable.

The statistics prepared by the committee show further that the immigrants excluded by the illiteracy test are those who remain for the most part in congested masses in our great cities. They furnish, as other tables show, a large proportion of the population of the slums. The committee's report proves that illiteracy runs parallel with the slum population, with criminals, paupers, and juvenile delinquents of foreign birth or parentage, whose percentage is out of all proportion to their share of the total population when compared with the percentage of the same classes among the native born. It also appears from investigations which have been made that the immigrants who would be shut out by the illiteracy test are those who bring least money to the country and come most quickly upon private or public charity for support.

The replies of the governors of twenty-six States to the Immigration Restriction League show that in only two cases are immigrants of the classes affected by the illiteracy test desired, and those are of a single race. All the other immigrants mentioned by the governors as desirable belong to the races which are but slightly affected by the provisions of this bill. It is also proved that the classes now excluded by law, the criminals, the diseased, the paupers, and the contract laborers, are furnished chiefly by the same races as those most affected by the test of illiteracy. The same is true as to those immigrants who come to this country for a brief season and return to their native land, taking with them the money they have earned in the United States. There is no more hurtful and undesirable class of immigrants from every point of view than these "birds of passage," and the tables show that the races furnishing the largest number of "birds of passage" have also the greatest proportion of illiterates.

These facts prove to demonstration that the exclusion of immigrants unable to read or write, as proposed by this bill, will operate against the most undesirable and harmful part of our present immigration and shut out elements which no thoughtful or patriotic man can wish to see multiplied among the people of the United States. The report of the committee also proves that this bill meets the great requirement of all legislation of this character in excluding the greatest proportion possible of thoroughly undesirable and dangerous immigrants and the smallest proportion of immigrants who are unobjectionable. . . .

I now come to the aspect of this question which is graver and more serious than any other. The injury of unrestricted immigration to American wages and American standards of living is sufficiently plain and is bad enough, but the danger which this immigration threatens to the quality of our citizenship is far worse. That which it concerns us to know and that which is more vital to us as a people than all possible questions of tariff or currency is whether the quality of our citizenship is endangered by the present course and character of immigration to the United States. To determine this question intelligently we must look into the history of our race. . . .

Such, then, briefly, were the people composing the colonies when we faced England in the war for independence. It will be observed that with the exception of the Huguenot French, who formed but a small percentage of the total population, the people of the thirteen colonies were all of the same original race stocks. The Dutch, the Swedes, and the Germans simply blended again with the English-speaking people, who like them were descended from the Germanic tribes whom Caesar fought and Tacitus described. . . .

By those who look at this question superficially we hear it often said that the English-speaking people, especially in America, are a mixture of races. Analysis shows that the actual mixture of blood in the English-speaking race is very small, and that while the English-speaking people are derived through different channels, no doubt, there is among them none the less an overwhelming preponderance of the same race stock, that of the great Germanic tribes who reached from Norway to the Alps. They have been welded together by more than a thousand years of wars, conquests, migrations, and struggles, both at home and abroad, and in so doing they have attained a fixity and definiteness of national character unknown

[In these omitted paragraphs Lodge argued that while the English were not a pure race ethnically, they had developed into a race "by conditions and events of the last thousand years." The invaders of England were all Germanic tribes. They had different names and spoke different languages but were "of one blood." In the course of centuries, they developed well defined mental and moral qualities. These same Englishmen settled the British colonies in North America. There they intermingled with Scotch-Irish, Germans, and French Huguenots—all singularly fine people—and Protestants with the highest moral qualities.]

to any other people. Let me quote on this point a disinterested witness of another race and another language, M. Gustave Le Bon, a distinguished French writer of the highest scientific training and attainments, who says in his very remarkable book on the Evolution of Races:

> Most of the historic races of Europe are still in process of formation, and it is important to realize this fact in order to understand their history. The English alone represent a race almost entirely fixed. In them the ancient Briton, the Saxon, and the Norman have been effaced to form a new and very Homogeneous type.

. . .

What, then, is this matter of race which separates the Englishman from the Hindoo and the American from the Indian? It is something deeper and more fundamental than anything which concerns the intellect. We all know it instinctively, although it is so impalpable that we can scarcely define it, and yet is so deeply marked that even the physiological differences between the Negro, the Mongol, and the Caucasian are not more persistent or more obvious.

When we speak of a race, then, we do not mean its expressions in art or in language, or its achievements in knowledge. We mean the moral and intellectual characters, which in their association make the soul of a race, and which represent the product of all its past, the inheritance of all its ancestors, and the motives of all its conduct. The men of each race possess an indestructible stock of ideas, traditions, sentiments, modes of thought, an unconscious inheritance from their ancestors, upon which argument has no effect. What makes a race are their mental and, above all, their moral characteristics, the slow growth and accumulation of centuries of toil and conflict. These are the qualities which determine their social efficiency as a people, which make one race rise and another fall, which we draw out of a dim past through many generations of ancestors, about which we can not argue, but in which we blindly believe, and which guide us in our short-lived generation as they have guided the race itself across the centuries. . . .

Such achievements as M. Le Bon credits us with are due to the qualities of the American people, whom he, as a man of science looking below the surface, rightly describes as homogeneous. Those qualities are moral far more than intellectual, and it is on the moral qualities of the English-speaking race that our history, our victories, and all our future rest. There is only one way in which you can lower those qualities or weaken those characteristics, and that is by breeding them out. If a lower race mixes with a higher in sufficient numbers, history teaches us that the lower race will prevail. The lower race will absorb the higher, not the higher the lower, when the two strains approach equality in numbers.

In other words, there is a limit to the capacity of any race for assimilating and elevating an inferior race, and when you begin to pour in in unlimited numbers people of alien or lower races of less social efficiency and less moral force, you are running the most frightful risk that any people can run. The lowering of a great race means not only its own decline but that of human civilization.

M. Le Bon sees no danger to us in immigration, and his reason for this view is one of the most interesting things he says. He declares that the people of the United States will never be injured by immigration, because the moment they see the peril the great race instinct will assert itself and shut the immigration out. The reports of the Treasury for the last fifteen years show that the peril is at hand. I trust that the prediction of science is true and that the unerring instinct of the race will shut the danger out, as it closed the door upon the coming of the Chinese.

Mr. President, more precious even than forms of government are the mental and moral qualities which make what we call our race. While those stand unimpaired all is safe. When those decline all is imperiled. They are exposed to but a single danger, and that is by changing the quality of our race and citizenship through the wholesale infusion of races whose traditions and inheritances, whose thoughts and whose beliefs are wholly alien to ours and with whom we have never assimilated or even been associated in the past. The danger has begun. It is small as yet, comparatively speaking, but it is large enough to warn us to act while there is yet time and while it can be done easily and efficiently. There lies the peril at the portals of our land; there is pressing in the tide of unrestricted immigration. The time has certainly come, if not to stop, at least to check, to sift, and to restrict those immigrants. In careless strength, with generous hand, we have kept our gates wide open to all the world. If we do not close them, we should at least place sentinels beside them to challenge those who would pass through. The gates which admit men to the United States and citizenship in the great Republic should no longer be left unguarded.

> O Liberty, white Goddess, is it well
> To leave the gates unguarded? On thy breast
> Fold Sorrow's children, soothe the hurts of fate,

Lift the down-trodden, but with hand of steel
Stay those who to thy sacred portals come
To waste the gifts of freedom. Have a care,
Lest from thy brow the clustered stars be torn
And trampled in the dust. For so of old
The thronging Goth and Vandal trampled Rome,
And where the temples of the Caesars stood
The lean wolf unmolested made her lair.

13

A HARVARD DEAN

"Popular" prejudices are sometimes bred in polite, enlightened, educated circles. The obtuseness of the English ruling classes toward the suffering of the Irish during the famine years, 1845 to 1851, has been partly traced to British politicians' unwavering faith in the doctrine of *laissez-faire*. German academic race theorists wrote books and drafted laws that provided the intellectual justification for the genocide of millions of Jews, Gypsies, and other "subhuman" peoples.

Nathaniel S. Shaler (1841–1906), a transplanted Kentuckian who became Dean of the Lawrence Scientific School at Harvard University, was widely known outside the university as a member of many study commissions and a prolific writer of books and magazine articles on topics of the day. He was one of those race-conscious intellectuals whose pro-Aryan theorizing established and gave respectability to the idea that the "new" immigration was inferior to the old.

A sort of "human relations" specialist in his day, Shaler prided himself on his ability to identify people of different nationalities by their features. The notion that this could be done was held by many educated Americans around the turn of the century and explains the prevalence, in books and magazines published from about 1885 to 1915, of photographs purporting to show "typical" immigrant faces.

Readers who have wondered about the connection between the conception of Negroes' caste status and the alleged racial inferiority of Southern and Eastern Europeans will not be surprised to learn that Shaler described Negroes as "the most interesting type of primitive man left in this world" in his book *The Neighbor*, published in 1904 as a "plea for a larger understanding" between men.

Shaler's article raises other questions. To what extent have ethnic conflicts taken the place of class conflicts in American history? If the peasants who emigrated to the New World were the passive, patient, home-loving, unambitious types Shaler observed, why did Henry Cabot Lodge detect so many dangerous radicals, anarchists, ultra-socialists, and brigands among them? Even though Shaler's views of the inferiority of some races are not acceptable today, what evidence is there to refute his conviction that democracy can flourish only in racially and ethnically homogeneous societies? Or his insistence that national harmony depends on shared ideals, including a common ethnic background? In short, are there clear-cut and satisfactory answers for all the disturbing questions about nationality, race, and ethnicity raised in this outspokenly partisan piece?

EUROPEAN PEASANTS AS IMMIGRANTS

Nathaniel S. Shaler

The question as to the limit which, in the interests of our States, may be set to the free commingling of various races cannot safely be dealt with by men who are moved by philanthropy alone. The unguided humanitarian gratifies himself by free giving to the street beggar, and fancies that his dole is true alms. The well-informed lover of his kind, perhaps with quite as much of the Christian spirit, gives nothing in ignorance, and helps only where he has made sure that his bounty will be so well bestowed that it will not lower the conditions of society. It is said of a distinguished English divine, a wise and beneficent man, that, when he came to die, he thanked God he had never given money to a street beggar. It seems to me that, in the larger work of the state, we are bound by the same limitations which should affect our personal charities. The commonwealth has no more right to do deeds of charity or hospitality in an unreasoning way than has the individual man. Even more than an individual, it is the keeper of a trust; for while an individual may hope that his misdeeds of this nature may die with him, the evil done by society, or its product, the state, is inevitably propagated from generation to generation.

FROM *The Atlantic Monthly* XXXVII (May, 1893), pp. 646–55.

We have suffered grievously from the folly of our predecessors in recklessly admitting an essentially alien folk into this land. In their greed for gain, they peopled half the continent with Africans, thus giving us a heritage of evil and perplexity the burden of which we are just beginning to appreciate. It may in the end turn out that through this insensate act they have imperiled the future of their own race in the land best fitted for its nurture. If the negroes, in certain parts of the United States, increase more rapidly than do the whites, the people of our own blood will be expelled from such districts. Where the black population becomes dominant, only the semblance of a democracy can survive; the body of the people will, as in Hayti, shape their society and their government to fit their inherited qualities. The alternative of such a condition is that the whites may, by their intellectual superiority and their cooperation with the abler negroes, maintain their authority in a forcible way. But what a wretched shadow of our ideal state this authority will be! In place of an association of true freemen, all by divine right equal heritors in the duties and the privileges of the citizen, we shall have the most vicious and persistent form of despotism, a race oligarchy.

History makes it plain that a race oligarchy almost inevitably arises wherever a superior and an inferior variety of people are brought together. We have a living example of these conditions in several of the Latin countries of the Americas. The peoples of these states, by a common and evident necessity, tend to the oligarchic system. They are made up of masters and servants. The forms of a democracy seem, indeed, to be well suited to such a despotism of race. Every part of the machinery may appear to operate substantially as it does in the best of our commonwealths, and yet the spirit and theory of our system have no more real place in such governments than in the Czar's dominions.

There are many things which go to show that the oligarchic form of society in our Southern States, brought about by the essential diversities of the white and black races, is already affecting the system of their government. The negro has little or no more place in the body politic than he has in the social system. One third of the population in that part of the country is excluded from the most educative duties of the citizen, those which should come to him through the trusts which his neighbors confide to his care. I am far from blaming the Southern whites for their action in summarily excluding the enfranchised race from political advancement. The ignorance of these Africans, their general lack of all the instincts of a freeman, have made this course, it seems to me, for the time at least, imperatively necessary. It is a very grave misfortune for us all that any part of our people have been thus separated from the ideals of a democratic government. On the other hand, it was a more desperate and immediate evil to have the Southern commonwealths converted into mere engines of plunder, as was the case during the so-called period of reconstruction, when the blacks controlled these States.

My reason for noting the facts above mentioned is that we may derive from them some sense of the vast body of evidence which goes to show that the presence of any considerable mass of alien people (alien, though they may have been born upon the soil) is, to a democratic state, a danger of the most serious sort. It inevitably leads to changes in the essentials of such a government. Under these conditions, the ideal commonwealth is impossible, and the spirit of the people inevitably tends toward despotic forms of administration.

Accepting the view that a true democracy cannot be maintained in the presence of a large alien class, we perceive that the main question which underlies the problem of immigration concerns the extent to which the foreign people we receive are already fit, or may readily be prepared, for incorporation into the body of American citizens. It is unreasonable to suppose that the foreigner can in any way be made a true citizen until he is in some measure engrafted on the social system from which the government springs. He must acquire the necessary motives through a natural process of enfranchisement; the mere forms of the court are idle mummery unless this work has been done. The novice must be made free to the current thought of the realm, which does not pass as easily as its coin.

To determine the difficulty of this naturalizing process necessary to give the stranger a sympathy with our institutions, we must consider the origin and nurture of the masses of people who come to us from the Old World. This is a very large task, for these immigrants are derived from many different countries, and represent the products of a great diversity of social conditions which have bred in them a singular variety of motives. To make even a general estimate of final value, it would be necessary for the observer to spend many years in assiduous travel, with the subject matter of this inquiry foremost in his mind. I am not aware that any investigator has deliberately undertaken this task. I therefore venture to set forth the results of some of my own studies, which appear to me to have a certain, though, I must confess, only a limited value.

As the considerations which I am about to present are important only in the measure of my opportunities of inquiry, it is fit that I should state what these chances have been. Within the last twenty-seven years, I have spent between four and five years in Europe, and have devoted a large part of that time to journeys afoot in Great Britain and on the Continent, through the regions which furnish the greater part of the immigrants who are now coming, and are likely in the future to come, to this country. As my wanderings have usually been made alone, they have naturally afforded a much more intimate acquaintance with the people of the land than is ordinarily obtained by travelers. All human beings interest me much, and especially those native to the soil; and I have always found it easy to secure at least a superficial relation with my neighbors in other lands.

The most striking impression which is gained by such opportunities of acquiring a knowledge of European folk concerns the nature of the peasant class. To an American who knows his own people by long and familiar contact, the European son of the soil, in his natural habitat, seems at once to be a very singular creature. The truly naturalized American, even of the lower grade, thinks and acts in a manner which is essentially common to all his kind, however far apart they may be in station or employment. We feel at once there are no essential or permanent differences of motive in the ranks of our society. We note peculiarities due to schooling or to occupation, and something of variety due to local conditions and to the inheritances which come therewith; but the fundamental motives of our men and women, be they rich or poor, from town or country, from North or South, are the same. They never have a sense of inferiority; never a grudge against those who, by one chance or another, occupy a place above them. Every American, born to the manner of his kind, feels the world to be open to him. He looks and wins his way upward; the dominant passion of his soul is to secure a better estate, if not for himself, at least for his children. Everywhere we find a great deal of talent among Americans in the lowest condition of life. All these well-endowed individuals have no sense of social restraint; they feel that they are free to go the way which their capacities may open to them. The whole of the social system in which they dwell is recognized as their own as soon as they can lay just claim to it. They are given to criticising this system, but they do so in a manner which shows that they do not regard it as something in its nature foreign.

The characteristic European peasant differs from the American laboring man in the motives which are of first importance in the composition of the citizen of a democracy. The peasant knows himself to be by birthright a member of an inferior class, from which there is practically no chance of escaping. He is in essentially the same state as the Southern negro. There is a wall between him and the higher realms of life. The imprisonment is so complete that he rarely thinks about the chances of escaping. Centuries of experience have bred in him the understanding that he is by nature a peasant, and that, save in rare instances, he can acquire no other station in the land of his birth. His only chance of considerable betterment is through the army or the Church; and even by these gates he can rarely pass beyond the limits of his class. It is characteristic of peasants that they have accepted this inferior lot. For generations they have regarded themselves as separated from their fellow-citizens of higher estate. They have no large sense of citizenly motives; they feel no sense of responsibility for any part of the public life save that which lies within their own narrow round of action. Within these limits they are controlled by habits and traditions of an excellent sort; they have indeed contrived for themselves a separate lower estate, divided from the rest of the people with whom they dwell as completely as though parted by centuries or by wide seas.

The isolation of the folk of the peasant class makes it impossible for them to develop any political quality whatsoever. They do not learn to associate their actions; they do not feel the province of individual effort in the control of common interests. They appear never to have that keen sense of what is going on beyond their vision which is the foundation of citizenly duty. The only relation with the ruling orders of society which they hold is either that of a blind respect or an equally blind antagonism. In general, the peasant not only exhibits no longing for preferment; he exhibits a perfect acquiescence in the lot which has been assigned him. To his mind, the head of the state is hardly further away than the lowest member of the superior class. Centuries of such breeding have, of course, checked the development of all those motives and aspirations which are the foundations of our democracy, and which are the life-breath of a true commonwealth. There are, however, other influences at work which tend still further to limit the grade of peasant life. Certain of these we shall have to note in some detail.

It is the most noteworthy, if not the most noticeable peculiarity of the laboring classes in Europe that they exhibit relatively little difference between man and man. Rarely, indeed, do we find any one born in the peasant caste who shows much individuality of mind.

At first, the uniformity in the character of these people was a puzzle to me; to any one who had become accustomed to the ongoing spirit of a democratic state, the fact that such folk in no wise chafe against their narrow bounds must be a matter for surprise. The only distinct desire which seems to exist among these people is for more opportunities for gain. Political preferment, a better social station, enlarged fields of action, are, not, as with us, the mainsprings of endeavor. The gainful motive, like many others which animate the peasant class, is singularly limited. Money is desired for its own sake. The peasant who attains fortune rarely alters his scheme of living. If the money be inherited, the family may continue to live the ancestral life, frowning on any effort of the children to turn from the laborious paths of their forefathers. A man of this kind becomes a true miser, in a way which is practically unknown, we may indeed say impossible, in a democracy. Such an instance of this vice as is pictured in Balzac's Eugénie Grandet may naturally develop in the peasant class.

It must be confessed that in the immediate view the plan of life of the peasant is more pleasing than that so often followed by the new-made rich of the democratic society. With us, the accession of wealth is nearly always valued for the chance it affords the possessor to lift his mode of living to what seems to him a better social level, which is most often a position he is not in a natural manner fitted to occupy. Yet the essential difference between a democratic and an aristocratic society is indicated by the conduct of the men who have come by money while they were members of the laboring class. The peasant has no social or political longings to satisfy, for the simple reasons that his inheritances and the traditions of his class supply him with none. The ordinary man of our democratic community, in his imagination, sees himself among the powers of the land. If he gains the means, he makes haste to assail the social leadership, and perhaps aims for a place in the federal Senate.

While the oftentimes absurd pretensions of the people who have suddenly gained wealth may amuse or distress us, we have to recognize their behavior as evidence of the sympathetic bond which is the strength of our state. To be strong, a democratic society such as ours needs to have its members aspiring for the fullest measure of life, eager for all the advantages of contact and influence which can be achieved. Only in this way can the preferment of the best men be secured. Where, as among peasant folk, there is no upward striving, the mass of the people is hardly more profitable to the best interests of the commonwealth than the cattle of the fields. It may swell the census and fill the ranks of armies, but its aid is lacking in all forms of social endeavor.

The absence of diversity in the intellectual quality of peasants is doubtless in part to be explained by the singular uniformity in their habitudes of existence, and by the fixed and secure conditions of their routine labor, and the caste distinctions which part them from the superior classes. There is, however, another series of influences which have long and effectively operated to lower and make uniform the mental and social qualities of this class in nearly all European countries. These conditions must be clearly understood before we can adequately account for the state of these people, or judge as to their fitness for the uses of American citizenship.

The most important group of causes which have stamped, in an indelible manner, the sign of inferiority on the laboring classes of the Old World may be briefly stated as follows. While the greater part of the hand laborers of the ancient societies of Europe have been denied community with the ruling folk, there have been two ways open by which the abler youths of both sexes, who were born in this class, could pass forth from it, never to return. These ways led to military service and to the orders of the Catholic Church. Entering the army, the man, particularly if he had in him the stuff to make a good soldier, found a permanent occupation. He commonly died in arms, or returned to his people only when too old to rear a family. If his ability was distinguished, he might win a rank which would remove him from the class whence he sprung. His descendants would retain his acquired station, and, despite all reverses of fortune, would seldom return to the order of peasants. Thus, every person of capacity who adopted the career of arms was likely to be lost to his people. In this way, for perhaps twenty generations, the lower classes of European people have been robbed of much of their strength.

Great in amount as has been this withdrawal of talent from the people on account of military pursuits, the Church has, at least during the last twelve or fifteen centuries, been a far more efficient means of impoverishing the peasant blood. While the army of the sword enlisted its hosts only from the men, and permitted them occasionally to leave descendants among their people, the army of the cross gathered its recruits from both sexes, and doomed them alike to sterility. On its altars were sacrificed not only the talents of the individual, but all the expectation of good progress which the able man or woman offers to society. It is not easy to conceive how efficient this system of selecting the able youth from the body of the people has been, or how effectively it is still carried on in certain parts of Europe.

Since the Church first possessed the lands of Europe, and organized its clerical system, more than twelve hundred years have elapsed. During this time the population within its control has probably averaged at least fifty million. Allowing that there has been a priest to each five hundred of these people, we have about a hundred thousand of the abler men of each generation withdrawn from the body of the people, the greater portion of them from the lower ranks of society. Each of these men searched among the children of his parishioners for the boys and girls of promise who might be taken into the ranks of the priesthood or into the various religious orders. We may fairly estimate that the persons who were thus withdrawn from the life of their time, and whose inheritances were lost to their people, numbered as much as one percent of the population. Although a part of this promise of the people was taken from the upper classes, the greater part of it was probably always, as at present, derived from the lower orders of society. Among the prosperous folk, there have ever been many classes of occupations tempting the abler youths, while among the laborers the Church has afforded the easiest way to rise, and that which is most tempting to the intelligent. The result has been, that while the priesthood and monastic orders have systematically debilitated all the populations of Catholic Europe, their influence has been most efficient in destroying the original talent in the peasant class.

The doctrine of inheritance is so little understood, and its application to the development of peoples so novel, that the full bearing of these influences exerted by the great celibate organizations of European states is not commonly appreciated. The researches of Mr. Francis Galton, and of the other investigators who have followed his admirable methods of inquiry, have clearly shown that the inheritance of qualities in man is as certain as among the lower animals. The cases are indeed rare where persons of conspicuous ability have been born of parents of inferior capacity. In practically all cases, it appears that talent of any kind does not suddenly originate among the lower orders of men. It rises gradually through generational development. At first the living spring of power is weak; it gathers volume in several fortunate successions of parent and child; and finally it appears in the strong tide of talent or genius. The first and noblest object of society should be to favor these beginnings of a higher life, and to preserve the inheritance, in the confident hope that it may gain strength with time. But the system of the two great organizations, the army and the Church, has operated in diverse measure, but with the same effect, to destroy these beginnings of capacity by the sword or by celibacy.

We are all familiar with the results obtained by the process of selection as it is exercised by the breeder on the cattle of our fields. By this simple means, the speed of the horse, as well as its size, has been greatly increased; the original rough and scanty wool of the sheep has been changed to the merino fleece; and the few savage instincts of the dog have been overlaid by a marvelous development of sagacity and affection, which has given a really human quality to the mind of that creature. Let us suppose, however, that the breeder had taken pains to select all the most powerful horses, and had devoted them to the carnage of the battlefield; that he had carefully destroyed all the lambs which possessed fine fleeces; that he had tolerated only the savage curs, or bred them alone for drawing burdens, disregarding all the intelligence and sympathy which they might exhibit. What would the condition of these domesticated animals now be? Certainly they would exhibit none of the qualities which give them value; they would, indeed, still be in their primitive state. Yet this is substantially the evil work which has been done by the most permanent of our social organizations. If they had been designed for the purpose, they could not have been more efficiently contrived to prevent the advance of the lower ranks of mankind.

It must not be supposed that this criticism of the army and the Church takes no account of the collateral advantages which have arisen from the selection which these establishments have made of the abler youth of each generation. The process has led to gains of great and permanent value. The art of war has much educational importance: it teaches men the principles of orderly association, and inculcated the motives of discipline. Through the development of the military art, the folk of our race gradually rose from savagery to feudalism, and thence to the higher ideals of the modern state. War is an evil arising from the nature of man, and its ills have diminished with every stage in the advance from the rude work of antiquity to the science of today. The Church needed all the forces it could command for the long combat which conquered paganism, and established the higher religious ideal of Christianity. The millions who have been in its active priesthood have been, as a whole, an army fighting in the cause of human advance. It is possible that these men could not have done their work so well save as celibates. The service demanded the fullest measure of devotion, which perhaps could not have been obtained from men who were influenced by domestic ties. If the sacrifice of the people's strength had been limited to those who entered the calling of the priest, the question of the balance of good and ill might be regarded as doubtful; but when we consider the hosts of able men and women in each generation withdrawn from the body of the people by the religious orders, we feel that there have been no adequate compensations for the sacrifice. The only sound apology for the system is to be found in the ignorance of its founders concerning the nature of man, — a plea which, in time, our descendants will, it may be, have to make for ourselves.

The extent to which this process of destroying the talent of the peasant class has affected the quality of the population in different parts of Europe varies greatly. It has doubtless been most effective in those regions where the Roman Church has had the most uninterrupted sway. The Latin countries, Italy, Spain, Portugal, and France, have felt the influence of the conditions imposed by the Roman Church, down to the present day. In the northern part of Europe, owing to the development of those forms of Christianity in which the clergy is not celibate, and in which the monastic order finds no important place, the greater part of the population has been, for many generations, exempt from this destructive influence.

The observant foot traveler in Europe may, at many points, observe differences in the conditions of the peasant class which are due to diversities in their history: thus, on the line between the western cantons of Switzerland and the neighboring parts of France. The difference in the quality of the laboring classes in these two fields is surprisingly great, and coincides exactly with the political line. On the east we have a vigorous and varied body of people, in their essential qualities like our own folk; on the west, characteristic peasants, such as give the economic strength of France, laborious, dull, substantially immobile people. So far as my experience goes, the peasantry of Germany and the Scandinavian countries is in a much higher state than that of southern Europe; there is, indeed, a distinct improvement visible as we go northward. In England there is but a remnant of the peasant folk, and this is vanishing before the process of advance on the lines of democratic culture.

It seems to me that where the above-described processes which have lowered the intellectual tone of the peasant class have done their full work, we cannot expect to find among the laboring people good material from which to make the citizens of a democracy. For that purpose we need not only a sound basis of moral character, — which, thanks to the Church, is often an admirable feature in the lower classes of Europe, — but also a considerable measure of native ability. A democratic society which has not the power to supply men of capacity from its lower ranks will soon cease to be a true democracy, and decline to the oligarchic state. It is the peculiar feature of our American population that ability is as well developed among the lower as among the higher grades of the people. This feature is shown in many ways; among others, by the endless religious movements. The condition where there are "fifty religions and but one sauce," though in some respects disagreeable, affords excellent proof of the intellectual quickness of the folk, even if it shows a strange defect in taste in other matters. The same inventive quality of the mind is also noticeable in the incessant stream of mechanical contrivances which comes from our laboring men of native blood. Neither of these indications of ability is discernible among the characteristic peasants of Europe. They have no desire to change the faith or the tools of their forefathers. The Italian of to-day uses substantially the implements which served the Roman of the same calling in the first century of our era. I have seen, within view of a main railway in Tuscany, in actual use, ploughs which contained not a particle of metal, and retained the classic form. It is not necessary that every American citizen should be a patentee, but the general existence of this inventive motive shows the wide distribution of the foreseeing and planning power which makes good citizens. Those who are inquirers in the matter of machines and creeds will, when called on, be ready for statecraft.

If the form of our government were such as permitted us to create or maintain a peasant class, the European people of this grade might be a valuable contribution to our population. Such folk are generally laborious, patient, and home-loving. In them the simpler virtues of men are very firmly implanted. They make an admirable foundation for any state which is ruled by a distinct upper class; which, in a word, has an aristocratic organization, whatever may be the name by which it designates its government. Thus, in France, where the political system is still, though founded on universal suffrage, aristocratic in essence, where there is little trace of an upward movement out of the peasant class, the orderly, laborious people of this grade constitute the strength of the state, restoring by their ceaseless toil and economy the vast waste of capital which that unfortunate country has suffered during the last twenty years. But our fathers did not, and we do not as yet, declaredly propose to found a state on such a purely laboring class. The only social order consistent with our commonwealth is one in which all men are not only equal before the law, but have an essential unity in their motives and aspirations. Just so far as we admit these peasant people to a place with us, we inflict on our life the impoverishment of citizenly talent which their own unfortunate history has laid upon them.

But I hear the optimist cry: "These people are essentially like ourselves; they will quickly respond to the stimulus of our free air. In one generation they will become thoroughly Americanized." I would ask the hopeful man to consider how long it would require to change himself or his descendants into the characteristic mould of body and mind of the peasant. Backward steps in the generations are always more easily taken than are those of advance, but all who have considered such changes will, I think, agree with me that it would take some centuries of sore trial to bring the characteristic American to the lower estate, and the chance is that the breed would perish on the way. Our country affords excellent instances to show how indelible long-inherited characteristics may become. The bodily characteristics, and to a great extent the motives, of our African folk have withstood the greatest climatic and social changes which any race has ever experienced within the historic period. Much of the peasant quality stays in the Germans of Pennsylvania, though they are from an excellent and relatively advanced original stock. Even if we take slight social peculiarities, we find them amazingly persistent among our eminently plastic people. At least one instance bearing on this point I may be permitted to give.

Much has been said concerning the unhappy spirit of battle which leads to so many homicides in certain parts of the South. It is a fair matter for wonder how a people, in general so like others of their time and race, should have this barbaric habit of killing their neighbors on slight provocation. The explanation seems to be that, in the Southern States, the social conditions induced by slavery have served to perpetuate in the white people the peculiar notions of personal honor which marked, and were indeed an essential concomitant of, the feudal system. The strong commands of the Christian faith, vigorous legislation, the pressure of public opinion brought to bear by their more advanced neighbors, have not served to stamp out this evil. So far, indeed, they seem to have made no distinct impression upon it. It remains a most striking example to show the singular permanence of motives among men. A like endurance of ancestral quality could, if space admitted, readily be shown in other parts of this country, among folk who have been thoroughly

Americanized, who have been exempt from the bondage of tradition in a measure which we cannot expect in the descendants of a peasant class.

Whoever will take care, in a dispassionate way, to consider the conditions of a peasant class will be led to doubt the profit of our present experiments which tend toward a reconstruction of our society on the new foundations which such people afford.

We should remember that our English race had won its way to the independent and vigorous social motives which are the characteristics of our democracy before they were transplanted to this country. The circumstances of that migration prevented the importation of a peasantry, and insured that the laboring class, except the Africans, should be formed of people who had already risen above the state of serfdom. The social conditions of the land tended to prevent the institution of a very distinct peasant class in the mother country, and they had made a development of such an estate quite impossible here. The result was that our original population retained, and in a way restored, the primitive social form of the Germanic race, or perhaps we had better say the Aryan variety of mankind. They were men who had never been slaves. Their stock had been but little pauperized by the army or the Church, or ground down by centuries of life in the conditions of a lower caste. Compare the origin and nurture of these freemen with those of the ordinary laborers of Europe, and we see at once the gravity of the danger which the mass of European immigration brings to us. The American commonwealth could never have been founded if the first European colonists had been of peasant stock. It is doubtful whether it can be maintained if its preservation comes to depend upon such men.

14

A POPULAR WRITER

 The Greenhorns, "the last ones over," have generally been suspected of being less able and valuable additions to the American people than those who founded the First Families. Like the new boy in school, they have also become the butt of many jokes. The comic redheaded Irishman in the person of bogtrotter Teague O'Reagan makes his American debut in the first installment of *Modern Chivalry,* an episodic tale published in Philadelphia in 1792.

But the indisputably greatest comic Irish figure in American journalism was Mr. Dooley, the creation of Finley Peter Dunne. Mr. Dooley presided over the bar of a saloon in Archey Road, listened patiently to the palaver of Hennessey, the incarnation of the stereotyped ignorant Irish day laborer, and expressed his own, liberal, compassionate, often incomparably witty opinions on problems of the day.

Dunne (1867–1936) was a Chicago journalist, city editor, baseball reporter, and prolific creator of dialect essays, many of them still justly famous for their shrewd observations about our politics, affectations, and, as in the essay reprinted here, prejudices of old immigrants toward the new. Hennessey's objection to new immigrants is ironic. The Irish had been received with misgivings wherever they appeared, and "No Irish Need Apply" notices were a living memory for many Americans when this piece was written. While the Irish shared some of the characteristics of old immigrants — they spoke English and arrived in large numbers before the Civil War — their poverty, lack of vocational specialization, and Roman Catholicism put them into a category with the new. In fact, from the sociological point of view, their status may be defined as intermediate between old and new immigrants.

IMMIGRATION

Finley Peter Dunne

"Well, I see Congress has got to wurruk again," said Mr. Dooley.

"The Lord save us fr'm harm," said Mr. Hennessy.

"Yes, sir," said Mr. Dooley, "Congress has got to wurruk again, an' manny things that seems important to a Congressman 'll be brought up befure thim. 'Tis sthrange that what's a big thing to a man in Wash'nton, Hinnissy, don't seem much account to me. Divvle a bit do I care whether they dig th' Nicaragoon Canal or cross th' Isthmus in a balloon; or whether th' Monroe docthrine is enfoorced or whether it ain't; or whether th' thrusts is abolished as Teddy Rosenfelt wud like to have thim or encouraged to go on with their neefaryous but magnificent entherprises as th' Prisidint wud like; or whether th' water is poured into th' ditches to reclaim th' arid lands iv th' West or th' money f'r thim to fertilize th' arid pocket-books iv th' conthractors; or whether th' Injun is threated like a depindant an' miserable thribesman or like a free an' indepin-dant dog; or whether we restore th' merchant marine to th' ocean or whether we lave it to restore itsilf. None iv these here questions intherests me, an' be me I mane you an' be you I mane ivrybody. What we want to know is, ar-re we goin' to have coal enough in th' hod whin th' cold snap comes; will th' plumbin' hold out, an' will th' job last.

"But they'se wan question that Congress is goin' to take up that you an' me are intherested in. As a pilgrim father that missed th' first boats, I must raise me claryon voice again' th' invasion iv this fair land be th' paupers an' arnychists iv effete Europe. Ye bet I must — because I'm here first. 'Twas diff'rent whin I was dashed high on th' stern an' rockbound coast. In thim days America was th' refuge iv th' oppressed iv all th' wurruld. They cud come over here an' do a good job iv oppressin' thimsilves. As I told ye I come a little late. Th' Rosenfelts an' th' Lodges bate me be at laste a boat lenth, an' be th' time I got here they was stern an' rockbound thimsilves. So I got a gloryous rayciption as soon as I was towed off th' rocks. Th' stars an' sthripes whispered a welcome in th' breeze an' a shovel was thrust into me hand an' I was pushed into a sthreet excyvatin' as though I'd been born here. Th' pilgrim father who bossed th' job was a fine ol' puritan be th' name iv Doherty, who come over in th' Mayflower about th' time iv th' potato rot in Wexford, an' he made me think they was a hole in th' break-wather iv th' haven iv refuge an' some iv th' wash iv th' seas iv opprission had got through. He was a stern an' rockbound la-ad

FROM *Observations by Mr. Dooley* (New York, 1902).

himsilf, but I was a good hand at loose stones an' wan day — but I'll tell ye about that another time.

"Annyhow, I was rayceived with open arms that sometimes ended in a clinch. I was afraid I wasn't goin' to assimilate with th' airlyer pilgrim fathers an' th' instichoochions iv th' counthry, but I soon found that a long swing iv th' pick made me as good as another man an' it didn't require a gr-reat intellect, or sometimes anny at all, to vote th' dimmycrat ticket, an' befure I was here a month, I felt enough like a native born American to burn a witch. Wanst in a while a mob iv intilligint collajeens, whose grandfathers had bate me to th' dock, wud take a shy at me Pathrick's Day procission or burn down wan iv me churches, but they got tired iv that befure long; 'twas too much like wurruk.

"But as I tell ye, Hinnissy, 'tis diff'rent now. I don't know why 'tis diff'rent but 'tis diff'rent. 'Tis time we put our back again' th' open dure an' keep out th' savage horde. If that cousin iv ye'ers expects to cross, he'd betther tear f'r th' ship. In a few minyits th' gates 'll be down an' whin th' oppressed wurruld comes hikin' acrost to th' haven iv refuge, they'll do well to put a couplin' pin undher their hats, f'r th' Goddess iv Liberty 'll meet thim at th' dock with an axe in her hand. Congress is goin' to fix it. Me frind Shaughnessy says so. He was in yisterdah an' says he: ' 'Tis time we done something to make th' immigration laws sthronger,' says he. 'Thrue f'r ye, Miles Standish,' says I; 'but what wud ye do?' 'I'd keep out th' offscourin's iv Europe,' says he. 'Wud ye go back?' says I. 'Have ye'er joke,' says he. ' 'Tis not so seeryus as it was befure ye come,' says I. 'But what ar-re th' immygrants doin' that's roonous to us?' I says. 'Well,' says he, 'they're arnychists,' he says; 'they don't assymilate with th' counthry,' he says. 'Maybe th' counthry's digestion has gone wrong fr'm too much rich food,' says I; 'perhaps now if we'd lave off thryin' to digest Rockyfellar an' thry a simple diet like Schwartzmeister, we wudden't feel th' effects iv our vittels,' I says. 'Maybe if we'd season th' immygrants a little or cook thim thurly, they'd go down betther,' I says.

" 'They're arnychists, like Parsons,' he says. 'He wud've been an immygrant if Texas hadn't been admitted to th' Union,' I says. 'Or Snolgosh,' he says. 'Has Mitchigan seceded?' I says. 'Or Gittoo,' he says. 'Who come fr'm th' effete monarchies iv Chicago, west iv Ashland Av'noo,' I says, 'Or what's-his-name, Wilkes Booth,' he says. 'I don't know what he was — maybe a Boolgharyen,' says I. 'Well, annyhow,' says he, 'they're th' scum iv th' earth.' 'They may be that,' says I; 'but we used to think they was th' cream iv civilization,' I says. 'They're off th' top annyhow. I wanst believed 'twas

th' best men iv Europe come here, th' la-ads that was too sthrong
and indepindant to be kicked around be a boorgomasther at home
an' wanted to dig out f'r a place where they cud get a chanst to
make their way to th' money. I see their sons fightin' into politics
an' their daughters tachin' young American idee how to shoot too
high in th' public school, an' I thought they was all right. But I
see I was wrong. Thim boys out there towin' wan heavy foot afther
th' other to th' rowlin' mills is all arnychists. There's warrants out
f'r all names endin' in 'inski, an' I think I'll board up me windows,
f'r,' I says, 'if immygrants is as dangerous to this counthry as ye
an' I an' other pilgrim fathers believe they are, they'se enough iv
thim sneaked in already to make us aborigines about as infloointial
as the prohibition vote in th' Twenty-ninth Ward. They'll dash again'
our stern an' rock-bound coast till they bust it,' says I.

" 'But I ain't so much afraid as ye ar-re. I'm not afraid iv me
father an' I'm not afraid iv mesilf. An' I'm not afraid iv Schwartzmeister's father or Hinnery Cabin Lodge's grandfather. We all come
over th' same way, an' if me ancestors were not what Hogan calls
rigicides, 'twas not because they were not ready an' willin', on'y
a king niver come their way. I don't believe in killin' kings, mesilf.
I niver wud've sawed th' block off that curly-headed potintate that
I see in th' pitchers down town, but, be hivins, Presarved Codfish
Shaughnessy, if we'd begun a few years ago shuttin' out folks that
wudden't mind handin' a bomb to a king, they wudden't be enough
people in Mattsachoosetts to make a quorum f'r th' Anti-Impeeryal
S'ciety,' says I. 'But what wud ye do with th' offscourin' iv Europe?'
says he. 'I'd scour thim some more,' says I.

"An' so th' meetin' iv th' Plymouth Rock Assocyation come
to an end. But if ye wud like to get it together, Deacon Hinnissy,
to discuss th' immygration question, I'll sind out a hurry call f'r
Schwartzmeister an' Mulcahey an' Ignacio Sbarbaro an' Nels Larsen
an' Petrus Gooldvink, an' we 'll gather to-night at Fanneilnoviski
Hall at th' corner iv Sheridan an' Sigel sthreets. All th' pilgrim fathers
is rayquested f'r to bring interpreters."

"Well," said Mr. Hennessy, "divvle th' bit I care, on'y I'm here
first, an' I ought to have th' right to keep th' bus fr'm bein' overcrowded."

"Well," said Mr. Dooley, "as a pilgrim father on me gran'
nephew's side, I don't know but ye're right. An' they'se wan sure
way to keep thim out."

"What's that?" asked Mr. Hennessy.

"Teach thim all about our instichoochions befure they come,"
said Mr. Dooley.

15
A LABOR LEADER

After the United States Immigration Commission issued its report in 1910, the president of the American Federation of Labor expressed organized labor's official support of immigration restriction. Samuel Gompers (1850–1924) was the English-born son of Dutch-Jewish immigrants who left London for the Lower East Side of New York in 1863.

As leader of the AF of L for over forty years he pioneered some of the disparaging attitudes against Orientals and eastern and southern Europeans which paved the way for the racialist quota laws of the 1920s. While he repeatedly disavowed "any vulgar prejudice" against foreigners, these disclaimers merely heightened the irony of his political alliance with Henry Cabot Lodge, the deeply racist Senatorial opponent of the new immigration.

Did Gompers want to prove that he was a "real" American by supporting the literacy test vetoed by three Presidents, and by campaigning for the virtual exclusion of "new" immigrants in the 1920s? Was it racial snobbism, fear of competition, anxieties over loss of status, or a combination of these feelings that motivated his opposition to admission of more recent arrivals, beginning with the Russian Jews who in the 1880s threatened his and his father's cigarmaker's trade? Was he convinced that the trade union's sole task was improvement of members' working conditions and wages, with no thought for broader social reforms for the masses of unskilled, unorganized, native and foreign, white and black laborers?

Historical records furnish no precise answers to such questions. They show, however, that nearly all American unions tended to exclude strangers and were in many ways organized like ethnic associations with benevolent purposes. Those who did not belong to the closed circle of insiders, whether American-born railroad engineers, Irish teamsters, British miners, or Jewish garment workers, were kept out.

IMMIGRATION — UP TO CONGRESS

THE A.F. of L. ON IMMIGRATION

Samuel Gompers

Resolution 77, passed at the annual convention held at Toronto, Ontario, November, 1909:

WHEREAS, The illiteracy test is the most practical means for restricting the present stimulated influx of cheap labor, whose competition is so ruinous to the workers already here, whether native or foreign; and

WHEREAS, An increased head tax upon steamships is needed to provide better facilities, to more efficiently enforce our immigration laws, and to restrict immigration; and

WHEREAS, The requirement of some visible means of support would enable immigrants to find profitable employment; and

WHEREAS, The effect of the Federal Bureau of Distribution is to stimulate foreign immigration; therefore be it

RESOLVED, By the American Federation of Labor in Twenty-ninth Annual Convention assembled, that we demand the enactment of the illiteracy test, the money test, an increased head tax and the abolition of the Distribution Bureau; and, be it further

RESOLVED, That we favor heavily fining the foreign steamships for bringing debarable aliens where reasons for debarment could have been ascertained at the time of sale of ticket.

FROM *American Federationist*, XVIII (January, 1911), pp. 17–21. Reprinted by courtesy of AFL *American Federationist*.

The final inning of the tug of war over immigration has now begun. In this contest tremendous forces are engaged. On the side of America are the upholders of two distinctive American sentiments, the maintenance of the American standard of living for our wage-working classes and the maintenance of American institutions as they are, unimpaired through the financial degradation of the working classes. On the pro-immigration side is the powerful immigration machine, composed of the transocean combine, with all its thousands of agents and other innumerable parasites, the bankers, padrones, etc., who are coining money out of the millions of immigrants coming in the course of years into this country from Europe.

The center of this tug of war has at last shifted to Congress. No longer is the discussion indefinite, casual, or partisan, or without an immediate object, conducted through the press and other insufficient agencies of information and debate. No longer, either, is it backed up merely by individual impressions or the partial investigations heretofore promoted by various private institutions. The Federal Government undertook four years ago the solution of the immigration question through scientific means. It set out to ascertain the undeniable facts and after three full years of research its commission has brought forward no less than forty volumes on the subject, covering every possible phase. Its recommendations it has brought forward in concise form in a separate pamphlet.

A reading of these recommendations confirms the facts of the case as they have been accepted by the American Federation of Labor after the serious study its members had given the question for decades. The local, and then the international unions, and finally the annual conventions of the American Federation of Labor itself, have had immigration up for consideration as one of the principal labor topics on literally thousands of occasions. The membership as a whole, from upholding the sentiments the great majority once entertained, namely, that this country could go on indefinitely absorbing the entire possible stream of immigration, have reluctantly, in view of the facts, passed over to the sway of the sentiment that their own good heartedness toward the immigrants and the laborers of the Old World was being exploited by large employers for the purpose of reducing wages as well as by the steamship combine and its myriad of parasites for the sake of their own profits. At last the great body of the American industrial wage-workers have come to see one fact above others, which is, that the immigrants are assimilated in America through the wage-working class. This means that the American born wage-earners and the foreign wage-earners who have been here long enough to aspire to American standards are subjected to the ruinous competition of an unending stream of men freshly arriving from foreign lands who are accustomed to so low a grade of living that they can underbid the wage-earners established in this country and still save money. Whole communities, in fact whole regions, have witnessed a rapid deterioration in the mode of living of their working classes consequent on the incoming of the swarms of life-long poverty stricken aliens. Entire industries have seen the percentage of newly arrived laborers rising, until in certain regions few American men can at present be found among the unskilled.

By the Commission's report it is shown that in many communities as high as 50, and even 70, per cent of the children in the public schools are the offspring of foreign fathers. This remarkable change in America, it must be kept in mind, is almost wholly in the wage working class. It was recognized by our wage-workers in many parts of the country that this radical change in population was taking place, and hence delegates to the trade union conventions began some years ago to give their testimony as to the need of restriction of the evidently assisted, or artifically promoted, immigration. Opposition to those who supported these views brought about a continual sifting and searching for the truth as it affected trade unionism and the general wage level. At work in advance of the investigators of the Immigration Commission were the representatives of labor as most deeply interested investigators in the cause of labor. Not only in a general way, but most strikingly in certain occupations and in certain districts of the country, what had been brought home to trade unionists as going on through immigration was the rapid change in the membership of the unions as well as in population. In no country on the face of the globe do such rapid transitions in industry and in population take place as in ours. Therefore, in time the general opinion among union men on immigration had come to be such as was expressed in the resolution passed at the Toronto Convention.

The United States Immigration Commission, after its protracted studies, perfectly agrees with this opinion. The Commission, as a whole, in its own words, "recommends restriction as demanded by economic, moral, and social considerations, furnishes in its report reasons for such restriction, and points out methods by which Congress can attain the desired result if its judgment coincides with that of the Commission."

There was but one dissenting voice on the Commission's report — that of Congressman William S. Bennet of New York, whose emphatic rejection on November 8 by his constituents was one of the remarkable features of the recent campaign. Mr. Bennet's minority report is brief and not very clear as to his reasons for finding every other member of the Commission of eleven members in the wrong. Since the date on which he sent it in however, he has found his proper place. On December 6 he sent a telegram to the President of the "Liberty Immigration Society," declaring that "immigration at the present time is not a menace, either mentally, morally, or physically." This telegram was published, with words of approval, by the foreign New York newspapers which draw much of their financial support from the large display advertisements of the steamship combine engaged in dredging Europe for emigrants.

The following is the most significant passage of the United States Immigration Commission's Report (page 39):

> The investigations of the Commission show an oversupply of unskilled labor in basic industries to an extent which indicates an oversupply of unskilled labor in the industries of the country as a whole, and therefore demands legislation which will at the present time restrict the further admission of such unskilled labor.
>
> It is desirable in making the restriction that —
>
> a. A sufficient number be debarred to produce a marked effect upon the present supply of unskilled labor.
>
> b. As far as possible, the aliens excluded should be those who come to this country with no intention to become American citizens or even to maintain a permanent residence here, but merely to save enough, by the adoption, if necessary, of low standards of living to return permanently to their home country. Such persons are usually men unaccompanied by wives or children.
>
> c. As far as possible the aliens excluded should also be those who, by reason of their personal qualities or habits, would least readily be assimilated or would make the least desirable citizens.
>
> The following methods of restricting immigration have been suggested:
>
> a. The exclusion of those unable to read or write in some language.
>
> b. The limitation of the number of each race arriving each year to a certain percentage of the average of that race arriving during a given period of years.
>
> c. The exclusion of unskilled laborers unaccompanied by wives or families.
>
> d. The limitation of the number of immigrants arriving annually at any port.

e. The material increase in the amount of money required to be in the possession of the immigrant at the port of arrival.

f. The material increase of the head tax.

g. The levy of the head tax so as to make a marked discrimination in favor of men with families.

All these methods would be effective in one way or another in securing restrictions in greater or less degree. A majority of the Commission favor the reading and writing test as the most feasible single method of restricting undesirable immigration.

The Commission also makes the following points in its report:

Further general legislation concerning the admission of aliens should be based primarily upon economic or business considerations touching the prosperity and economic well-being of our people.

The development of business may be brought about by means which lower the standard of living of the wage-earners.

Aliens convicted of serious crimes within a period of five years after admission should be deported.

So far as practicable the immigration laws should be so amended as to be made applicable to alien seamen.

Any alien who becomes a public charge within three years after his arrival in this country should be subjected to deportation.

The Commission also believes that in order "to protect the immigrant against exploitation, to discourage sending savings abroad, to encourage permanent residence and naturalization, to secure better distribution of alien immigrants throughout the country," the States should enact laws strictly regulating immigrant banks and employment agencies, and that aliens who attempt to persuade immigrants not to become American citizens should be made subject to deportation, and that the Division of Information should co-operate with the States desiring immigrant settlers.

At the recent St. Louis Convention of the American Federation of Labor the President in his report called the attention of the delegates to the fact "that a veritable flood of bills" designed to check immigration had been introduced in the last session of Congress, and the report of the Executive Council on the President's report expressed the hope that this flood of bills and the work of the Immigration Commission would result "in the enactment of legislation which will protect the workers in this country from the unfair competition resulting from indiscriminate immigration."

On behalf of American labor, it is to be said that the action of the trade unions in this country on this most delicate international question involves a step that touches the heart of every man contemplating it. That step, the advocacy of exclusion, is not prompted by any assumption of superior virtue over our foreign brothers. We disavow for American organized labor the holding of any vulgar or unworthy prejudices against the foreigner. We recognize the noble possibilities in the poorest of the children of the earth who come to us from European lands. We know that their civilization is sufficiently near our own to bring their descendants in one generation up to the general level of the best American citizenship. It is not on account of their assumed inferiority, or through any pusillanimous contempt for their abject poverty, that, most reluctantly, the lines have been drawn by America's workingmen against the indiscriminate admission of aliens to this country. It is simply a case of the self-preservation of the American working classes. Changes are constantly going on in Europe for the uplift of the men of labor, and it can well be believed that each country in Europe is in position today to solve its own labor questions in the way best for itself. A fact now obvious to labor in this country is that American labor and European labor have both been made the subject of a colossal bunco game played by avaricious exploiters of the poor. The sounding phrase "protection to American labor" has of recent years been a standing insult to the intelligence of American wage-earners, with millions upon millions of new-comers arriving here through promoted immigration. Considering the opportunities now existing in Europe for the advance of the working classes, the net gains to be made on the whole by European immigrants to this country at the present time are to be questioned. The manifold acute sufferings of immigrants, their sacrifices to enable them to come to America, the trials of the ocean voyage, the discouragements in seeking work in the United States — in getting a foot-hold in the wage-working ranks, in the oppression they suffer at the hands of employers, and in their sickness and death rate — all these drawbacks serve to counter-balance much of whatever success may at last come to them. Of the 30 to 40 per cent of the immigrants who return to Europe, an enormous number go back, by the evidence of the Commission, defeated, disheartened, ruined.

It is not necessary here to dilate on many of the inhuman features of immigration, statements as to which have been so hotly disputed in the many articles published in American periodicals in recent years. Suffice it to say that the Immigration Commission's Report in its summary gives reason to believe that the most sensational charges against steamship companies and other monster plunderers of the poor ever made in the yellowest of the magazines come near to official substantiation.

The Commission says:

The old immigration movement was essentially one of permanent settlers. The new immigration (since 1882) is very largely one of individuals, a considerable proportion of whom apparently have no intention of permanently changing their residence, their only purpose in coming to America being to temporarily take advantage of the greater wages paid for industrial labor in this country. This, of course, is not true of all the new immigrants, but the practice is sufficiently common to warrant referring to it as a characteristic of them as a class. From all data that are available it appears that at least 40 per cent of the new immigration movement returns to Europe and at least 30 per cent remains there. This percentage does not mean that 30 per cent of the immigrants have acquired a competence and returned to live on it. Among the immigrants who return permanently are those who have failed, as well as those who have succeeded. Thousands of those returning have, under unusual conditions of climate, work and food, contracted tuberculosis and other diseases; others are injured in our industries; still others are the widows and children of aliens dying here. These, with the aged and temperamentally unfit, make up a large part of the aliens who return to their former homes to remain (p. 16, "Brief Statement").

As a class the new immigrants are largely unskilled laborers coming from countries where their highest wage is small compared with the lowest wage in the United States. Nearly 75 per cent of them are males. About 83 per cent are between the ages of 14 and 45 years, and consequently are producers rather than dependents. They bring little money into the country and send or take a considerable part of their earnings out. More than 35 per cent are illiterate, as compared with less than 3 per cent of the old immigrant class (p. 16).

It should be stated, however, that immigration from Europe is not now an absolute economic necessity, and as a rule those who emigrate to the United States are impelled by a desire for betterment rather than by the necessity of escaping intolerable conditions. This fact should largely modify the natural incentive to treat the immigration movement from the standpoint of sentiment and permit its consideration primarily as an economic problem (p. 17).

Comparatively few immigrants come without some reasonably definite assurance that employment awaits them, and it is probable that as a rule they know the nature of that employment and the rate of wages. A large number of immigrants are induced to come by quasi labor agents in this country, who combine the business of supplying laborers to large employers and contractors with the so-called immigrant banking business and the selling of steamship tickets.

Another important agency in promoting emigration from Europe to the United States are the many thousands of steamship ticket agents and sub-agents operating in the emigrant furnishing districts of southern and eastern Europe. Under the terms of the United States immigration law, as well as the laws of most European countries, the promotion of emigration is forbidden, but nevertheless the steamship-agent propaganda flourishes everywhere. It does not appear that the steamship lines as a rule openly direct the operations of these agents, but the existence of the propaganda is a matter of common knowledge in the emigrant-furnishing countries and it is fair to assume is acquiesced in, if not stimulated, by the steamship lines as well. With the steamship lines the transportation of steerage passengers is purely a commercial matter; moreover, the steerage business which originates in southern and eastern Europe is peculiarly attractive to the companies, as many of the immigrants travel back and forth, thus insuring east-bound as well as west-bound traffic (p. 17).

There are annually admitted, however, a very large number who come in response to indirect assurance that employment awaits them. In the main these assurances are contained in letters from persons already in this country who advise their relatives or friends at home that if they will come to the United States they will find work awaiting them. On the other hand, it is clear that there is a large induced immigration due to labor agents in this country, who, independently or in co-operation with agents in Europe, operate practically without restriction. As a rule only unskilled laborers are induced to come to the United States by this means (p. 21).

There have been established at a number of our important ports societies who, with the permission of the immigration authorities, send representatives to meet incoming aliens whose friends and relatives fail to call for them. In case these immigrants need advice or a place where they can remain in safety for a few days, these societies furnish such aid and permit them to come to the homes which have been established for that purpose. These societies and homes have usually been founded by and are under the direction of societies connected with some religious body. In a number of instances they receive subventions from foreign governments, inasmuch as they care for the immigrants of the countries concerned.

As the welfare of the immigrants, especially young women, might be materially affected by the care exercised by the representatives of these homes, it seemed wise to investigate their methods of work and the condition of their homes. The results were surprising. While in a number of cases the societies were doing excellent work and the homes were giving due attention to the welfare of the young women placed in their charge, securing them positions and afterwards seeing that the positions were those suitable for the girls, in a number of instances it was found that the managers of the homes had apparently deceived the directors and supporters of the societies and were making of the homes mere money-making establishments for the managers. In a few cases, in order to promote their own financial advantage, the managers overcharged the immigrants, permitted the immigrant homes to remain in a filthy condition from lack of care, and even were ready to furnish to keepers of disreputable houses young girls as servants in such houses. The Commission called the attention of the Immigration Commissioner at Ellis Island and of the authorities at Washington to these abuses. In a number of cases vigorous action was taken and representatives of seven societies were forbidden access to the immigrant station until a complete change in the management had been brought about (p. 23).

A large proportion of the southern and eastern European immigration of the past twenty-five years has entered the manufacturing and mining industries of the eastern and middle western States, mostly in the capacity of unskilled laborers. There is no basic industry in which they are not largely represented and in many cases they compose more than 50 per cent of the total number of persons employed in such industries. Coincident with the advent of these millions of unskilled laborers there has been an unprecedented expansion of the industries in which they have been employed. Whether this great immigration movement was caused by the industrial development or whether the fact that a practically unlimited and available supply of cheap labor existed in Europe was taken advantage of for the purpose of expanding the industries can not well be demonstrated. Whatever may be the truth in this regard it is certain that southern and eastern European immigrants have almost completely monopolized unskilled labor activities in many of the more important industries (p. 29).

The effect of the new immigration is clearly shown in the Western Pennsylvania fields, where the average wage of the bituminous coal worker is 42 cents a day below the average wage in the Middle West and Southwest. Incidentally, hours of labor are longer and general working conditions poorer in the Pennsylvania mines than elsewhere. Another characteristic of the new immigrants contributed to the situation in Pennsylvania. This was the impossibility of successfully organizing them into labor unions. Several attempts at organization were made, but the constant influx of immigrants to whom prevailing conditions seemed unusually favorable contributed to the failure to organize. A similar situation has prevailed in other great industries (p. 30).

These groups have little contact with American life, learn little of American institutions, and aside from the wages earned profit little by their stay in this country. During their early years in the United States they usually rely for assistance and advice on some member of their race, frequently a saloon keeper or grocer, and almost always a steamship ticket agent and immigrant banker who, because of superior intelligence and better knowledge of American ways, commands their confidence. After a longer residence they usually become more self-reliant, but their progress toward assimilation is generally slow (p. 30).

Space prevents us from giving further quotations. It is to be hoped that all intelligent unionists will write to their representatives in Congress for copies of the "Brief Statement of the Conclusions and Recommendations to the Immigration Commission," issued last month from the Government Printing Office and which can be had for the asking. Let every active unionist and every local union also see to it that this information has its proper and due influence on the public through the local newspapers and on the local representative in Congress.

Now is the time to be wide awake! It was well enough to promote discussion of the question and to follow up through the years the development of public opinion on the subject, but now is the hour for action. Remember the forces we are obliged to encounter, and let the campaign be quick, sharp, and brief. The enemy has everything to gain through procrastination of our law-givers in dealing with the subject.

16

AN ANTHROPOL-OGIST

Franz Boas (1858–1942) was one of the fathers of American anthropological studies, the founder of comparative linguistics, and an influential teacher of a whole generation of American anthropologists.

In 1910, he completed his famous study of the changes in bodily form of the children of immigrants, in which he demonstrated that "the head form, which has always been considered one of the stable and permanent characteristics of human races, undergoes far-reaching changes due to the transfer of the people from European to American soil.... We are compelled to conclude that when [bodily features] change, the whole bodily and mental makeup of the immigrants may change."

Boas' work was one of the volumes in the Reports of the Immigration Commission which had been appointed in 1907 under the chairmanship of Senator Dillingham. The widely quoted report figured prominently in the debates leading to the Johnson Act of 1921, which ended unrestricted immigration.

Though Boas emphasized the "great plasticity of human types," the Commission's Report paid little attention to his findings and discussed differences between "old" and "new" immigrants as if racial temperaments and, by implication, mental and moral differences between men, were and remained fixed in "blood" and heredity.

The last two pages of Boas' paper, omitted here because of space limitations, deal with the question of Negro physical and mental makeup. Boas concluded that while differences in character and specific aptitudes may exist, there is "no proof whatever that these differences signify any appreciable degree of inferiority of the Negro...."

By reporting that the American environment was recasting the most persistent hereditary traits of immigrants from widely different racial and ethnic backgrounds, that there was emerging a common American type with an "American face," Boas indirectly attacked the nativist assumption that racial fixity prevented assimilation of alien, non-Anglo-Saxon groups.

The following address was delivered to the American Association for the Advancement of Science, Baltimore, 1908.

RACE PROBLEMS IN AMERICA

Franz Boas

The development of the American nation through amalgamation of diverse European nationalities and the ever-increasing heterogeneity of the component elements of our people have called attention to the anthropological and biological problems involved in this process.

I propose to discuss here these problems with a view of making clear the hypothetical character of many of the generally accepted assumptions. It will be our object to attempt a formulation of the problems, and to outline certain directions of inquiry, that promise a solution of the questions involved, that, at the present time, can not be answered with scientific accuracy. It is disappointing that we have to accept this critical attitude, because the events of our daily life bring before our eyes constantly the grave issues that are based on the presence of distinct types of man in our country, and on the continued influx of heterogeneous nationalities from Europe. Under the pressure of these events, we seem to be called upon to formulate definite answers to questions that require the most painstaking and unbiased investigation. The more urgent the demand for final conclusions, the more needed is a critical examination of the phenomena and of the available methods of solution.

Let us first represent to our minds the facts relating to the origins of our nation. When British immigrants first flocked to the Atlantic coast of North America, they found a continent inhabited by Indians. The population of the country was thin, and vanished comparatively rapidly before the influx of the more numerous Europeans. The

FROM *Science*, XXIX (May 28, 1909), pp. 839–49. Reprinted by permission of the publisher.

settlement of the Dutch on the Hudson, of the Germans in Pennsylvania, not to speak of other nationalities, is familiar to all of us. We know that the foundations of our modern state were laid by Spaniards in the Southwest, by French in the Mississippi Basin and in the region of the Great Lakes, but that the British immigration far outnumbered that of other nationalities. In the composition of our people, the indigenous element has never played an important role, except for very short periods. In regions where the settlement progressed for a long time entirely by the immigration of unmarried males of the white race, families of mixed blood have been of some importance during the period of gradual development, but they have never become sufficiently numerous in any populous part of the United States to be considered as an important element in our population. Without any doubt, Indian blood flows in the veins of quite a number of our people, but the proportion is so insignificant that it may well be disregarded.

Much more important has been the introduction of the Negro, whose numbers have increased many fold so that they form now about one eighth of our whole nation. For a certain length of time the immigration of Asiatic nations seemed likely to become of importance in the development of our country, but the political events of recent years have tended to decrease their immediate importance considerably; although we do not venture to predict that the relation of Asiatics and white Americans may not become a most important problem in the future. These facts, however, are familiar to all of us and stand out clearly to our minds.

More recent is the problem of the immigration of people representing all the nationalities of Europe, western Asia and northern Africa. While until late in the second half of the nineteenth century the immigrants consisted almost entirely of people of northwestern Europe, natives of Great Britain, Scandinavia, Germany, Switzerland, Holland, Belgium and France, the composition of the immigrant masses has changed completely since that time. With the economic development of Germany, German immigration has dwindled down; while at the same time Italians, the various Slavic peoples of Austria, Russia and the Balkan Peninsula, Hungarians, Roumanians, east European Hebrews, not to mention the numerous other nationalities, have arrived in ever-increasing numbers. There is no doubt that these people of eastern and southern Europe represent a physical type distinct from the physical type of northwestern Europe; and it is clear, even to the most casual observer, that their present social standards differ fundamentally from our own. Since the number of new arrivals may be counted in normal years by hundreds of thousands, the question may well be asked, What will be the result of this influx of types distinct from our own, if it is to continue for considerable length of time?

It is often claimed that the phenomenon of mixture presented in the United States is unique; that a similar intermixture has never occurred before in the world's history; and that our nation is destined to become what some writers choose to term a "mongrel" nation in a sense that has never been equaled anywhere.

When we try to analyze the phenomena in greater detail, and in the light of our knowledge of conditions in Europe as well as in other continents, this view does not seem to me tenable. In speaking of European types, we are accustomed to consider them as, comparatively speaking, pure stocks. It is easy to show that this view is erroneous. It is only necessary to look at a map illustrating the racial types of any European country — like Italy, for instance — to see that local divergence is the characteristic feature, uniformity of type the exception. Thus Dr. Ridolfo Livi, in his fundamental investigations on the anthropology of Italy, has shown that the types of the extreme north and of the extreme south are quite distinct — the former tall, short-headed, with a considerable sprinkling of blond and blue-eyed individuals; the latter short, long-headed and remarkably dark. The transition from one type to the other is, on the whole, quite gradual, but, like isolated islands, distinct types occur here and there. The region of Lucca in Tuscany and the district of Naples are examples of this kind, which may be explained as due to the survival of an older stock, to the intrusion of new types, or to a peculiar influence of environment.

Historical evidence is quite in accord with the results derived from the investigation of the distribution of modern types. In the earliest times we find on the peninsula of Italy groups of heterogeneous people, the linguistic relationships of many of which have remained obscure up to the present time. From the earliest prehistoric times on, we see wave after wave of people invading Italy from the north. Very early Greeks settled in the greater part of southern Italy and Phoenician influence was well established on the west coast of the peninsula. A lively intercourse existed between Italy and northern Africa. Slaves of Berber blood were imported and have left their traces. Slave trade continued to bring new blood into the country until quite recent times, and Livi believes that he can trace the type of Crimean slaves who were introduced late in the Middle Ages in the region of Venice. In the course of the centuries, the migrations of Celtic and Teutonic tribes, the conquests of the Normans, the contact with Africa, have added their share to the mixture of people on the Italian peninsula.

The fates of other parts of Europe were no less diversified. The Pyrenaean Peninsula, which at present seems to be one of the most isolated parts of Europe, had a most checkered history. The earliest inhabitants of whom we know were presumably related to the Basques of the Pyrenees. These were subjected to Oriental influences in the Pre-Mycenaean period, to Punic influences, to Celtic invasions, Roman colonization, Teutonic invasions, the Moorish conquest, and later on to the peculiar selective process that accompanied the driving-out of the Moors and the Jews.

England was not exempt from vicissitudes of this kind. It seems plausible that at a very early period the type which is now found principally in Wales and in some parts of Ireland occupied the greater portion of the islands. It was swamped by successive waves of Celtic, Roman and Anglo-Saxon migration. Thus we find change everywhere.

The history of the migrations of the Goths, the invasions of the Huns, who in the short interval of one century moved their habitations from the borders of China into the very center of Europe, are proofs of the enormous changes in population that have taken place in early times.

Slow colonization has also brought about fundamental changes in blood as well as in diffusion of languages and cultures. Perhaps the most striking recent example of this change is presented by the gradual Germanization of the region east of the Elbe River, where, after the Teutonic migrations, people speaking Slavic languages had settled. The gradual absorption of Celtic communities, of the Basque, in ancient times the great Roman colonization, and later the Arab conquest of north Africa, are examples of similar processes.

Intermixture in early times was not by any means confined to peoples which, although diverse in language and culture, were of fairly uniform type. On the contrary, the most diverse types of southern Europe, northern Europe, eastern Europe and western Europe, not to mention the elements which poured into Europe from Asia and Africa, have been participants in this long-continued intermixture.

There is, however, one fundamental difference in regard to the early European migrations and the modern trans-Atlantic migration. On the whole, the former took place at a period when the density of population was, comparatively speaking, small. There is no doubt that the number of individuals concerned in the formation of the modern types of Great Britain were comparatively few as compared with the millions who come together to form a new nation in the United States; and it is obvious that the process of amalgamation which takes place in communities that must be counted by millions differs in character from the process of amalgamation that takes place in communities that may be counted by thousands. Setting aside social barriers, which in early times as well as now undoubtedly tended to keep intermingling peoples separate, it would seem that in the more populous communities of modern times a greater permanence of the single combining elements might occur, owing to their larger numbers, which make the opportunities for segregation more favorable.

Among the smaller communities the process of amalgamation must have been an exceedingly rapid one. After the social distinctions have once been obliterated, pure descendants of one of the component types decrease greatly in number, and the fourth generation of a people consisting originally of distinct elements will be almost homogeneous. I shall revert to this phenomenon later on.

It might be objected to this point of view, that the very diversity of local types in Europe proves the homogeneity of race types — as, for instance, of the northwestern European type, the Mediterranean type, the east European type, or the Alpine type; but it must be remembered that we have historical proof of the process of mixture, and that the relative number of component elements is sufficient to account for the present conditions.

I think we may dismiss the assumption of the existence of a pure type in any part of Europe, and of a process of mongrelization in America different from anything that has taken place for thousands of years in Europe. Neither are we right in assuming that the phenomenon is one of a more rapid intermixture than the one prevailing in olden times. The difference is based essentially in the masses of individuals concerned in the process.

If we confine our consideration for the present to the intermixture of European types in America, I think it will be clear, from what has been said before, that the concern that is felt by many in regard to the continuance of racial purity of our nation is to a great extent imaginary. The history of Europe proves that there has been no racial purity anywhere for exceedingly long periods, neither has the continued intermixture of European types shown any degrading effect upon any of the European nationalities. It would be just as easy to prove that those nations that have been least disturbed have lacked the stimulus to further advance and have passed through periods of quiescence. The history of Spain might be interpreted as an instance of an occurrence of this kind.

The question as to the actual effects of intermixture will not, however, be answered by a generalized historical treatment such as we have attempted here. The advocates of the theory of a degradation of type by the influx of so-called "lower" types will not be silenced by reference to earlier mixtures in Europe, the course of which can no longer be traced in actual detail for we do not know to what extent actual intermarriages have taken place, and what the development of families of mixed descent as compared with those of pure descent has been. It seems necessary that the problem should be approached from a biological standpoint. It seemed well, however, to gain first a clearer view of the historical relations of our problem. A knowledge of the events of the past tends to lay our apprehensions, that make the problem exciting, and which for this reason fill the observer with a strong bias for the results which he fears or desires.

Two questions stand out prominently in the study of the physical characteristics of the immigrant population. The first is the question of the influence of selection and environment in the migration from Europe to America. The second is the question of the influence of intermixture. A beginning of a thorough study of the former question was made as early as the time of the civil war, when Gould and Baxter, in their statistics of the enlisted soldiers, proved that the immigrant representatives of European nations were always better developed than the corresponding people in Europe. It has not been possible, up to the present time, to learn whether this difference is due to better development here or to a process of selection, by which the weaker elements are eliminated before leaving their home country. It would be easy to ascertain the facts by an investigation of the arriving immigrants. That there is good reason to suppose that more favorable social surroundings in the United States have much to do with the better development of the immigrants is proved by the anthropometrical statistics collected by Bowditch in Boston and by Peckham in Milwaukee, who found that the children growing up in America are better developed than European children. Although much additional material has been collected on the old lines, the fundamental questions which are involved in this investigation have never received adequate attention. Statistics which I had occasion to collect recently seem to show that the development of children of immigrants is the better the longer their parents have been in the United States. I presume this merely suggests that the economic well-being of the immigrants increases, on the whole, with the length of their stay here, and that the corresponding better nutrition of the children results in better physical development. Whether, however, the whole change can be explained adequately in this manner is open to doubt. It is quite possible that the type may undergo certain changes due to environment.

In how far types must be considered as stable is a question in regard to which there is still considerable diversity of opinion. Investigators like Kollmann maintain the absolute stability of the types now existing; while, on the other hand, indications are not absent which suggest a changeability of types, at least in certain respects. It would seem that stature may be considerably influenced by long-continued more or less favorable environment. There are investigators who maintain that the more or less energetic use of the jaws may influence the form of the head, owing to the pressure brought about by the muscles, which tend to compress the skull laterally. On the other hand, we have very clear evidence that features, like the form of the head, the form of the face and stature, are inherited from generation to generation with great persistence. As long as these questions are still so far from being settled, it seems necessary to take into consideration the possibility of a change of type in the immigrants, due to the new surroundings in which they have been placed. Some anthropologists in America have even gone so far as to claim that the geographical environment affects the European in such a way that he begins to resemble the Indian type. I have failed to find, so far, even a trace of evidence on which this opinion can be based.

The only indication that I can offer which might suggest an influence of environment is an observation which I made a number of years ago in Massachusetts, where I found that the variability of type was remarkably low, considering the mixed composition of the population — a variability which is less than the corresponding values obtained in Europe. But a sporadic observation of such a character is, of course, entirely insufficient to solve a problem of this magnitude. It would seem to my mind that one of the most important and fundamental investigations that have to be made in regard to the question of the biological assimilation of immigrants is a thorough discussion of the sameness or change of type of the second and third generations.

It has often been observed that the local types which have developed in America show a considerable amount of individualization. Some of this may very well be due to the influence of environment. It might be, for instance, that the tallness of the people of Kentucky is due to the limewater of that area. This would be in accord with the observations made by Roese in Gotha, who found that the stature in that city had changed with the introduction of hard water. It will certainly be possible to carry through this inquiry among a people like the Italians or Swedes, where the anthropometrical conditions of the home country are fairly well known, while for many other nationalities parallel inquiries in Europe and in America would be necessary. Even if, by extended inquiries into the physical characteristics of the descendants of immigrants, the modifications of their type should become well known, the problem would still remain. In how far do these types increase in a pure state after their migration, in how far do they tend to become extinct, and what tendency they have to mix with the rest of the population. It seems best to defer a discussion of this question until after consideration of the influence of race intermixture.

Here we may consider again the physical effect of intermixture and the propagation of mixed types independently. I regret to say that the available information in regard to this point is, if anything, more meager than that relating to the modification of types after their migration into this country. The fundamental question that must be asked is, whether the mixture of two distinct types of man tends to produce an intermediate homogeneous type in which certain of the characteristics of the parents appear blended, or whether the resultant tends to exhibit reversion to the parental types. This reversion may again be two-fold. We may either find a complete reversion to one of the component parental types, or we may find a mixture of traits, some resembling the one parent, some the other parent. Obviously this question is most intimately related to the whole study of Mendelian inheritance, which occupies such a prominent place in the work of modern biologists. So far, the results obtained from a study of human types are few in number. I believe the earliest observation in regard to this subject was made by Felix von Luschan, who found as early as 1884 that the inhabitants of the south coast of Asia Minor, who are the descendants of intermarriages between a short-headed type of the central parts of Asia Minor and of the long-headed south coast type — a mixture which has continued for thousands of years — show clear evidence of alternating inheritance. In 1895 I was able to show (utilizing fairly extended observations) that the mixed blood resulting from unions of American indians and whites shows, in regard to certain traits, a clear tendency to reversion to either parental type; while in other respects (for instance, in stature) new characteristics seem to develop. A recent inquiry into heredity among east European Jews shows that here also the children show a tendency to revert either to the father's or to the mother's type. This result is interesting, because it bears upon unions inside a fairly uniform type of man. Other observations relate to the inheritance of abnormal traits, all of which seem to suggest, if not true Mendelism, at least the occurrence of alternating inheritance. However, the observations on mixtures of Indian and white have shown that while alternating inheritance may be found in regard to such traits as the form of the head and face, the development of the bulk of the body follows different laws. Notwithstanding these observations, the whole problem of the effects of race intermixture upon the various characteristic traits of human types is entirely unsolved.

It is not too much to say that the whole work in this field remains to be done. We do not know what weight to give to the small differences of types such as are found in Europe, and whether these differences are sufficiently great to be considered important as compared with the differences between individuals of the same geographical type but belonging to opposite ends of the local series. We must not forget that the people of Europe in each locality are very variable, and that we may find (for instance, in Scotland) considerable numbers of individuals who will differ from one another more than do the average individuals of, let me say, Scotland and southern Italy. The question of the effects of intermixture of types can, therefore, not be treated entirely separately from the question of intermarriages among people belonging to the same locality. And it is worth considering whether the remoteness of blood relationship in different parts of Europe, as compared to the closer blood relationship inside of a narrow territory, may not outweigh all the influences of the differences of geographical types. The whole question seems to be most complex, and worthy of the most detailed and thorough study; but I do not venture to predict the anatomical and physiological effects of intermixture without a most painstaking investigation, which has not been made up to this time.

Considering our lack of knowledge of the most elementary facts that determine the outcome of these processes, I feel that it behooves us to be most cautious in our reasoning, and particularly to refrain from all sensational formulations of the problem, that are liable to add to the prevalent lack of calmness in its consideration; the more so since the answer to these questions concerns the welfare of millions of people.

The problem is one in regard to which speculation is as easy as accurate studies are difficult. Basing our arguments on ill-fitting analogies with the animal and plant world, we may speculate on the effects of intermixture upon the development of new types — as though the mixture that is taking place in America were in any sense, except a sociological one, different from the mixtures that have taken place in Europe for thousands of years; looking for a general degradation, for reversion to remote ancestral types, or towards the evolution of a new ideal type — as fancy or personal inclination may impel us. We may enlarge on the danger of the impending submergence of the northwest European type, or glory in the prospect of its dominance over all others. Would it not be a safer course to investigate the truth or fallacy of each theory rather than excite the public mind by indulgence in the fancies of our speculation. That these are an important adjunct in the attainment of truth, I do not deny; but they must not be promulgated before they have been subjected to a searching analysis, lest the credulous public mistake fancy for truth.

If I am not in a position to predict what the effect of mixture of distinct types may be, I feel confident that this important problem may be solved, if it is taken up with sufficient energy and on a sufficiently large scale. An investigation of the anthropological data of people of distinct types — taking into consideration the similarities and dissimilarities of parents and children, the rapidity and final result of the physical and mental development of children, their vitality, the fertility of marriages of different types and in different social strata — such an investigation is bound to give us information which will allow us to answer these important questions definitely and conclusively.

The final result of race mixture will necessarily depend upon the fertility of the present native population and of the newer immigrants. It has been pointed out repeatedly that the birth-rate of Americans has declined with great rapidity, and that in the second and third generations of immigrants the same decline makes itself felt. It will therefore be important to know what the relation of fertility of different types may be.

If the fertility of foreigners continues high without a corresponding higher death-rate of children, we may anticipate a gradual increase of the physical influence of the more fertile type. The immigration of the divergent types of southern and eastern Europe is, however, so recent, that this question can not be answered until at least twenty years more have elapsed.

No less important than the fertility of each immigrant type by itself is the question, in how far they tend to intermarry. The data presented in our census reports do not give a clear insight into this tendency among various nationalities. The difficulties of collecting significant statistics on the problem are very great. They appear particularly clear in the case of Italians. Married men from Italy come to the United States, earn some money, and go back to rejoin their families. They may come again, and, when conditions are propitious, they may finally send for their families to follow them. Thus we find among the Italian immigrants very large numbers who were married before they came here. It seems almost impossible to separate the contingent of couples married before their arrival here from those married after their arrival, and the chief point of interest to us lies in the intermarriages of children born in this country. It is natural that in large cities, where nationalities separate in various quarters, a great amount of cohesion should continue for some time; but it seems likely that intermarriages between descendants of foreign nationalities are much more common than the census figures would make it appear. Our experience with Americans whose grandparents immigrated into this country is, on the whole, that most social traces of their descent have disappeared, and that many do not even know to what nationalities their grandparents belonged. It might be expected — particularly in Western communities, where a rapid change of location is common — that this would result in a rapid mixture of the descendants of various nationalities. This inquiry, which it is quite feasible to carry out in detail, seems indispensable for a clear understanding of the situation.

It is somewhat difficult to realize how rapidly intermixture of distinct types takes place, if the choice of mates is left entirely to accident. I have made this calculation; and I find that in a population in which two types intermingle, and in which both types occur with equal frequency, there will be in the fourth generation less than one person in ten thousand of pure descent. When the proportion of the two original types is as nine to one, there will be among the more numerous part of the population only eighteen in one thousand in the fourth generation that will be of pure blood. Taking these data as a basis, it is obvious that intermixture, as soon as the social barriers have been removed, must be exceedingly rapid; and I think it safe to assume that one hundred years from now, in the bulk of our population, very few pure descendants of the present immigrants will be found.

Unfortunately, however, we do not know the influence of racial cohesion. Obviously this is one of the fundamental points that ought to be known in order to gain a clear insight into the effect of recent immigration. The data collected by our census and by other agencies do not contain this information, which is one of the most urgent desiderata for an understanding of the composition of the American population. I may therefore express the hope that this question may be included in the census to be organized next year, or may be otherwise provided for by an inquiry to be undertaken under the auspices of the government. Without this information, the whole discussion of the effect of intermixture will remain speculative.

No material whatever is available to answer the question whether mixture of types is favorable for the physical development of the individual, or unfavorable. Statistics collected in the Argentine Republic tend to show that with a mixture of similar types, but from remote countries, considerable changes in the proportions of the sexes develop. Observations on half-breed Indians show that a type taller than either parental race develops in the mixed blood; that the fertility of the mixed blood is increased; and I can not find any evidence that would corroborate the view, so often expressed, that the hybrid of distinct types tends to degenerate.

17
A REPRESENTATIVE OF INDUSTRY

 About 1910 the foreign born made up approximately 60 percent of the American labor force in basic industries such as iron and steel manufacture, construction work, coal, iron and copper mining, and oil refining. Undoubtedly some native-born workers were right when they blamed the immigrant for stealing their jobs. Some influential economists held that the availability of a cheap, fluid pool of unskilled labor enabled the native-born worker to move up the economic and occupational ladder.

Taking the long view, these economists pointed out that except for the Negro imprisoned at the bottom of the industrial pyramid by caste and color bars, the native workman's rise would probably have been slower if there had not been a constant replenishment of unskilled labor at the bottom of the Northern labor pool. Other economists argued that the steady flow of unskilled immigrants into the country allowed manufacturers to reduce the number of skilled, highly paid mechanics and replace them with low-paid, less skilled immigrants manning improved labor saving machinery.

Figures about the effect of immigration on wages and employment in the United States have been manipulated to support those who desired completely unrestricted immigration, those who wished to regulate the flow, and those who thought that only "undesirables," however that term was defined, ought to be excluded.

Today many economists, though by no means all, think that some skilled mechanics *were* displaced by immigrants who worked at dull, routinized jobs tending labor saving machinery. But some hold that many more natives and old immigrants moved into supervisors' and skilled mechanics' slots as the labor force expanded, with recently arrived immigrants filling the lowest-paying jobs shunned by native labor. Statistics show that working conditions and hours of labor improved gradually over a period of decades during which immigration, old *and* new, increased, was nearly cut off, then resumed at different rates. Wages have remained lowest, working conditions improved least, and labor unions were least effective in the American South, where immigration had the least impact.

Until recently historians of labor saw immigrant restriction laws after 1882 as a series of labor and nativist victories in the face of opposition from business groups like those represented here by an Indianapolis firm. But recent studies have shown that business publications and business interests were not uniformly opposed to the restriction of immigration. Some blamed immigrants when the economic system failed to produce its expected returns. Some favored admission of more skilled laborers in preference to the unskilled. In the main, businessmen in the 1920s did not defend the policies they had favored for nearly a century.

The following account, by a foreman in charge of maintenance at Milholland Machine Company, Indianapolis, Indiana, presents the position of many industrialists and skilled American supervisory workers before the great crash of 1929, when *laissez-faire* and the "iron law" of supply and demand were still thought by many to be the sole determinants of industrial life and economic progress.

WHY FOREIGNERS ARE NEEDED IN STEEL PLANTS

PRACTIAL EXPERIENCES WHICH INDICATE THEIR USEFULNESS AND SUGGEST THE WISDOM OF MODIFYING THE IMMIGRATION LAWS

How many American citizens, American-born, who are now crying out against the invasion of the foreigner, have witnessed this foreigner at work around the furnaces of a great steel mill? How many of these same patriots would have been willing to change places with him, had they seen him in action? And, if so, what would have been the wage asked? Then who are the individuals responsible for the cry against the high price of steel and steel products?

I have worked in the great mills at Gary and before the blazing furnaces of Pennsylvania, and my opinions are purely personal ones, formed as a result of experience. I was employed at Gary a few years ago, when labor was plentiful and choice jobs were not to be had. In a great plant of this kind "pull" avails little, and a man must play his part in the great machine efficiently in order to get on.

One day I had a letter from a friend, stating that he was out of work and wanted a job. Could I do anything for him? He was willing to do anything. I had known Bill for a long time. We had been farmer boys together, and I had always known him to be a good hard worker. I went to the superintendent of my department the next morning and asked him to hire Bill. The superintendent told me that he was "full up," but if I guaranteed Bill to be a good man, I could tell him to come ahead and he would make a place for him.

I wired Bill at once including carfare. Two days later he arrived, and I shared my room with him. I stood good for his meals at the restaurant and gave him some money for carfare to his work. The superintendent gave Bill a job at labor; the best he had at the time, but he gave him the preference and a soft job. Instead of being put to work with a gang of "foreigners" shoveling sand, he was

George Walter

FROM *Iron Age*, CXII (August 9, 1923), pp. 331 – 2. Reprinted by permission of the publisher.

given a job thawing out cars of sand with a steam hose. Fifteen minutes were required on this job to set the nozzles for an hour's thawing. This hour was then Bill's own. It gave him plenty of opportunity to go inside and get warmed up if he got cold. The first three nights Bill set his hose lines for the first time, and then went inside and slept the remainder of the night.

IT WAS A HUNKIE'S JOB

At the end of a week, the superintendent told me that Bill "couldn't stand the cold, but that he didn't mind heat." So he had transferred him to the rail mill. Two days later I found a note pinned to the bed saying that Bill hadn't come to "take a 'hunkie's' job"; he had at least expected a job fit for a white man, and he "had quit cold." After I had finished paying the bill at the restaurant and explaining to the superintendent that Bill had changed some, I decided that Bill was right. "It was a hunkie's job because the hunkie was the only one who could be trusted to do it."

Bill's case is only one of thousands, and it is because of this that the great steel industries have come to depend so much upon the foreigner. The foreigner comes to this country with little or nothing. His head is full of ideas of big money easily obtained. Friends soon place him to rights and, as soon as he realizes that he must work and work hard to get his big money, he goes to work. Long hours and hot furnaces do not deter him; he wants the money and gets it. His work is well done because he knows that his job depends upon it.

He believes that seven or eight years over these furnaces will break his health, unless he is possessed with a super-physique, but he has no intention of doing this. A few years' hard work and frugal living, and he has saved considerable money. It requires considerable money, however, to live in the United States; so he either sets up a little business of his own or goes home.

This business he owns in its entirety. If it fails he alone is the loser. None of his friends has borrowed money sunk in the deal. But his business does not fail. He assured himself of that before he opened up. He works, his wife works and his children work helping to keep shop. Bye and bye he has put enough by to open another shop, and so it goes. Had he had the least doubt of success, he would have returned home, where his few thousands would have lasted him a lifetime. There he would have told "how he done it" and more would have come over to fill his place and prevent a shortage of help.

SPENDING MONEY IN EUROPE

Who spends the more money in Europe, the returned foreigner or the American tourist? Then why do we cry because American export business is so far below that of other countries who must depend upon export business for their very existence? We want to sell the foreigner the finished product of our factories, and yet we tell him blandly that he must not come over here and help make these products, even though he has sold his household goods to purchase his passage. The "quota is full" means just what it says, but the foreigner must spend his last few dollars and travel thousands of miles to the gates of Ellis Island to find it out. Then at the expense of the steamship company he is returned to his native land to see others living in his old home and others in his old place at the mills.

I have seen men in steel mills working entire shifts with wet towels bound around their foreheads. Smoke and soot gummed up with sweat ran down the bare blistered shoulders of the men at the soaking pits, spitting blue dust from their mouths as they shoveled it into the pits below. Small wonder that the cry should be, "This is no white man's job." Nevertheless this job is necessary to the production of steel, and the men who do it, though they may not be Americans, are white. Also many of them are embryo Americans. For years the steel interests have been bending their efforts toward Americanizing these toilers, and their efforts to a large degree have been fruitful. The allegation that the steel industries are un-American is false; they are decidedly American and have proved it, but they must get their work done to exist, and the foreigner seems to be the only dependable laborer available for the job.

AGITATING FOR MORE MONEY

Many who do not consider the steel industry in their attacks upon the foreigners make the complaint that they are responsible for low wages. But the steel interests will tell you different. Here is the bitter that comes with the sweet. The greater per cent of the foreigners are continually agitating for more money. When it is offered, nothing can stay the dropping of tools but an attractive counter offer.

"Me quit, boss."

"How come quit, John?"

"Me ketchim more money 'nother place."

"Yeah, and ketchim more work, too."

"No matter more work. Ketchim more money, plenty more money; me quit. Tomorrow me ask new boss give my friends job. Mebbe whole gang quit."

And the whole gang will quit unless the boss is wise and makes a raise. These men stick together and try to get for their friends as good as they have themselves. They are not afraid to recommend their friends, because they *know that they will do a full day's work for a day's pay.* They won't go to sleep on the job, as Bill did, not very often. They want more money, though, and when they get it their American brother gets it, too, but he seldom realizes the part the foreigner played in getting it. When they strike, they strike until the day of settlement. Others may take their places or they may go to work elsewhere, but they won't sneak in through the back gate.

Steel wants and must have the foreigner. Steel is ready and willing to deal with the strike question among the foreigners. Then why not let down the bars a little and let steel have its labor and at the same time hold steel responsible for the good behavior of its imported product?

18

A SOCIOLOGIST

The introduction to this anthology calls attention to the mixture of idealistic, nationalistic, economic, social, and perhaps personal motives by which historians have tried to account for remedies offered by proponents of immigration restriction. By the first decade of this century, a majority of those who were concerned with the quality of American life probably agreed that restriction of the total numbers of immigrants and plans for their assimilation and integration were desirable and inevitable goals of any revision of our immigration policy.

Opponents of the legislation proposed in the 1920s and eventually passed by Congress as the Acts of 1921 and 1924 objected generally not to numerical limitation on arrivals but to the assumptions, frequently heard even on the floor of Congress, that the new immigrants from southern and eastern Europe lacked native potentials for contributing to the country's material and cultural advancement.

Quite narrow conceptions of Americanism and notions of superior and inferior racial inheritances were widespread even among sociologists, historians, and other academically trained students of population and migration.

Henry Pratt Fairchild (1880–1956) taught sociology at New York University and was chairman of its graduate department from 1938 until his retirement in 1945. In one of his books, published in 1926, *The Melting Pot Mistake,* he called for the "exercise of a wholly different type of control over the public utterances of aliens from that imposed upon citizens" and described unrestricted immigration as slowly, insidiously, irresistibly "eating away . . . all form and symmetry, all beauty and character, all nobility and usefulness" in American life and nationality.

He presented the paper reprinted here at the annual meeting of
the American Sociological Society in 1912. In it, he conveniently
summed up the chief contemporary objections to the new immigration
and described one of the many schemes suggested for its curtailment.

THE RESTRICTION OF IMMIGRATION

*Henry Pratt
Fairchild*

There are enough people in the United States who believe that there
is something wrong with our present method of handling immigration, to furnish an audience, ready made, to one who has a remedy
to propose. It is no longer necessary to go over the long line of
argument to prove that evils exist. For this very reason, perhaps,
there has been a wide variety of schemes of reform presented, each
with its followers.

Nevertheless, the student of social affairs who is accustomed
to regard public problems in the light of established laws and fundamental principles, approaches such a question as the regulation
of immigration with extreme reluctance. It is such a tremendous
movement, and cuts straight across all social relations with such
an unsparing inclusiveness, as to inspire him with a feeling of rev-
erential awe, rather than a desire to intermeddle. In a human problem of such complexity, one can never foresee with accuracy what
the unknown factors will be, nor be certain that some of the latent
springs of human conduct will not break out to upset his best laid
plans. Yet the immigration problem is not one which can be let
alone. It is a dynamic question, which demands attention and decision. If we settle the matter by determining to do nothing, we thereby
make a decision, for which we may be more accountable than if
we took some positive stand. And in this country, immigration will
not be let alone. Somebody must make decisions, and frame policies,
and if the social scientists hold aloof, it will be done by selfish
interests and quack politicians.

More than this, it is an immediate problem. Things are happening with alarming rapidity, and what is to be done must be done

FROM *American Journal of Sociology,* XVII (March, 1912), pp.
637–46.

speedily. These are the reasons which justify the presentation of this paper, in which it is proposed to suggest certain improvements in our method of handling the immigration situation in this country.

One thing we may be sure of — any remedy ought to bear some immediate relation to the evils which it contemplates remedying. Before proceeding to the outline of the proposed new scheme, it will be profitable to glance hastily over the most important of the evils charged against immigration, and the foremost remedies which have been suggested, with a view to determining to what extent the latter promise direct relief from the former. The chief objections to the present immigration situation may be summarized under eight heads, each with a convenient catch-word to fix it in memory, as follows:

1. We have too many immigrants. A million a year of the peasants of Europe is more than this country can safely undertake to look after. This may be called the "numbers" objection.

2. The immigrants are poorly distributed. The great majority of them settle in the most densely populated states, and in the most congested sections of the largest cities of those states. The agricultural regions, which particularly want them, get very few of them. This is the "distribution" objection.

3. The immigrants are poorly assimilated, or not assimilated at all. This is in large measure due to the faulty distribution, and to excessive numbers. There is great danger to the country in the growing heterogeneity of population, which results from ever increasing numbers of immigrants, of widely diverse races, who form compact colonies in our great cities, and come in slight touch with American life. The "assimilation" objection.

4. The competition of alien laborers, accustomed to a low standard of living, is lowering the wages and standard of living of the American workman — at the very least, it is preventing them from rising. The "standard of living" objection.

5. Immigration seriously increases the amount of pauperism and crime in the United States, through the admission of large numbers of aliens of bad moral character, or low economic ability. The "pauperism and crime" objection.

6. The present immigration movement is not a natural one, but is stimulated and fostered by transportation companies, labor

agents, and other interested parties. Immigrants come with mis-conceptions and delusions, and without any natural fitness for American life, and as a result many of them suffer bitter hard-ships, and add nothing to the life of this country. The "stimula-tion" objection.

7. Many — perhaps most — of the immigrants enter the country as conscious law-breakers, since a very large proportion of them knowingly evade the contract-labor provision of the law. Thus they begin their American life with a spirit of indifference or hostility to law, which augurs ill for their future usefulness to the country. The "illegal entrance" objection.

8. Immigration, as at present conducted, is proving of no real and lasting benefit to foreign nations. The stimulus given to the birth rate by the fact of emigration prevents any relief of congestion, and the other apparent benefits of emigration are offset by positive evils. The difference in economic level between the United States and foreign countries is gradually being obliterated, at the expense of the United States, and without bettering the other nations. The "foreign countries" objection.

Not all of the foregoing charges have as yet been adequately proved. Some of them perhaps never can be. But they contain the germ of the most important criticisms of the present system, and any proposed remedy ought to promise relief for at least two or three of them.

Among the principal remedies suggested for the problem under consideration the following stand out prominently:

1. The literacy test. This had received perhaps more attention than any other single remedy, and had a host of adherents. It would certainly meet the numbers objection. Since more than a quarter of the immigrants over fourteen years of age can neither read nor write, the strict application of the literacy test would probably cut down the total immigration to an approximately equal degree. It is difficult to see how the literacy test would be of any avail in meeting the distribution, standard of living, stimulation, or illegal entrance objections. It might help to a limited degree in securing better assimilation (No. 3), and it is claimed that literate immigrants are somewhat less prone to pauperism and crime than illiterate ones (No. 5).

2. Consular, or other inspection abroad, either at the port of embarkation, or in the native village of the immigrant. This might

secure a somewhat better enforcement of the existing law, and obviate some of the hardships of the rejected immigrant. It is hard to see how it could materially affect any one of the foregoing objections.

3. Requiring immigrants to come up to a certain physical standard, such as is required for recruits to the army. This would probably remedy the numbers objection to a considerable extent, but would hardly meet any of the others. Our immigrants are already as free from physical and mental diseases and weaknesses, and abnormalities, as a rigid examination can make them.

4. A minimum wage requirement for aliens, making it illegal to employ any alien for less than a specified wage. This is aimed directly at the standard of living objection. It hardly touches any of the others. It is, furthermore, highly impracticable and unjust, as it would impose an *ex post facto* basis of admission. No immigrant could possibly know before he left home what wage he might be sure of unless he was under contract, which is legally prohibited, nor could the examining inspectors tell anything about it. It is hard to see what would be done with aliens who could not earn the specified wage, unless they were supported at public expense, which would subject them to deportation, and would multiply the "tragedy of the rejected immigrant" a hundred fold.

Other suggested remedies, mentioned in the Report of the Immigration Commission, are as follows:

5. The limitation of the number of immigrants of each race.

6. The exclusion of unskilled laborers unaccompanied by wives or families.

7. The limitation of the number of immigrants arriving annually at any port.

8. The material increase in the amount of money required to be in the possession of the immigrant, or of the head tax.

9. The levy of the head tax so as to make a marked discrimination in favor of men with families.

All of these last five remedies, except the very last, are designed primarily to meet the numbers objection, and would be effective to a greater or less extent. Those which aim to discriminate in favor of men with families might also have some effect in meeting the assimilation objection, as families are much more likely to come in touch with Americanizing influences than single individuals. They might, however, operate to aggravate the pauperism and crime objection, as men might be induced to bring over their families when they were really not able to do so, and later fall into pauperism, or be led into crime.

Looking over this list of remedies it becomes apparent that the only objection which most of them seem likely to meet to any considerable extent is the "numbers" objection. The mere reduction in the number of immigrants is very probably desirable, and might be accomplished in a variety of ways. Most of the remedies, however, fail absolutely to touch directly the great problems of distribution, assimilation, the degrading competition of low standards of living, pauperism and crime, unnatural immigration, and evasion of law, to say nothing of the somewhat idealistic problem of really bettering foreign nations. The scheme of regulation which is now to be discussed aims to touch directly every one of these objections. It will seem to many visionary and impractical, to others too drastic and revolutionary — it at least has the merit of having some connection with the evils which it aims to remedy.

The first change involved in the proposed plan is for the government to recognize frankly its responsibility for aliens after they have been admitted and to take charge, officially and authoritatively, of the distribution of immigrants in this country. Hitherto we have tacitly assumed that if sufficient care is exercised in the matter of admission, our duty is done, and the mere fact of residence in this country will bring to the immigrant all of those advantages which he is seeking, and the United States will secure all the benefit possible from his presence. We are tardily learning the utter falsity of this assumption. To promote better distribution, the government should make it its business to ascertain where immigrant labor is actually needed, and where it can be supplied without injuring economic and social conditions — the two ideas are nearly correlative — and should see to it that the immigrants go there, and not elsewhere. To accomplish this, the aid of state and local boards should be enlisted. These agencies should furnish to the government authorities a statement of the number of immigrants who are desired in various sections, the nature of the work they are desired to do, and the wages they may expect. Private employers should be encouraged to state their needs to such boards, or directly to the federal authorities, and make known how many immigrants they wish to employ. All such requests should be investigated, and given official approval before they are acted upon.

All of these requests, and this information, would be compiled and tabulated, and the officials of foreign governments should be supplied with the lists of places, the numbers of immigrants desired, wages, etc. Prospective immigrants should then be required to select the places to which they wished to go before emigrating. A small proportion might possibly be allowed to emigrate without any specified destination — a sort of floating representation.

To aid in the carrying out of this provision, passports should be required of all immigrants, bearing the approval of the foreign nation of the emigration of the individual, and stating the destination which the immigrant has chosen in this country.

Under this system, the greater number — if not all — of the arriving immigrants would come with their destination already picked out, and approved of by the United States government. The government should then see that they get there. The immigrant should not be discharged from authority until he has reached his specified destination. Inspectors should accompany the immigrant trains, and turn their charges over to state and local officials, who should be held responsible for their safe delivery.

In addition to the direct and obvious advantage of securing a more rational distribution, these provisions would also result in encouraging the immigrant to make a more careful study of conditions in America before he left home, and to choose his destination on the grounds of the need of his services, rather than because some friend or relative lived there. This would help to do away with much of the ignorance and misconception which characterize so many of the immigrants today. The passport provision, furthermore, would require the foreign government to scrutinize each would-be emigrant, and this, if conscientiously done, would tend to limit the number of inadmissibles who annually reach our shores.

It may seem that this arrangement would tend to encourage the immigration of contract laborers. There is no doubt that it would. In fact, one part of the proposed plan under discussion is the entire repeal and abolishment of the contract labor clause of the immigration law. It is one of the greatest absurdities of our present legislation, that it assumes and implies that the most desirable immigrant is the one who knows absolutely nothing about what work he is going to do in this country, or whether he will be able to find any. It puts a premium upon ignorance and lack of foresight. If we should see a group of our own fellow-citizens starting out for some foreign country with such a hazy idea of their prospects there, we should brand them as most shiftless and foolhardy. This section of our laws has been made necessary so far, because the government has not hitherto taken control of the number of immigrants, nor of their distribution, nor felt any responsibility for the condition of the immigrant after landing. Under the proposed system, the government should not only allow, but encourage, the making of contracts with prospective immigrants, by state and local boards of public works, and by private employers. But every contract should be made under the approval of the government, witnessed by an official stamp of some kind. The government authorities should also establish a minimum wage for each locality or industry, below which contracts must not be made. Any contract which lacked the official seal, or named a wage below the fixed minimum should be *ipso facto* null and void. Any immigrant, party to such a contract, should be subject to deportation, and the employer to punishment.

To facilitate the making of legal contracts, the government should provide printed forms, stating the place, the name of the employer, the occupation, conditions of labor, and wage, leaving a blank for the name of the immigrant. By this means, employers of labor who found themselves unable to secure an adequate supply of labor at a fair living wage in this country could send their agents to foreign countries, and secure laborers in an open and above-board, legal way, accomplishing the same end that they achieve by underhand and illegal methods, through the assistance of unscrupulous labor agents and contractors. The great difference would be that under the new system the wage agreed upon would have to be such as met with official sanction. If employers did not find it worth while to engage foreign labor under such conditions, it would simply show that there was no real need for laborers in the country, and would work to the advantage of the workmen already here.

The plan, as thus far outlined, contains three main propositions:

1. government control of the distribution of immigrants;

2. requirement of passports for admission;

3. the abolition of the contract labor clause, and the encouragement and government control of labor contracts with aliens, at a minimum wage.

These three provisions meet most of the stock objections which have been outlined. They meet directly the distribution, and therefore the assimilation, objection. The abolition of the contract labor clause, in connection with the minimum wage, meets the standard of living objection. The requirements of a passport, coupled with better distribution, would mitigate the dangers of pauperism and crime. The diminution of the power of the labor agent, and the various runners, would tend to make the movement a more natural one. This would also be furthered by requiring the immigrant to choose a specific destination out of a long list recommended by the United States government. The abolition of the contract labor clause would remove the greatest temptation to illegal entrance, for the majority of immigrants. The proposed plan does not contemplate removing any of the restrictive tests now employed, except the contract labor clause.

The only objections not thus far provided for are the numbers objection and the foreign countries objection. In regard to these, it should be noted first of all, that there is nothing in the three propositions which have been put forth, which is inconsistent with most of the important plans for reducing numbers, or which would prevent them from being applied together. There is, however, another method of meeting directly the two remaining objections, which harmonizes especially well with the rest of the proposed plan. It would be a decided innovation, and the attempt to introduce it might meet with insuperable obstacles of a political and administrative nature. At first sight it presents a decided aspect of impracticability. Nevertheless, it is interesting from a theoretic standpoint, and might prove more possible of application than at first seems probable. Briefly stated, it is as follows:

> The immigration of unskilled laborers to this country should be restricted to a single foreign nation, or group of nations, each year. Let it be understood, by international agreement, that in one year, only immigrants from Germany would be admitted, the next from Italy, the next from Austria-Hungary, etc. Nations which send only small contingents of immigrants should be grouped, either with each other, or with one of the larger countries. Passports to unskilled immigrants from other nations should not be recognized, with the possible exception that each nation might be allowed, every year, a small number of immigrants, to be chosen by the foreign nation, to cover exceptional cases. The United States government could then maintain a special force of inspectors, who should make their headquarters in the nation whose turn it was, year by year, and help to direct and facilitate the movement from that end.

This provision would manifestly help to cut down numbers, for it is not at all likely that ever, in a single year, would as many immigrants arrive from any single country, or group of countries, as now come from all countries. It would also give foreign nations a chance to utilize emigration, consciously and advisedly, for their own benefit. There is every reason to believe that the popular idea that a regular emigration from a country tends to relieve congestion, is a fallacy. Rather does it seem probable that population increases at least as fast, in a country with a large emigration, as if there was none at all. On the other hand, a sudden and extensive emigration, limited in time, may result in cutting down population, and giving the standard of living time to rise before the forces of reproduction have filled up the gap. Under the proposed plan, any foreign nation which believed that a large emigration of its citizens would be a benefit both to those who went and those who stayed — as for instance, on the occasion of the introduction of some important labor-saving machine — could make arrangements with the United States to take its turn at such a time. If foreign nations did not care to do their part in such an arrangement, or if the natives did not wish to leave, the immigration problem would be happily solved for us, without any responsibility on our part.

Against the plan thus outlined, a host of objections, criticisms, doubts, and queries arrays itself. Of these, no one can be more conscious than the writer. Yet the same can be said of almost any human device or project. The validity of such a proposition must rest upon searching analysis and criticism, and ultimately upon trial. The pressing and immediate nature of the immigration problem in the United States justifies the proposal of any seriously conceived plan, which claims to rest on scientific principles.

When the western hemisphere was opened up to settlement by Europeans, the ratio between men and land was altered for all civilized nations. There were opportunities for the permanent betterment of the human race such as had never before been equaled. They demanded the highest degree of human wisdom in their utilization, in order that they should not be squandered. The responsibility for the choicest portion of this new world was laid on the people of the budding nation of the United States. In our modern days of conservation, we are learning, almost too late, how recklessly these resources were dissipated. Vast treasures of forest, mine, river, and fertile plain, which, under proper management, might have been made to serve the race for all time to come, were ruthlessly wasted. Today we are busily engaged in trying to save what is left.

The human aspects of the situation are similar. The United States, above all other lands, has offered the theater for the highest evolution of the human species, for the development of a people who should help to draw all other races up to a higher plane of living. The duty of the United States is not to herself alone, but to all the world. The problem of immigration is but a part of the great conservation movement. It has to do with the conservation of the American people, and all that it stands for.

19

AN ECONOMIST

Professor Roy L. Garis taught from 1921 until 1946 in the economics department at Vanderbilt University. In 1927 he published *Immigration Restriction,* an expanded version of the arguments presented here. While he had acquired a thorough knowledge of immigration history, he also was determined to prove the inferiority of "new" immigrants. He therefore omitted or dealt disingenuously with evidence that weakened or refuted his central thesis. For instance, the Alien and Sedition Laws of 1798, passed by the Federalist faction to stifle Republican opposition, in Garis' version were "favored" by Jefferson as a warning "against the evils of excessive immigration." In reality, the Jeffersonians called these Acts despotic and unconstitutional. Jefferson, as President, pardoned those convicted under the Sedition Act, while Congress restored their fines with interest.

Because Garis' data is limited to anti-immigrant sentiments and actions, it does not reveal the efforts of real estate promoters, Western and Southern state immigration boards, and railroad agents to lure hundreds of thousands of settlers here. He diligently catalogued every effort to exclude immigrants but did not mention Democratic party platform promises from 1840 through 1856 to maintain "an asylum for the oppressed of every nation," or Republican party planks in 1868 and 1872 pledging to encourage immigration. He did not point out that the Contract Labor Law of 1864 *legalized* rather than forbade recruitment of foreign labor by American employers. He left out of his account the welcome extended to foreigners by writers like Ralph Waldo Emerson and Walt Whitman.

As a consequence of his single-minded focus on anti-immigration sentiment, Garis presented a distorted interpretation of American attitudes towards newcomers. He was right when he noted that opposition to immigrants was common throughout American history. But today it is obvious that immigrants have for three hundred years come for almost identical reasons: for riches, for land, for peace, for freedom, for a chance to lead a new, better life. The society receiving them was indeed a changing, evolving one. And while "old" and "new" immigrants differed culturally and religiously, they came for the same variety and mixture of reasons. Within a generation or two or three, nearly all adapted equally well to American conditions and traditions.

Of course there was a case to be made for limiting immigration and improving the laws which selected immigrants. No formula devised even by the most fair-minded Congress would have pleased all. What Garis asked for, however, was exclusion of entire classes of immigrants on racial and ethnic grounds alone. Like other nativists, he objected to the presence of cultural differences. To eliminate these, he was prepared to exclude the law-abiding, able, and needy along with the criminal and unwell entirely on the basis of national and racial origins. It would be instructive to compile a list of prominent Americans who (or whose parents) would have been ineligible for entry if the nativists' formulas for excluding immigrants had been applied since 1900.

AMERICA'S IMMIGRATION POLICY

Roy L. Garis

The important provisions of the Immigration Act of 1924, signed by President Coolidge on May 26, are:

1. it preserves the basic immigration law of 1917;

2. it retains the principle of numerical limitation as inaugurated in the act of May 19, 1921;

3. it changes the quota basis from the census of 1910 to the census of 1890;

4. it reduces the quota admissible in any one year from three to two per cent.;

FROM *The North American Review*, CCXX (September, 1924), pp. 63–77. Reprinted by permission of the publisher.

5. it provides a method of selection of immigrants at the source rather than to permit them to come to this country and land at the immigration stations without previous inspection;

6. it reduces the classes of exempted aliens;

7. it places the burden of proof on the alien to show that he is admissible under the immigration laws rather than upon the United States to show that he is not admissible; and

8. it provides entire and absolute exclusion of those who are not eligible to become naturalized citizens under our naturalization laws.

While it was evident from the beginning that no law would please all, yet it is safe to say that at least eighty per cent. of the American people approve of the new provisions in the Act of 1924. The sources of opposition were and still are:

1. Those who believe that the law is not sufficiently restrictive. For the most part this opposition was not a stumbling block.

2. Those who believe that the law does not admit enough common laborers to do the rough work of the United States.

3. Those who, while pretending to favor restriction, really want anybody and everybody except the insane, the criminal and the diseased, so that they may proceed to reap dividends from their particular lines of endeavor, whether the lines be mills, factories, steamships, newspapers of various languages, or the like, in addition to bondsmen, some lawyers, common crooks, and others who daily exploit the newly arrived alien.

4. Those of an international mind, who think that migrations should not be impeded, except possibly from China, Korea, Japan and India.

5. Those who for religious, racial, or family reasons desire more of their own to be residents of the United States.

6. Those who have been led to believe that the United States can go throughout the world handpicking bricklayers here, plasterers there, gardeners elsewhere and farmers at another place, and bring them, without thought of families, to our States; in other words, selection, distribution and supervision.

In order to expose further the character of this opposition, it is highly desirable and profitable that we analyze our traditional immigration policy to see if we have permanent legislation worthy of the name.

Three times in our history the exercise of the Presidential veto prevented the enactment by Congress of legislation that would restrict immigration by the application of a literacy test. These vetoes were by Presidents Cleveland in 1897, Taft in 1913, and Wilson in 1915. It is clear that both President Cleveland and President Wilson considered restriction of immigration to be contrary to our traditional policy, for each viewed a simple literacy test as "a radical departure" from such a policy. However, President Wilson stated, "If the people of this country have made up their minds to limit the number of immigrants by arbitrary tests and so reverse the policy of all the generations of Americans that have gone before them, it is their right to do so. But I do not believe that they have." These statements are deserving of serious consideration, solely that we may secure a proper focus on the facts of the situation as it exists today.

A great deal of cant and hypocrisy is being preached at the present day as to the motives that lie back of the attitude of the American Government and the American people toward immigration of the past. "A political asylum" "a haven of refuge," "a welcome to the oppressed," "a home for the persecuted" — these and like phrases are all fine, high-sounding expressions, and we believe in them as did our forefathers. But the fact is, they express a secondary and not the primary cause underlying the action of our people and Government toward the alien.

This primary basis has always been what might be called selfish altruism. We have welcomed the immigrant, not because he was an alien, not because he was escaping religious or political persecution, not because he was down-trodden and oppressed, but primarily and essentially because we believed his coming here was for our own good as a people and as a nation. We have welcomed him only so long as, and no longer than, we believed this. When we had been made to realize that his arrival was dangerous and fraught with injury to us, we objected to his coming and took steps to prevent it — even from colonial times. And once having taken a step forward — once having put up a bar — we have never let it down again or taken a step backward.

Accepting for the moment as a fact the statement that a certain line of action has become our traditional policy, we can certainly successfully contend that mere precedent is not good argument in itself for the continuation of such a policy. The American people have never worshipped at the shrine of tradition, they have never made of precedent a fetish. There is no justification for continuing in one direction simply because that is the way we have been going.

Our problem is not a question of consistency in following out a supposed traditional policy in regard to immigration, but it is a problem of the application of intelligence and the saving grace of common sense to the same economic and social phenomenon operating under entirely different conditions. These may or may not require the adoption of the same traditional policy; they may involve a complete reversal of that policy. It is the height of folly to maintain that our immigration problem today is the same and demands the same treatment as that of a generation or generations ago simply because it has the same word name. Conditions are fundamentally different and, what is even more important, we have had an opportunity through experience to become acquainted with certain facts which should enable us to approach the solution of the present aspects of the immigration problem with a greater degree of intelligence.

In the above and for the moment, we granted that there has been a traditional policy of virtually unrestricted, free immigration — a policy which, President Wilson clearly perceived, could be reversed if the American people so desired. The only question in his mind was that he was not sure that the people desired "to reverse the policy of all the generations of Americans that have gone before." Were he President today I am sure that Mr. Wilson would say that the American people have reversed what he conceived to be their traditional policy.

But has America, until the last decade, welcomed the immigrant with open arms and wild enthusiasm, as the advocates of free immigration declare? What has been her real traditional policy? What have been the views of the leaders of American thought from colonial days?

Between 1714 and 1720 fifty-four ships arrived in Boston with immigrants from Ireland. They were carefully scrutinized by the Puritan exclusionists. Cotton Mather wrote in his diary on August 7, 1718: "But what shall be done for the great number of people that are transporting themselves thither from ye North of Ireland?" John Winthrop, speaking of twenty ministers and their congregations that were expected the same year, said: "I wish their coming over do not prove fatall in the End." They were not welcome, and so most of them moved on beyond the New England settlements.

The Scotch-Irish came in such large numbers to Pennsylvania that James Logan, the Secretary of the Province, wrote to the Propri-

etors in alarm in 1729: "It looks as if Ireland is to send all its inhabitants hither, for last week not less than six ships arrived, and
every day two or three arrive also." Not being welcome, these too
pushed on to the frontier.

In 1717 the British Government entered on the policy of penal
transportation, and thenceforth discharged certain classes of felons
upon the Colonies. New England escaped these "seven year passengers." It is estimated that between 1750 and 1770 twenty thousand
convicts were exported to Maryland alone. The Colonies bitterly
resented such cargoes, but their self-protective measures were regularly disallowed by the selfish Home Government.

Benjamin Franklin, in a personal letter dated Philadelphia, May
9, 1753, wrote concerning the Germans of Pennsylvania: "Unless
the stream of importation could be turned from this to other Colonies,
they will soon outnumber us, that all the advantages we will have
will in my opinion be not able to preserve our language, and even
our government will become precarious."

From what has been said above it is evident that conditions
in Pennsylvania were by no means exceptional. Professor McMaster
says of the same period: "Diverse as the inhabitants of the States
were in occupations, they were not less diverse in opinions, in
customs, and habits. Differences of race, differences of nationality,
of religious opinions, of manners, of tastes, even of speech, were
still distinctly marked."

It is evident then that all of the Colonies received their share
of human chaff despite their vigorous protests. But the important
thing to note is that the thoughtful people of those days were against
immigration even when there was land in abundance and opportunity
beckoned on every hand.

The "yellow streak" in the population faded rapidly, for many
of these men belonged to the class of the unfortunate rather than
to the vicious and were the product of a passing state of society.
No doubt the worst felons were promptly hanged, so that those
who were transported — despite the protests of Virginia and the other
Colonies — were such as excited the compassion of the court in an
age that recognized nearly three hundred capital offenses. When
we consider the fact that many were the victims of bad surroundings
rather than born malefactors; that the larceny of a few shillings was
punishable by death, and that many of the victims were deported
because of religious differences and political offenses, or kidnapped
and brought over to be sold as indentured servants, then the stigma
of crime is erased. Under the regenerative stimulus of opportunity

many of these persons reformed, and, therefore, one does not wonder that some of these transported persons rose to places of honor and distinction in the Colonies and that many of them became respected citizens. Opportunity beckoned then, but today the immigrant's labor is considered no more than any other commodity to be bought at the lowest price, while opportunity is like a jack-o'-lantern or like the pot of gold at the foot of the rainbow.

But be that as it may, before passing on, I desire to point out again the opposition in all the Colonies to the coming of new immigrants — an opposition which was so bitter that the new immigrants either themselves moved on to the frontier which was ever moving westward, or else forced the original inhabitants to do so. But today there is no frontier!

Very early in the legislation of our Federal Congress, in fact as early as 1798, statutes were enacted affecting the alien. The most important of these were the Alien and Sedition laws, both of which had for their object the removal of aliens from the United States. The Alien Law authorized the President, without trial, to order out of the country "any aliens he shall judge dangerous to the peace and safety of the United States" and, if they remained, to imprison them "so long as, in the opinion of the President, the public safety may require." In order that no alien might escape, sea captains were to make reports in writing of the names, ages, and places of birth of all foreigners brought over in their ships.

That early legislation was severe on the foreigner is attested by another law passed in 1798. A new Naturalization Act raised the period of necessary residence in the United States from five to fourteen years and provided that foreigners seeking naturalization must declare their intention five years before the time for obtaining papers. Even more stringent than these laws was another enacted in the same year which gave to the President the right, in case of war declared or invasion threatened, to seize, secure, or send away all resident aliens, whether natives or adopted citizens, of the hostile nation.

When we recall the conditions existing at the time of these acts — a young Republic with a new form of government surrounded by avowed and hostile enemies — there was some justification for this severe attitude toward foreigners in this country. Washington, Jefferson, and other founders of our Government favored such legislation and warned the country against the evils of excessive immigration.

These acts indicate clearly a hostile attitude by our Federal

Government in its youth toward foreigners. Historical facts thus refute the contention of the past and present advocates of unrestricted immigration that we have always welcomed the immigrant with outstretched arms. Unable to protect themselves in colonial days, the States took drastic measures against foreigners almost from the beginning of their independence. Reference to these early statutes is important in that they were based upon conditions which have given tone and color to so much of the opposition that has manifested itself toward the immigrant at different periods in our history.

As early as 1804 a proposal in Connecticut to extend the franchise brought from the Federalists the charge that "never yet has an extension of the franchise failed to bring with it those triple horrors: Catholics, Irishmen, and Democratic rule." "Give to every man a vote and the ports of Connecticut would be crowded with ships swarming with patriots and rapparees fresh from the bogs of Erin, elections would be decided by the refuse of jails and gibbets, and factious men from Ireland would inflict on Connecticut just such a government as they have already inflicted on Delaware, on Pennsylvania, on New York."

In 1807 immigrants were characterized as "the vagabonds and wandering felons of the universe." Dire prophecies as to the submerging of our institutions, and the inevitable downfall of the Republic, abounded in the newspapers at the time so many Irish Catholics were coming to the United States. Through the sections of the country where the Irish settled, anti-Catholic riots were not infrequent, even necessitating at times the calling out of troops. In New York City at the spring elections of 1834 complaint was made by the Whigs that gangs of Irishmen "armed with stones and bludgeons drove them from the polls, attacked their committee in its own room, put the Mayor, Sheriff, and posse to flight and terrorized the city." In Boston in 1837 a mob attacked and sacked the houses of the Irish. There were also anti-foreign riots of more or less serious proportions in Cincinnati, Philadelphia and other cities. In Cincinnati the rioting was directed primarily against the German element.

In 1819 Congress enacted a law providing for an enumeration of arriving aliens, this being the first action on record of legislative attention to the subject of immigration itself. Opposition to immigration was soon crystallized. In 1838 the House of Representatives instructed its Judiciary Committee to consider the propriety of passing a law prohibiting the importation into this country of vagabonds and paupers.

The antagonistic attitude of a considerable part of the public manifested itself in the political parties of the time in what has come to be called the nativistic movement or "Native Americanism." Immigration and its effects became an issue of the very first importance and was the cause of one of the most remarkable movements in American history. The Native American Association, formed in 1837 in Washington, sought to cherish native American sentiment, to exclude foreign opinions and doctrines, to exclude foreigners from office under the State and Federal Governments, and to procure a repeal of the naturalization law. The opposition to foreigners holding office was quite general. In 1835 the platform of the Native Americans in New York stated: "Elevate no person of foreign birth to any office of honor, trust, or profit in the United States."

Immigration was a prominent issue in the election of 1844 which made James K. Polk President of the United States over Henry Clay. In the Pierce-Scott Presidential campaign of 1852 Scott was accused of "nativism" and this was a factor in his defeat. The historian, Rhodes, states that "this is the first Presidential campaign in which we light upon those now familiar efforts to cajole the German and Irish citizens," and ever since then the foreign vote has played an important part in deciding great questions of American policy.

In 1854 the opposition to immigration as manifested in the Native American movement became known as the "Know-Nothing Party," its official title being the American Party. Their cry now began to be Washington's famous order, "Put none but Americans on Guard Tonight." The country was shaken to its depths, yet all this agitation and opposition by the American public proved futile in the direction of restricting the volume of immigration, for the great, almost limitless West was still to be settled. There was still a frontier, still plenty of land, the immigrants were for the most part still willing to go West and settle on the land, while opportunity still beckoned.

Although the opposition to immigration was not strong enough to place any restrictive measures on the Federal statute books prior to the Civil War, yet a number of States legislated on the subject of immigration. As early as 1847 New York passed laws dealing with the situation. Massachusetts, California, Louisiana and other States also took action. However, the Supreme Court of the United States declared a number of these laws unconstitutional, and in a case in 1882 it stated that the subject of immigration "had been confided to Congress by the Constitution, and that Congress can more appropriately and with more acceptance exercise it than any other body known to our laws, State or National." From the very moment when this decision of the Supreme Court was handed down the Government embarked upon a national policy of regulating immigration.

The act of March 3, 1875, prohibited the immigration of alien convicts and of women brought in for purposes of prostitution. Under date of May 6, 1882, Congress passed and the President approved an act "to regulate immigration" by which was suspended for ten years the coming of Chinese laborers to our shores — a suspension not yet removed. The act of February 26, 1885, prohibited the importation of laborers under contract. The act of February 15, 1893, granted additional quarantine powers and imposed additional duties upon the Public Health Service. By 1907 there were as many as sixteen classes of aliens being denied admittance to the United States, and to these the act of 1907 added others. A number of other important acts were passed prior to the act of February 5, 1917, which, among other important restrictions, made provision for the literacy test. On May 11, 1922, an act was approved extending the act of May 19, 1921 — the so-called 3 per cent. law — to and including June 30, 1924.

It was admitted by all that this 3 per cent. law was a makeshift, temporary, war measure to stem the tide of those unfortunates of Europe who were beginning to pour into this country in order to escape the misery and burdens which they had inherited from the World War. By extending this act to June 30, 1924, Congress had time to work out more or less permanent legislation to take the place of the somewhat arbitrary, unscientific restriction of a quota based upon the census of 1910. The country is virtually back to normal conditions. It was high time for us to face the problem fearlessly and frankly before Congress adjourned in June.

Our review so far has made it evident that from colonial times the American people have opposed the coming of immigrants into this country when they had to associate with them and enter into competition with them; that so long as there was plenty of land — a frontier — and the immigrants were willing to go to it, the problem was not acute; that the young Republic was forced in self-defense to pass drastic laws against the aliens; that with the passing of the years in the last century the opposition to immigrants became more and more crystallized and found expression in one restrictive measure after another until prior to the Act of 1924 less than 400,000 immigrants could enter the United States in any fiscal year under the 3 per cent. law; and lastly but most important of all, that once having passed a restrictive measure, the American people have never repeated it, but have expressed themselves time and time again to be in favor of more severe measures of restriction.

If America can be said to have had a traditional immigration policy, it has certainly not been one upholding free and unrestrictive immigration. On the other hand public opinion in America has upheld a policy of increasing restriction and this, if anything, has been her traditional policy. The American people want restriction, strict, severe restriction. The bars must be put up higher and more scientifically. Practical results are demanded. Does the Act of 1924 take steps in this direction? Does it grant what the public wants in concrete terms?

In the first place and without question, the American people wanted the Act of 1917 excluding certain classes to be continued and strengthened — the most important of these classes being idiots, imbeciles, feeble-minded persons, epileptics, insane persons, paupers, beggars, vagrants, persons afflicted with disease, criminals, polygamists, anarchists, persons likely to become a public charge, illiterates, etc. Such persons as these must be excluded even though they might be eligible for admittance under every other provision of the law. The Act of 1924 continues and strengthens the exclusion of such classes.

In the second place and beyond doubt, public opinion is opposed to the so-called "new" immigration and desired its restriction to the lowest possible minimum.

At the present time European immigration to the United States may be divided into two groups, the "old" and the "new." The "old" immigration extended from the beginning of our national history to about the year 1890 and was derived chiefly from Great Britain and Ireland, Germany, and the Scandinavian countries. Thus practically all the immigrants to 1890 were predominantly Anglo-Saxon-Germanic in blood and Protestant in religion — of the same stock as that which originally settled the United States, wrote our Constitution and established our democratic institutions. The English, Dutch, Swedes, Germans, and even the Scotch-Irish, who constituted practically the entire immigration, were less than two thousand years ago one Germanic race in the forests surrounding the North Sea. Thus being similar in blood and in political ideals, social training, and economic background, this "old" immigration merged with the native stock fairly easily and rapidly. Assimilation was only a matter of time and this was aided by the economic, social and political conditions of the country. Even though those who were already here objected to others coming in, yet once in they soon became Americans, so assimilated as to be indistinguishable from the natives. Furthermore, in comparison with the present-day immigration it was relatively small in volume, while the abundance of free land and our need for pioneers prevented the rise of any serious problem.

In the period centering about the year 1880, and in particular in the decade 1880–1890, there was a distinct shift in the immigration movement. Whereas before 1890 most of our immigrants had been Anglo-Saxons and Teutons from Northern Europe, after 1890 the majority were members of the Mediterranean and Slavic races from Southern and Southeastern Europe. The great bulk of this "new" immigration has its source in Russia, Poland, Austria, Hungary, Greece, Turkey, Italy and the Balkan countries. It is in connection with this "new" immigration that the present immigration problem exists. Its solution challenges our attention.

As Professor Commons says: "A line drawn across the continent of Europe from northeast to southwest, separating the Scandinavian Peninsula, the British Isles, Germany, and France from Russia, Austria-Hungary, Italy, and Turkey, separates countries not only of distinct races but also of distinct civilizations. It separates Protestant Europe from Catholic Europe; it separates countries of representative institutions and popular government from monarchies; it separates lands where education is universal from lands where illiteracy predominates; it separates manufacturing countries, progressive agriculture, and skilled labor from primitive hand industries, backward agriculture, and unskilled labor; it separates an educated, thrifty peasantry from a peasantry scarcely a single generation removed from serfdom; it separates Teutonic races from Latin, Slav, Semitic, and Mongolian races. When the sources of American immigration are shifted from the Western countries so nearly allied to our own, to Eastern countries so remote in the main attributes of Western civilization, the change is one that should challenge the attention of every citizen."

The racial proportions of incoming aliens having thus undergone a remarkable change since 1890, the result has been "a swift and ominous lowering of the general average of character, intelligence, and moral stamina," with the result now that the situation is "full of menace and danger to our native racial stream and to our long-established institutions." The advocates of free and unrestricted immigration refute such a contention by pointing out that the same has been said time and time again for over a hundred years. They point to members of the old immigration and say that all that these needed was an opportunity. They go to great trouble to compare the present "new" immigration with the types which came to us prior to 1890, in order to establish their contention that the present "new" immigration is no worse than the former. However, I desire to point out in this connection a thought which I have not found expressed in the arguments answering the above contentions of the advocates of free immigration. It is simply this — that the comparison of the present "new" immigration with the lower types which came to us prior to 1890 is wasted energy. The vital thing for us today is not whether the present "new" immigration is equal to, superior to, or lower than the immigration of 35 years ago, but how does it compare with the "old" immigration of *today?* According to every test made in recent years and from a practical study of the problem, it is evident beyond doubt that the immigrant from Northern and Western Europe is far superior to the one from Southern and Eastern Europe.

In the Act of 1924 Congress adopted a suggestion of the writer that a simple and practical solution of the problems created by the "new" immigration — a solution based on scientific and historical facts — would be to adopt the census of 1890 instead of 1910 or 1920 as the basis for permanent legislation and future percentage laws. It is true that the 3 per cent. law based on the census of 1910 was primarily quantitative, but it was nevertheless qualitative to the extent that it kept from our shores millions of undesirables which this country could afford to do without. The two per cent. law based on the census of 1890 limits qualitatively to a much higher degree as well as numerically within safe boundaries. It closes the doors to all but a few thousand "new" immigrants each year. It will give us time to educate and assimilate those now here (a task of gigantic proportions, requiring many years). And yet such a plan does not exclude to a detrimental point those immigrants from Northern and Western Europe who might desire to come and who are easily assimilated. Such a provision is eminently fair and equitable, and yet it raised a storm of protest among the nationals whose quotas it reduced. But this is the invariable effect of any legislative proposals that are frankly framed for the benefit of America and Americans rather than for Europe and Europeans. And yet, as in the case of any bill, the character of the opposition may be the strongest kind of evidence of intrinsic merit.

There are many industries in this country which are dependent upon foreign labor if wage scales and working hours of past years are to prevail. Native American labor will not work twelve-hour shifts when eight-hour jobs can be had. Americans will not be satisfied with the living conditions or the fare that the foreign-born laborer is satisfied with.

The solution of the labor shortage in these industries is either a revised schedule of employment or a free entry of labor from foreign countries. Yet to open the gates again to the common labor of foreign lands would be to surrender much of what we have gained. It would but add to our domestic problems, since the great majority of this class are unfitted for citizenship.

Some industries have not kept pace with other American industries either in working hours or wages. A labor shortage in such industries will probably be a direct result of this condition. The thinking man comes to regard such industries as a place to seek employment only when all other places fail, and to be left as soon as a job can be obtained elsewhere. A revision of standards in some of our industries is what is needed right now. Happily some have seen the handwriting on the wall and are taking such a step. American industries can get all the labor they need if they will give labor a square deal and cease treating it as a commodity.

Indeed, the time is opportune for Americans to insist on an American policy, regardless of what our employers of cheap labor and our foreign born want. We have catered to them too long already and in consequence have been throwing away our birth-right. The vital thing is to preserve the American race, as far as it can be preserved, and build it up with Nordic stock; intelligent, literate, easily assimilated, appreciating and able to carry on our American institutions. The percentage law based on the census of 1890 will in time automatically bring about such a result.

In a recent letter to me, the Hon. Roger W. Babson stated: "Of course I am in favor of an extension of our Immigration Service to the points of embarkation on the other side." Perhaps no other provision in the Act of 1924 has met with such general approval as the one which provides for a form of examination over seas. For several years it seemed impossible to work out a practical method and one satisfactory to the nations in whose ports such inspection takes place. Under the new law both non-quota and quota immigrants are required to file their written application under oath in duplicate before the United States consul in their country for an immigration certificate. These applications go fully into their past records, their family history, and into their mental, moral and physical qualifications. This process now enables us to weed out in advance those not qualified for entrance into the United States. A satisfactory examination there procures an immigrant certificate for admission here, provided that the quota has not been exhausted. However, the certificate does not exempt the immigrant from a final inspection and medical examination at the port of entry. The immigrant is subject to deportation if he or she fails to measure up to the Act of 1917.

The law provides that not more than ten per cent. of the total number of certificates allotted to each country may be issued in any one month, and a certificate is void four months after the date of issuance. The counting of these certificates is made abroad. A no more constructive provision could be imagined than this, for it eliminates the racing of steamships into the ports of entry on the first day of each month, it eliminates the necessity of immigrants being forced to return to Europe due to exhausted quotas, and at the same time it gives our consuls the power to prevent obviously undesirable aliens from coming to America.

The provision in the law abrogating the gentlemen's agreement with Japan, and excluding all Japanese laborers from the United States because of their ineligibility for citizenship, has been the subject of world discussion. Under this gentlemen's agreement Japan, not the United States, determined what and how many Japanese laborers could come to America. It was inevitable that this arrangement should be ended and Congress was within its rights in ending it, although it might have accomplished it in a more diplomatic manner.

It has been my purpose to explain briefly those provisions of the new law which have been subject to the most discussion in order to make clear that each provision is but a logical step forward in our traditional policy of increasing restriction of immigration in a more humane, scientific and constructive manner. The Secretary of Labor, Mr. Davis, said in a recent address, "There should be some immigration of the right kind, but we, not Europe, will say who shall come or we will not let any come." Certainly in the Act of 1924 we have taken important steps forward in the right direction toward permanent legislation worthy of the name.

BIBLIOGRAPHICAL ESSAY

References shown here should be useful for studying immigrants and immigration during the period covered in this book and, in some cases, to the present time. It is *not* a complete bibliography of any aspect of the subject. Books and articles mentioned elsewhere in this book are generally not repeated here.

For basic bibliographies and concise summaries reflecting recent research and new interpretations in immigrant history, the pamphlet by Franklin D. Scott and Richard Beringer, *Emigration and Immigration* (2nd edition, 1966; Service Center for Teachers of History of the American Historical Association, 400 A. Street, SE, Washington, D.C. 20003), is first-rate. *A Report on World Population Migrations as Related to the United States of America* (George Washington University, Washington, D.C., 1956) includes a section, "New Peoples and Old Problems, 1880–1921." Moses Rischin, *An Inventory of American Jewish History* (1954) and the earlier volumes of the *American Jewish Yearbook* refer to various aspects of the new immigration. Maldwyn A. Jones, *American Immigration** (1960) emphasizes the similarities rather than the differences between old and new immigrants. It is a readable introduction to the entire history of immigration to America.

Oscar Handlin, *The Uprooted** (1951); *Race and Nationality in American Life** (1957); and *The American People in the 20th Century** (1963) are basic for a grasp of the immigrant experience and the immigrants' impact on American life and culture. For a "Critique of *The Uprooted*," see Rudolph J. Vecoli's article in *The Journal of American History*, LI (December, 1964), 404–17, also reprinted in *Study Master Notes* #704, *The Uprooted*.

The most complete collection of documents and reports illustrating historical, social, and legal aspects of "old" and "new" immigration

To conserve space, data concerning the publisher's name and place of publication have been omitted for all but a few titles.

Books available in paperback editions are shown with an asterisk [*] following the title.

Articles available in the Bobbs-Merrill Reprint Series are shown with a double asterisk [**] following the title.

211

is Edith Abbott's *Immigration, Select Documents and Case Records* (1924); it omits documents relating to Asiatic immigration. *Historical Aspects of the Immigration Problem, Select Documents,* by the same editor (1926) covers the period before 1882. Shorter collections are Michael Kraus, *Immigration, the American Mosaic** (1966); Oscar Handlin, *Immigration as a Factor in American History** (1959); and Moses Rischin, *American Immigration* (forthcoming).

The localized history pamphlets published by Teachers College Press of Columbia University on various nationality groups provide serviceable introductions for beginning students.

Articles, book reviews, and notices of books dealing with immigration, ethnic groups, and urban topics may be found in *The International Migration Digest* and periodicals published under the auspices of various ethnic, national, and religious groups. Among the better known are *Norwegian-American Studies, Swedish Pioneer Historical Quarterly, German-American Review, Polish-American Studies, Journal of Negro History, Phylon, American Jewish Archives, Quarterly of the American Jewish Historical Society,* and *Jewish Social Studies.* Names and addresses of ethnic historical societies are given in volume I, *Encyclopedia of Associations; National Organizations of the U.S.A.* (Gale Research Co., Detroit).

Localized ethnic and immigrant associations promoting historical activities are listed in *American Association for State and Local History Directory of Historical Societies and Agencies in the U.S. and Canada.*

The forty-one volumes of the *Reports of the U.S. Immigration Commission* are the result of the most extensive survey of the subject of immigration. Serious students will want to examine at least the abstracts of the commission's reports and the *Dictionary of Races or Peoples* prepared for it. Jeremiah W. Jenks and W. Jett Lauck, *The Immigration Problem* (1911, and later editions) is a summary of the material assembled by the Commission. The anti-new immigration bias of its conclusions and recommendations is analyzed in Handlin's *Race and Nationality in American Life,* cited above. Isaac A. Hourwich, *Immigration and Labor* (1912) is a reply to economic arguments advanced by the commission.

Henry Pratt Fairchild, *The Melting Pot Mistake* (1926) is typical of the views of a "liberal" racist. Madison Grant, *The Passing of the Great Race* (1916) represents the rabid, "Aryan," anti-democratic racist mentality. Other studies of the "new" immigration informed by a balanced view, not carried away by the rhetoric of "beaten men from beaten races," are John P. Gavit, *Americans by Choice* (1922);[1] William C. Smith, *Americans in the Making* (1939); Constantine Panunzio, *Im-*

---

[1] Gavit's book is one of ten volumes issued as the Carnegie "Americanization Studies" in the early 1920s. The books, which deal with the immigrant's adjustment problems to American institutions and life, have been reprinted, with new introductions, under the general editorship of Dr. William S. Bernard of the Brooklyn College Center for Migration Studies.

migration Crossroad (1927); and Peter Roberts, *The New Immigration* (1912). Social anthropologists analyze the Little Italys, Little Bohemias, and Polack Towns of "Yankee City" in W. Lloyd Warner, *The Social Systems of American Ethnic Groups* (1945). Harry Jerome, *Migration and Business Cycles* (1926) studies the relationship between fluctuations in employment and corresponding ebb and flow of migration.

There are numerous histories and sociological studies of separate nationalities and ethnic groups. William I. Thomas and Florian Znaniecki, *The Polish Peasant in Europe and America* (1927); Robert F. Foerster, *The Italian Emigration of Our Times* (1919); and Theodore Saloutos, *The Greeks in the United States* (1964) are among the best; other titles can be found under appropriate subject headings in library catalogs.

Andrew F. Rolle's *The Immigrant Upraised, Italian Adventurers and Colonists in an Expanding America* (1968) is an important reminder that the impressionistic, pessimistic interpretation of the immigrants' experience set forth movingly in *The Uprooted* does not invariably fit the lives of all immigrants. Those who moved west, Rolle concludes, who settled on the newer lands beyond the Mississippi River, found life there a challenging adventure, not an alienating, uprooting experience. They competed on equal terms with native-born Western settlers for positions at the top of the wealth and status ladder, suffered little discrimination or alienation, and believed the fluid social order of the West allowed a man, whether vintner, miner, homesteader, businessman, or banker, to go as far as his talents would take him.

The influence of the ethnic press, foreign-language radio stations, societies, parishes, schools, colleges, and the home in the perpetuation of immigrant languages is examined in Joshua A. Fishman, *Language Loyalty in the United States* (1966). Robert E. Park, *The Immigrant Press and Its Control* (1922) deals with an important Americanizing agency.

The romanticization of the East European village which has become an ancestral myth for some American Jews is corrected in Lucy S. Dawidowicz's *The Golden Tradition: Jewish Life and Thought in Eastern Europe* (1967). Stephen Birmingham's *Our Crowd: the Great Jewish Families of New York** (1967) includes accounts of the reception of Eastern European Jews by their established Americanized German-Jewish coreligionists. Allon Schoener (ed.), *Portal to America: The Lower East Side, 1870–1925* (1967) contains superb photographs and selections from contemporary newspapers and magazines. Ronald Sanders' *The Downtown Jews* (1969) is a fact-crammed study of the Yiddish press, theater, labor movement, and American Zionism.

Immigrant girls lured into prostitution are discussed in George K. Turner, "The Daughters of the Poor," which appeared originally in *McClure's Magazine;* excerpts are reprinted in Harvey Swados, *Years of Conscience: The Muckrakers** (1962). Egal Feldman's "Prostitution, the Alien Woman and the Progressive Imagination," *American Quarterly,* (Summer, 1967), probes the relationship between the "new" immigration, organized prostitution, and the Progressive movement. Allen F. Davis, *Spearheads of Reform* (1967) describes activities of settlement house workers among immigrants in Boston, Chicago, and New York.

The mixture of various ethnic groups is described in Rudolph J. Vecoli, *The People of New Jersey* (1965). Victor R. Greene, *The Slavic Community on Strike* (1968) reexamines the stereotype of Slavic work-force passivity by describing Slavic hard-coal miners' role in the union-ization of the anthracite industry. Saloutos, *They Remember America* (1956) is a study of Greek-Americans who returned home and their influence there.

Biographies and autobiographies recreate the immigrants' lives and provide opportunities for comparative studies. For instance, Samuel Gompers and Sidney Hillman both were immigrants and labor leaders, yet utterly different in their concern for the new immigrant, the Negro, and the poor white. Other life stories of "new" immigrants or their children are M. E. Ravage, *An American in the Making** (1917); Ludwig Lewisohn, *Up-Stream* (1922); Alfred Kazin, *A Walker in the City** (1951); Constantine Panunzio, *The Soul of An Immigrant* (1921); and Pascal D'Angelo, *Son of Italy* (1924). Cecyle S. Neidle has collected excerpts from the observations of immigrants and refugees in *The New Americans* (1967). Annotated lists of biographies and autobiographies are found in Maurice R. Davie, *World Immigration* (1949); William C. Smith, *Americans in the Making* (1939); Louis Kaplan (comp.), *A Bibliography of American Autobiographies* (1961); Harold U. Ribalow (comp.), *Autobiographies of American Jews* (1965); and Richard G. Lillard, *American Life in Autobiography** (1956). *Children of the Uprooted** (1966), by Oscar Handlin consists of 34 selections, about half of them drawn from fiction, in which the children of immigrants have their say.

Fiction often reveals the intensely human side of emigration and settlement. Upton Sinclair, *The Jungle* (1906); Pietro Di Donato, *Three Circles of Light* (1960); and Abraham Cahan, *The Rise of David Levinsky** (1917) are classics. Otis W. Coan and R. G. Lillard, *America in Fiction: An Annotated List of Novels That Interpret Life in the United States, Canada and Mexico* (1956) should be consulted for additional titles.

The "contributions" of newer immigrants to American writing, fine arts, advertising, films, theatre, and other products of mind and im-magination are difficult to chart. Among the better treatments are chapters in R. E. Spiller (ed.), *The Literary History of the United States* (1956); Merle Curti, *The Growth of American Thought* (1951); Marcus L. Hansen, *The Immigrant in American History** (1940); Oscar I. Janowsky (ed.), *The American Jew: A Reappraisal* (1964); and H. L. Mencken, *The American Language* (4th edition and Supplements, abridged, with anno-tations and new material by Raven I. McDavid, Jr., 1963), "Foreign Influences Today," pp. 251–66, and *passim*.

The bibliography in David F. Bowers (ed.), *Foreign Influences in American Life** (1944), is useful, as are George W. Pierson's assessment of the influence of migration on national character, "The M-Factor in American History,"** *American Quarterly,* (Summer, 1962), and Nathan Glazer's discussion of the relationship between immigrant influences and high and low culture, "The Immigrant Groups and American Culture," *Yale Review,* XLVIII (Spring, 1959), 382–97.

Daniel Bell, "Crime as an American Way of Life,"** *Antioch Review,* (Summer, 1963), dares to ask what ethnic groups might have contributed to crime and quasi-legal "business" in the United States. Folkways-Scholastic Records sell a 12" long-playing record of Lithuanian Folksongs in the U.S.A. (Cat. No. #4009). Vanguard Records issued Morris Rosenfeld's "Songs of the Ghetto," with good historical notes. Laura Fermi, *Illustrious Immigrants* (1968) deals with the intellectual migrations from Europe in 1930–1941 but her "notes toward an evaluation" are suggestive for earlier periods.

The "new" immigration since World War II is analyzed and described in *Annals of the American Academy of Political and Social Science,* CCCLXVII (September 1966).

The distribution of "Negro and Foreign-Born Population in 1900" and the "Density of Population in 1900," two maps in the *Atlas of American History,** E. W. Fox (ed.), Oxford University Press, N.Y., 1964), show how few of the foreign-born settled in the South and that areas where the immigrants were perceived as problems were the older, eastern areas with the greatest population density.

How the children of immigrants capitalized on their "marginal status" to deliver the immigrant vote, served as quasi-social workers to immigrants, and familiarized the newcomers with representative government is delightfully told in *Plunkitt of Tammany Hall,** as recorded by William L. Riorden (1963; with an introduction by Arthur Mann). The latter's *LaGuardia, A Fighter Against His Times, 1882–1933** (1959) is a study of a "marginal man" who made the most of the hyphen.

For the tangled history of nativist opinion and action and racism as they affected new immigrants, Thomas F. Gossett, *Race: The History of an Idea** (1965) and John Higham, *Strangers in the Land** (1965) are indispensable. Professor Higham's essay, "Immigration," in C. Vann Woodward (ed.), *The Comparative Approach to American History** (1968) opens up the international dimension for the theme of American migration history.

Many long-out-of-print studies and documents relating to new immigrants are included in *The American Immigration Collection* reprint series (Arno Press and The New York Times).